T0271693

THE
GREEN
BULLET

THE
GREEN
BULLET

THE RISE, FALL AND RESURRECTION OF ALEJANDRO VALVERDE AND THE CORRUPTION OF SPANISH CYCLING

MATT RENDELL

SEVEN DIALS

First published in Great Britain in 2023 by Seven Dials
an imprint of The Orion Publishing Group Ltd
Carmelite House, 50 Victoria Embankment
London EC4Y 0DZ

An Hachette UK Company

1 3 5 7 9 10 8 6 4 2

A CIP catalogue record for this book is
available from the British Library.

ISBN (Hardback) 9781474609746
ISBN (eBook) 9781474609760
ISBN (Audio) 9781409180876

Typeset by Input Data Services Ltd, Bridgwater, Somerset

Printed in Great Britain by Clays Ltd, Elcograf S.p.A.

MIX
Paper from
responsible sources
FSC® C104740

www.orionbooks.co.uk

In memory of Steve Docherty and Rob Llewelyn.

Contents

Abbreviations

AFLD: *Agence française de lutte contre le dopage*, French anti-doping agency

AIGCP: International Association of Professional Cycling Teams

CAS: Court of Arbitration for Sport in Lausanne, Switzerland

CERA: Continuous Erythropoiesis Receptor Activator, third-generation EPO

CNCDD: *Comité Nacional de Competición y Disciplina Deportiva*, the competent body for doping matters within the RFEC

CONI: *Comitato Olimpico Nazionale Italiano*, Italian Olympic Committee

Cyclistes professionnels associés, Association of Professional Cyclists

CSD: *Consejo Superior de Deportes*, Spain's national sports council

EPO: recombinant erythropoietin (the laboratory-produced version of the hormone that triggers production of red blood cells)

ESADE: *Escola Superior d'Administració i Direcció d'Empreses*, Higher School of Business Administration and Management

Federazione Ciclistica Italiana, Italian Cycling Federation

FMSI: *Federazione Medico Sportiva Italiana*, Italian Sports Medical Federation

GC: general classification

IESE: *Instituto de Estudios Superiores de la Empresa*, a business school attached to the University of Navarre in Pamplona

IGF-1: Insulin-like Growth Factor-1

IMF: International Monetary Fund

IMIM: *Institut Municipal d'Investigació Mèdica*, part of the Hospital del Mar in Barcelona

NAS: *Nucleo Antisofisticazione e Salute*, the food and medicine unit in the Public Health Command of the Italian Carabinieri

RFEC: *Real Federación Española de Ciclismo*, Royal Spanish Cycling Federation

SECOMA: *Sección de Consumo y Medio Ambiente*, the Consumption and Environment Section of the Guardia Civil

TUE: Therapeutic Use Exemption

UCI: *Union cycliste internationale*, International Cycling Union

UCO: Guardia Civil's Central Operational Unit

Ufficio di Procura Antidoping – Comitato Olimpico Nazionale Italiano, the office of CONI's anti-doping prosecutor

USADA: United States Anti-Doping Agency

Epigraph

Books. Don't buy them without advice from a Catholic of real knowledge and discernment. It's so easy to buy something useless or harmful.

Josemaría Escrivá de Balaguer y Albás,
The Way, Aphorism 339

You never knew our previous commander nor are you acquainted with the society within which his thoughts took shape; you're limited to seeing the world through the eyes of a well-educated European, all caught up within the web of liberal democratic ideology . . .

Franz Kafka, 'In the Penal Colony'

Introduction

Rare Bird

There is a theory that living in a world entirely made or modified by humans, with human purposes constantly reflected back at us, has changed the way our brains work, allowing the left hemisphere, which breaks reality down into abstractions and sees only what it sets out to, to take over. The many crises of our age – the climate emergency and mass extinction, but also urban gridlock, the obesity epidemic, the scramble for resources, and our own inability to discern other, better ways of living – may be the direct consequences.

I sometimes think that cycling, and the immersion in nature and the landscape it makes possible, is a form of last-gasp self-medication, despite the bike itself being a mechanical, left-hemisphere sort of creation, and the tendency, even outside the professional sport, to talk about cycling in left-hemispheric terms: VAMs and VO2 maxes, watts per kilo, metabolomic pathway analyses, and so on.

Perhaps, to generations who feel they have lost control over their lives – to whom all these crises make tomorrow seem so uncertain – numbers, data, statistics seem to promise something you can depend on. At such times, Alejandro Valverde, *Bala* (not a lame journalistic invention but common usage, short for *Bala verde*, the green bullet, from the breathtaking velocity of his sprint and the identical pronunciation of *b*s and *v*s in most varieties of Spanish) meets a need.

1

His career stats would be impressive in any sport. Take that prestigious trio of races clustered every year around his birthday, 25 April: the Amstel Gold Race around Maastricht and the south-east corner of the Netherlands; the Flèche Wallonne, from Charleroi to the top of the Chemin des Chapelles in the town of Huy in central Belgium; and the convoluted odyssey through the hills from Liège to Bastogne and back a little further to the east. Titles every rider wants. Only Alejandro Valverde has triumphed in five Flèches Wallonnes, or stood on the podium after nine editions. With four Liège–Bastogne–Liège wins, he lies second on the all-time list, one short of the Cannibal himself, Eddy Merckx, although, in podium finishes, Valverde, with seven, is Merckx's equal. At the Amstel Gold Race, Eddy outshines Ale with two victories in a race Valverde never won, having had to settle for second place in 2013 and 2015, and third in 2008. Even so, Bala's total of nineteen podiums in all of the Ardennes classics makes him Merckx's superior, Eddy having accumulated, in his remarkable career, 'only' fifteen top-threes in the prestigious triptych.

Yet, to call Valverde, as we must, one of the very best classics riders in cycling history, barely begins to describe him. His skillset was so complete that, on his day, as well as riding away from the purest climbers (Roberto Heras, Denis Menchov, Carlos Sastre) in the mountains, and limiting his losses to the great time trial specialists (and not all of the eight time trials he won in his career were uphill), he could even, at the end of a hard race, beat the best sprinters (Erik Zabel, Stuart O'Grady, Oscar Freire, Tom Boonen) on the flat. This made any bonus seconds on offer at stage finishes as good as his, which in turn made him a master of one-week racing, as three Voltas a Catalunya, two Critériums du Dauphiné and a Vuelta al País Vasco prove. In the stage races closest to his home town of Murcia, the Vuelta a Murcia itself and the Vuelta a Andalucía, he holds the outright record with five overall wins in each, while at the nearby Volta a la Comunitat Valenciana he is the joint record holder with three.

In the great three-week tours, his record is equally remarkable. True, he won only one Grand Tour title, at the Vuelta Ciclista a España in 2009, but, by finishing third in the 2015 Tour de France, and again at the 2016 Giro d'Italia, he became one of only twenty riders in cycling history to have made the podium in all three Grand Tours. Rummage more deeply among the statistics and you find that, of all the professional cyclists who have ever lived, only Bala has finished twenty Grand Tours in the top ten. Twelve of these were his home tour, the Vuelta a España, a record for that race. Ten of his Vuelta top-tens were also top-fives (also a record), and seven of these were podium finishes (that 2009 win plus three second places and three thirds – another record).

That said, he admitted, 'Three-week races are punishing. They mean a lot of days at your maximum, staying focused. I always end up having one bad day. I'm at my best in one-week or one-day races.'

Anything the numbers fail to convey, the comparison with Merckx makes clear: Alejandro Valverde was not just extravagantly gifted as a competitive cyclist but an all-time great – in the estimation of the statistics website procyclingstats.com, the seventh greatest cyclist in history.

Having said all that, Bala himself has always been averse to numbers. He says he only ever knew his win total because other people were always banging on about it on social media. In another context, where technology allows riders to know their power output in real time, he has always preferred riding on sensation.

He is living proof that there are more forms of wisdom than the left-brain hemisphere is ready to admit. However we try to fix it in data sets, the world never stops changing, and that applies to the past too. The moment we stop revising our conclusions is the moment we give up trying to make sense of the world. Any reader of Franz Kafka knows this. In one of his short stories, the inhabitants of an impossibly remote village in China suffer a strange confusion of present and past, mistaking the latest news from the outside world for ancient history, while filling their daily gossip with tales of long-ago abominations. In Kafka's telling, the journey from the capital to the furthest ends of the empire takes so long that proclamations issued centuries before by long-dead emperors are delivered as if published the previous day – a bewildering perspective, but a strangely familiar one. Kafka was writing before the age of live feeds and rolling news, yet he captures our experience rather vividly. By teatime every day, the morning headlines sometimes feel like the remote past. At the same time, the mass of granular detail buries the broad arc of history, making it almost impossible to make sense of the present. In a wider perspective, today's audacious interpretations make the past more fascinating than ever. You never know what's going to happen there.

Early in Kafka's unfinished novel *The Trial*, the protagonist, Josef K., whose full name we never know, faces detention for reasons that are never made clear. He rushes back to his room to look for his identification papers, but all he can find is his bicycle licence. Bala too spent his long career struggling to preserve his freedom to roam. And he too was a kind of genius. Like a violinist who thinks with the fingers, the bow, and the feedback loop of sound created and sound perceived, or a potter, whose thoughts are formulated by the hands, the wheel, the clay itself, the athlete's mind unifies brain, body and equipment – ball, bat, bike – in what has been called the distributed mind.[1] Bala was a brilliant exponent.

He was an author of sorts too, although the paradoxes, riddles, accusations, unfinished narratives and mind-bending differences of interpretation that characterise Kafka's tales, were not for him. Rather, Bala was a virtuoso in the neat, self-contained, zero-sum narratives that fill the sports pages: the hopeful start, the tactical choices, the decisive move, the concluding joy or sorrow of triumph or defeat. But both dealt in long time spans. By his retirement at the end of 2022, Valverde, born in 1980, resembled a swift-heeled emissary from another era.

Mind, if Kafka had written about characters as warm, helpful, polite, empathic and uncomplicated, as well adjusted, as Bala, he would have been a different writer. Attached to his family and roots, unchanged by success, a perpetual child for whom cycling, that most punishing of sports, always remained a form of play, magnanimous in victory, generous in defeat, liked and admired in the peloton, an inveterate prankster, a leader and, above all, a winner, Valverde is almost as far from Kafka and his cast of over-complicated masters of confusion and missed opportunities as it is possible to imagine. His destiny might even have been determined by his character.

His extraordinary freedom from debilitating rumination had the proportions of a superpower. Instead of agonising over his failure to win the Tour de France, Bala regarded his 2015 podium finish as one of his finest achievements. After defending his third place on the climb to Alpe d'Huez on the penultimate stage, before the Spanish radio reporters who used to swarm him like bees on every finish line, he wept, 'I've been chasing this all my career. I've done it at last.'

With them, and with everyone who interviewed him down the years, Valverde was almost unfailingly patient, attentive and amusing, even as he caught his breath. Self-deprecating, too. Discussing his greatest one-day rival, Paolo Bettini, before the 2008 world championships, he admitted: 'If we finish together, I can beat him. The problem is, he's so switched on when he races. Much more than me.'

Or consider this exchange from a recent documentary film in which Bala appears alongside multiple Grand Tour winners Pedro Delgado and Miguel Indurain. Delgado, now an accomplished broadcaster, asks him a characteristically thoughtful question:

DELGADO: We were three-week specialists, and in our day it was said that you had to arrive with the desire to win. We absolutely had to, whereas you always arrive having already taken your quota of classics and stage wins. I wonder if you start the three-week tour season with the feeling that you have already met your obligations, without the sensation we used to have that it was all or nothing.

VALVERDE: Now you say that, it's possible. For instance, in this Vuelta a España [2018] I won two stages in the first week. At the time, I wasn't planning to compete for the overall, but when you see yourself up there, you start fighting for it. But it is true that, in the last week, when you have to give everything, the people who are really fighting for the GC [general classification] have something extra that I don't, and when the suffering starts, I find I can't do it and I come off the gas. And when you come off the gas, it's over.

It is hard to think of another fabulously successful sportsman so frank about his shortcomings, or so open to speculation about the content of his unconscious. And he still finished fifth.

Or take that pre-2008 worlds interview, in which, after comparing himself to Bettini, he admitted: 'When you are always chasing so many objectives, you get distracted over the course of three weeks, and you lose focus . . . What I have to do is identify a single goal, focus only on that and forget about everything else.'[2]

The implication was that he would find it difficult.

Another dimension of his psyche is suggested by the nude photoshoot he took part in for *Interviú* magazine in 2003, the hair implant in 2015, more naked photography the following year for *Quo* magazine, and the pet parrot he named Figura ('star', 'celebrity') and trained to repeat the words 'champion' and 'handsome' at him. But name anyone as successful in their field who is free of vanity. And Bala's is not of the arrogant variety.

His sense of place is well known. He belongs in his home town, Murcia, 400 kilometres south-east of Madrid, 200 kilometres south-west of Valencia, like a rare bird endemic to a single habitat. He complains about the tax rate – 'an outrage, forty-something per cent' – but he has never been tempted to look abroad for a tax haven. 'I've thought about going to Andorra to pay less tax, but in the end I don't want to leave here, I want to stay in Murcia.

'My parents still live in [the village of] Las Lumbreras where I was born. I live six or seven kilometres away. Becoming famous or better known abroad has never been an incentive for me. This is where I feel most comfortable and that's how I perform best. It's the same reason I don't leave Murcia for Andorra. I need to be in my environment. Here is my family, the best climate, and my training group.'

There is wisdom in his recognition that he already has what he needs to be happy and at his athletic best.

Yet Murcia is the subject of mockery in other parts of Spain. The Murcian yokel, whose speech other characters find incomprehensible, is a stock character in Spanish stand-up and comic sketches. A talk show host recently elicited applause from his studio audience when a guest suggested he had a hint of Murcian in his voice, and he retorted, quick as a flash, 'A Murcian accent? Please. That's worse than an STD.'[3]

Indeed, a nickname that attached itself to him when he was a junior, *Torrente* ('torrent' or 'flood'), seems to derive from the relentless flow of his energy until you discover it comes from *Torrente, el brazo tonto de la ley* ('Torrente, the Stupid Arm of the Law'), a 1998 comic movie of questionable taste in which the main character, Torrente, is a sort of overweight Spanish counterpart to *The Naked Gun*'s Frank Drebin. A sequence in Movistar Team's advertorial film series *The Least Expected Day* (the editor might have labelled it 'Bala breaks wind in car') suggests that Bala shares Torrente's toilet humour. The team's

Latin American sponsors found the episode offensive, although the public explanation is simply that their speaking voices bear a certain similarity.

More concrete matters distance Murcia from the rest of Spain. Many local families have interests in the production of grapes, citrus and stone fruit. Yet the arid plain on which the city stands, the so-called *Huerta de Murcia* (literally, the Murcian orchard or vegetable patch), depends for its irrigation on major engineering projects. While Murcians regard water as a right, outsiders struggle to understand the madness of trying to grow fruit in a desert.

But Bala has never sounded defensive. If cordiality is a virtue in a public figure, as it surely is, he deserves public recognition. He received it in May 2018 when Murcia city council made him an *Hijo Predilecto* (favourite son). He was, said the nomination, 'an ambassador for Murcia, which, as his homeland, has been present in every headline, interview or event in which he has been the protagonist'.

His training group – as Bala calls it, his *grupeta murciana* – is his court: a bunch of friends, some professional cyclists (José Luis Martínez, Eloy Teruel), others amateur (his brother Juan Francisco, José the barber), his physiotherapist, Juan Carlos Escámez, and others who gather outside Murcia's Iglesia del Carmen, just south of the river, opposite the Floridablanca Garden to ride with him. On a typical day Alejandro rolls up with his Guardia Civil escort and an hour or so already in his legs. From there, they might ride to Señor Ángel's snack-bar in Librilla, 25 kilometres south-west of Murcia, for elevenses of *jamón* on toast, before intervals on the climbs of the Sierra Espuña 20 kilometres further on, and then a food stop at Alhama de Murcia on the way home. Such straightforward routines gave him four years as the world's number one rider, one as world number two, two more as world number three, and one each as numbers four and five.

His athletic longevity is revered too. Midway through his career, beaten by the veteran Chris Horner into second place in the final time trial and the overall classification of the 2010 Vuelta al País Vasco (Tour of the Basque Country), Valverde commented, 'This year he has been very strong. I hope I'm riding like that when I'm 38.'[4]

He was: in 2018, at the same age, he won the mountain stage of the UAE Tour; a stage, the points standings and the overall classification at the four-day Route d'Occitanie; and two stages and the points classification at the Vuelta a España, before going to Innsbruck for his tenth road world championships. It was likely to be his last chance, and the course, with a punishing ascent and a long, fast finishing straight, suited him perfectly. After nearly seventeen years at the very highest level, he had already won six world championship medals, two silver, four bronze – two more medals than any other rider in history – and had never finished outside the top ten. The question was, would his long history of near misses impair his judgement?

Two hundred and forty-nine punishing kilometres ridden, nine more to come, and the road tilts skywards. Romain Bardet, twice a podium finisher in the Tour de France, makes a jolting acceleration. The former track and field star Michael Woods, the WorldTour's only four-minute miler, continues the move. Only one other rider can follow: Bala, 38 years, five months, and counting, but still with the hunting instincts of a wolf. Approaching a tight left-hand bend, five kilometres from the finish line, he drifts to the front, partly for safety – these corners require good positioning – and partly to ensure that the chaser, the Dutchman Tom Dumoulin, will have to expend valuable energy if he is to rejoin them. Dumoulin finally bridges across with 1.6 kilometres to go. Woods responds with a testing change of pace. Then, with 1,300 metres remaining, Bala takes over. There are four riders in the move now, and only three medals, and, as the fastest finisher among them, it is Bala's race to lose, a thought he must banish.

Approaching the *flamme rouge* marking one kilometre to go, he positions himself beside the right-hand barrier so that the attacks can only come from one side, using all the expertise he acquired at the other end of his career, when, as an eighteen-year-old track sprinter, already the Spanish champion in the kilometre, he travelled to Havana, Cuba, for the 1998 world junior track championships. Combining endurance events with sprinting even then, he finished seventh in the team pursuit and eighth in the kilometre, proving his versatility, although his real genius, it was clear, lay in road racing.

Every second and a half he glances back. Dumoulin's attack comes just before his fourth look, but Bala sees it early and, rising out of the saddle, unleashes a burst of speed. The Dutchman has no choice but to desist. Tired after his solitary chase, Dumoulin knows now that he will not be the 2018 world road champion. Over the next fifty seconds, Bala, still hugging the barrier, looks over his shoulder no fewer than fifteen times. It is the supreme demonstration of the racer's art.

In the post-race interview, he says, 'It was a very long sprint. They left all the responsibility to me. When there were three hundred metres to go, I said to myself, "It's my distance. Full gas to the finish line."'

Much later, he reflected, 'In the heat of the moment, you are trying to keep as calm as possible. I knew I had started my sprint early, but, when I see it on TV now, I think, "It's far *too* early." I'm more nervous watching it on TV than I was at the time. All the years of your sporting life pass in a second.'

It was the 123rd win of his career as a professional cyclist. Only one world champion has been older: Joop Zoetemelk, the Dutchman, five months Bala's senior.

With his new world title, Bala was often paired up for TV interviews with a fellow Murcian, the Supersport 300 world champion Ana Carrasco, the first woman to win a solo motorbike world title. The social networks shook with laughter because 'Murcians talk funny', although the telling detail came on the evening of his victory, when the teammates who had supported him broke the strict diet of the elite endurance athlete by ordering celebratory hamburgers and chips. When they tried to tempt the new world champion into doing the same, he just said, 'I don't like burgers', and carried on with his customary plate of rice.

The discipline is as deeply engrained in him as his self-knowledge and imperturbability. These are undoubtedly the personal attributes that permitted him to cope with the pressures associated with his position in Spanish sport, under which those rather confected records and deceptively simple sporting narratives readily deconstructed themselves into something less composed. After all, his impressive career statistics were achieved despite missing the 2009 Tour de France, having his results from the first four months of 2010 wiped out, and then being suspended for the rest of 2010 and the whole of 2011, during the part of his sporting life when he might have been at his strongest.

His problems could be said to have begun on Wednesday 24 March 2004, when the Spanish sports daily *As* (the word means 'ace') published the first instalment of a long interview with one of Bala's ex-teammates, the former Kelme-Costa Blanca rider Jesús Manzano, who explained the team's internal doping system in greater detail than could possibly have been invented by someone with no professional pharmacological training, even if the Spanish Cycling Federation and Higher Sports Council somehow professed to find him unconvincing, and a perfunctory investigation dismissed his allegations.

Even so, two years later, Manzano's confession led to a small surveillance operation surrounding a doctor well known in Spanish cycling. The mission, codenamed *Operación Puerto* ('Operation Mountain Pass'), eventually spawned several huge investigations, revealing what looked like a Spanish national blood-doping programme with inbuilt deniability.

When the doctor, Eufemiano Fuentes, was finally arrested on 23 May 2006, the only unambiguous name found among his personal effects was Valverde's, written in longhand beside four abbreviations, Ale, Manc, Vino and Popo – not that it took a genius – on the back of a Silken Hotels business card tucked inside a black leather wallet. The Hotel Puerta de Madrid, which belongs to the chain, remains a popular overnight stopover with cyclists and cycling journalists.

Among nearly a hundred blood bags stored inside a freezer in the doping doctor's apartment, a bag containing plasma was found marked with the number '18'. Two documents found in the same residence gave a list of codenames: the number 18 corresponded to 'VALV. (Piti)'. A newspaper article about Bala appeared mentioning a dog that he called Piti. The suspicion that enveloped him could have been dispelled in an instant with a DNA test, but Valverde's legal team spent years fighting to ensure it never took place, which spoke volumes.

Even so, in the twenty-thousand-word case summary submitted before the 2006 Tour de France to competitive cycling's world governing body, the *Union cycliste internationale* (UCI), the French Minister of Sport Jean-François Lamour and the race organisation, he went unmentioned. Nor did his name appear anywhere in the 360-page sentence issued after the Operación Puerto trial in April 2013, or the eighty-four pages of the appeal court judgment in June 2016, more than ten years after the investigation began. Nor, indeed, in any of the eleven thousand pages that made up the thirty-six volumes of the investigation and the eight folders of annexes containing the documentary evidence – phone records, diaries, doping calendars and other exhibits. He was as absent as the footballers, boxers, tennis players and track and field stars whom Fuentes also claimed to be treating.

Operación Puerto dragged on and on from its 2006 inception. Judicial proceedings officially started two years and two months after Manzano's revelations, on 10 May 2006. The trial instructions were issued two years and eight months later, on 30 January 2009. That summer, the Tour de France director Christian Prudhomme complained that Operación Puerto continued to 'contaminate the sport four years after its beginning'. But it had barely started.

The DNA test eventually took place on 2 February 2009. It proved that the plasma was Valverde's. After the sports system handed him a nineteen-month worldwide suspension from May 2010 to January 2012, resentment might have consumed him. Instead, he came back as good as before, if not better, and, in any case, months before 31 July 2012, when the judge finally began hearing evidence in the criminal case built around Operación Puerto. The trial of Eufemiano Fuentes and associates finally took place from 28 January to 2 April 2013. By then, one of the accused had succumbed to Alzheimer's disease and another had taken his own life. Before sentencing at the end of April 2013, the legal teams representing the accused asked for the excessive duration of the investigation to be taken into consideration.

The purely legal considerations left many questions unanswered. If bag eighteen contained plasma, the clear, liquid part of the blood, what had happened to the corresponding red cells, the part of the blood that delivers oxygen to the muscles and improves athletic performance? It was not hard to imagine. But it would also be illuminating to know what passed through Valverde's mind in 2006 when he learned, first, that Fuentes had kept one of his blood bags from two years before, and, second, that it was now in the hands of the police.

Why did he think Fuentes hadn't destroyed the blood bags, and the documents that mentioned it? Did he imagine that the doctor thought of it as a form of insurance policy: if Bala is protected, I am protected; if I go down, Bala comes with me? Or did he suspect that Fuentes kept it as material proof of his own importance, as the chemical assistant of the world's best cyclist?

I never got the chance to ask.

Cards on the table: I worked for Movistar Team briefly, from late 2015 to early in 2016. It did not end well. In May 2015, in Sanremo, the first stage finish at the Giro d'Italia, Juan Pablo Molinero, one of the managers of Abarca Sports, the company which runs Movistar Team, offered me a job. No one outside Spain wrote about Movistar Team, he said. I spoke Spanish, I knew and got on with their stage race leader, Nairo Quintana, second in the 2013 and 2015 Tours de France, and victorious in the 2014 Giro. I was known and liked (half-right) and I could give the team something it sorely needed: accessibility. It made sense.

I had other reasons to accept the offer. Despite spending much of my time speculating about riders' motives, I had no personal experience of team culture. In this sense, I found the distancing required by journalistic ethics to be partly self-defeating. In addition, given the likelihood that Nairo, the world's most prominent sportsman of indigenous heritage, would win the Tour soon, it was a unique opportunity. It was also true that, to someone who has preferred whim to financial responsibility as the star to guide him through life, the chance of a company pension had its attractions. So, after months of emails back and forth, I called twenty years' worth of freelance clients to let them know I was no longer available, and joined Movistar Team as *chef de presse*.

In November 2015, at the pre-season training camp in Pamplona, the newcomers – two Spanish neo-pros, an experienced Colombian, and me – were instructed to put on a kind of tunic and an item of headwear resembling a serviette knotted in each corner, stand on a stool, introduce themselves to the room and make everyone laugh. When my turn came, after several adolescent anecdotes, I thought that an audience who spent a lot of its time on a team bus might appreciate a clever Bob Monkhouse gag that had gone round after his demise. It had the additional virtues of brilliance and brevity: 'When I die, I hope I go peacefully, in my sleep, like my father, not screaming in terror like his passengers.'

Not a titter.

A few minutes later, a number of riders and staff patted my shoulder gently and said, 'So sorry about your father.'

I should have known then.

At no point in our negotiations had Bala been mentioned. Even so, at that pre-season gathering, I found him to be one of those instinctively helpful people who open doors when your hands are full and pick things up when you have dropped them, always with a smile. A pleasure to be around. And prompt, too. In advance of the media day, I handed each rider an intricate timetable of his press obligations the following day, conceived to allow three dozen journalists some quality time with two dozen cyclists. Then everyone headed into Pamplona for the only dinner of the year where the entire team ate together. Food was followed by a night on the tiles. Riders were still returning to the hotel at five and six o'clock in the morning. My detailed schedule was history before it even started. Some riders disappeared completely the following day. Not Bala: he was in the gym at 7.30 a.m. and the hotel lobby in good time for his 9.15 a.m. press conference, dressed, breakfasted, beaming. He ran the show himself, as always.

Before starting the job, I had not asked for, but had been given (and I quote) 'absolute autonomy' in a number of areas. In practice, one press proposal that met with my approval ran contrary to Abarca's 'global strategy'. Another, I learned a few days later, clashed with 'company policy'. Later still, I was informed of a 'special agreement' that limited photographers' access to the riders and made a third project impossible. Furious, I demanded the exact wording of all three novel protocols in twenty-four hours. I probably left them with no alternative. I was convened for a meeting at a Madrid hotel. My team BlackBerry had been disconnected before my buttocks touched the chair. Before they left it, I had no job, no clients and no income. After five months in the job, I left Movistar for one of the older age group niches in the modern precariat.

But the question still stood: why was no one outside Spain writing about the team? Part of it was the same reason I came unstuck.

Spain is different. It is not a land of ponderous philosophical systems like Germany or France, or the industrial revolution, like Britain, but a place of mystics, poets, plaintive flamenco and painters who stare into the abyss. If its geniuses are from long ago – Seneca, Averroes, Cervantes, Velázquez, the architects of Granada and Seville – more recently it has given the world novelists, filmmakers and architects, even if much of the outside world thinks only of blue skies so reliable, they merit the tourist slogan 'Everything Under the Sun'.

It is a land of empty spaces traversed by deserted roads, and of different species of silence: calm, like the quiet of its hidden coves and beaches; contemplative, like the meditations of its pilgrims; windswept, like the landscapes of Don Quixote's windmills; tense, as in the moment before the striker of one of its great football teams takes a penalty; knowing, like the agreements between politicians and functionaries who abuse public power for private gain; duplicitous, like the furtive signs between the members of secretive organisations; deathly, like the unmarked mass graves of the Franco era.

The holidaymaker on the beach, the student in the library or art gallery, the foreign employee in his first months working for a Spanish cycling team, cannot tell these silences apart, if he notices them at all.

According to one of the most dogged investigators into corruption in Spain, Operación Puerto fits a pattern. In his monumental book *El fango: Cuarenta años de corrupción en España* ('Dirt: Forty years of corruption in Spain'), the former magistrate

Baltasar Garzón writes, 'No one has ever been afraid to be corrupt in Spain. As something that has always been taken as read, corruption has not traditionally bothered the average citizen. This indifference has allowed its roots to grow deep and solid, and to sustain a structure of interests that is very difficult to bring down.'[5] In Garzón's view, the justice system has contributed to this situation. 'Judgments that are laid down after long years of delay [accompanied by] laughable sentences, incomprehensible dismissals or shelving of cases, unacceptable collusions and connivance . . .'

But corruption is not always about power and self-enrichment. For the vulnerable, it can be a necessary survival mechanism. And if, as the neuroscientists assure us, we perceive the world not as it is, but as it is useful to us,[6] such accommodations are not necessarily conscious. Certainly, the Church offered the followers of the dictator Franco a religion that saw behind every sin its imminent forgiveness, and behind every sinner, punctual redemption, as if the trespass was the necessary portal allowing grace to enter our lives, and was therefore to be welcomed.

It is caricature, of course, as always when part of a culture is taken for the whole. Pat McQuaid, the president of cycling's world governing body, the Union cycliste internationale, did this in January 2007 when, in connection with Operación Puerto, he spoke of a clash in the fight against doping between two cultures, the Anglo-Saxon and the 'mafia Western European'.[7] The latter 'accept certain practices', he said, 'because of the way they deal with everything else in life'.

McQuaid concluded, 'It is very important that at the end of the day the Anglo-Saxon approach wins out, because if it doesn't, then the sport is doomed.'

In a newspaper article that appeared during the 2012 Tour de France, in a slightly different context, Bradley Wiggins weighed in with, 'I don't care what people say, the attitude to doping in the UK is different to in Italy or France.'[8]

His column appeared the day David Millar, post-suspension, won the stage. It was the forty-fifth anniversary of Tom Simpson's death on Mont Ventoux after mixing alcohol and amphetamines. And it is worth remembering the final report of a British parliamentary inquiry in March 2018 ('Combatting doping in sport'):

> [I]n 2012, we believe that th[e] powerful corticosteroid [triamcinolone] was being used to prepare Bradley Wiggins, and possibly other riders supporting him, for the Tour de France. The purpose of this was not to treat medical need, but to improve his power to weight ratio ahead of the race ... [W]e believe that drugs were being used by Team Sky, within the WADA rules, to enhance the performance of riders, and not just to treat medical need.[9]

Every nation believes it is alone in having a sure grasp on reality, and laughs at foreigners for thinking differently. And, since the culture we inherit through the accident of birth supplies us with intuitions about what we can get away with, every country has its own preferred forms of corruption. To take one example, the *Financial Times* hoped in March 2022 that Putin's attack on Ukraine would bring to an end 'the warm home the British establishment and its financial system provide for dirty money from the post-Soviet sphere and elsewhere'. So this book makes no attempt to score nationalistic points.

In any case, the most active and enterprising anti-doping authorities during the twenty years after 1990 were not Anglo-Saxon. Operación Puerto was discovered by diligent Spanish detectives, and taken up by the Italian Carabinieri who, armed with a full-blooded national anti-doping law since December 2000, listened in to telephone calls, tapped email accounts and pursued far-reaching anti-doping investigations. It was an Italian investigation that caught Alejandro Valverde, and, as we will see, Spanish–Italian cooperation that led to the downfall of Lance Armstrong.

*

That said, of all sports, cycling has no choice but to ingratiate itself with the politicians, local, regional and national. At the top of the cycling pyramid, the annual three-week tours, though privately owned, perform a quasi-diplomatic role for their host nations of Italy, France and Spain. Heads of state and industry appear beside race directors, and great cities offer the international peloton the freedom of their streets. In the best of times, they showcase their nations' towns, villages, landscapes and transport infrastructure. In the worst of times, they have a state-recognised role in relaunching the national economy, as we saw in the aftermath of the Covid-19 lockdowns.

Lower down, the sheer inconvenience of town-centre starts and road closures obliges public bodies to weigh the unavoidable costs against the benefits of a day of euphoria as cycling's international roadshow comes to town. It has plenty going for it: even without the influx of outsiders, their purse strings loosened by the holiday atmosphere, the competitors alone are numerous enough to provide local hotels and restaurants, whose proprietors invariably constitute an influential lobby, with an overnight bonanza. By granting nearby beauty spots a few seconds of airtime, television coverage promises local tourism a boost. The decision makers get their moment on the post-race podium, handing out the prizes, reflecting the race winner's glory. If the photograph makes the next day's papers, all the better.

In sporting matters, then, the dividing line between the state and the private sector can easily blur, without much damage being done. But sport can get too close to politics, and this book explores some examples of what can go wrong when it does, including circumstances where sports sponsorship was used to distract attention away from bad behaviour, years before the word 'sportswashing' had ever been coined.

As for Bala, was he Chance the Gardener, walking on water between the powerbrokers and the delinquents, oblivious to the rapacity, the dishonesty, the lack of principle? Or was he part of the conspiracy – and not just part, but at its very heart?

Five years after my Movistar adventure, two cycling magazines, the British publication *Procycling* and the wonderful Italian monthly *Alvento*, asked me to interview Bala for retrospective features. I bumped into him on the way to a race – the Abu Dhabi Tour in February 2021, I think – and, obliging as ever, he said he would be happy to sit down with me. To set it up, I contacted his publicist, who passed my request on to the team, who never replied, much as expected.

With no interview, I could never write those retrospectives and earn the income they would have generated. Movistar, *mil gracias*. Instead, my research turned into this book. I started and finished it waiting for their response.

Given frank, honest, uninhibited input from Bala, it would no doubt be very different. Alejandro is the expert on his own story. Only he knows the perspectives within which he sees it. But how much openness could I have expected? Revising the entire press record, I have found not a syllable in which he meaningfully addresses the subject of his doping, beyond a few baffling exercises in uncoupling words from meanings ('We have to unite and say, "Thus far and no further"'; 'I believe the time will come when this will all be over'; 'Let's see if little by little we can change things'. It was not for lack of asking. Ettore Torri, the anti-doping prosecutor of the Italian Olympic Committee, lamented in frustration that Valverde and his lawyers refused, in any of their many encounters, to discuss any substantive details of the case, addressing only procedural matters.

So perhaps we overestimate the importance of the set-piece, sit-down interview. The danger lurks therein of writing an official, approved biography – and what would be the point of that? So, the quotations in this book come from media reports written at the time, or soon afterwards, unless otherwise stated.

As well as judgments and legal documents mentioned earlier, I have consulted the work of the following journalists, among others: Pablo de la Calle in *El Mundo*, José Carlos Carabias in *ABC*, Javier de Dalmases in *Mundo Deportivo*, José Andrés Ezquerro and Juan Gutiérrez in the pages of *As*, Fernando Llamas in *Marca*, and the reporters at the Murcian newspapers *La Verdad* and *La Opinión de Murcia*. I am gratefully indebted to all of them, and, especially, to the brilliant Carlos Arribas of *El País*. The reluctant but acute and meticulous chronicler of Operación Puerto (and the author of a biography of Luís Ocaña that may be the best cycling book ever written), Carlos's texts underlie every page of this work. I of course consulted him before starting: any intention on his part to write a book about either Alejandro Valverde or Operación Puerto would have made this one pointless in all ways except, perhaps, one: *El País* being part of the same economic bloc as Movistar's owner, the telecommunications colossus Telefónica,[10] its reporters may have a little less freedom to adopt an independent stance.

Of course, all errors in what follows are my own, whether of fact or of interpretation. And interpretation has to take into account the changing role of sport. No longer, almost a quarter of the way into the twenty-first century, a straightforward vehicle for Corinthian values, and far more complicated than war minus the shooting, it has everywhere become a testbed for ideas about values – selfishness and altruism, merit and chance, justice and freedom – that we explore in the suspended reality of sport, then put to use in our understanding of the world and ourselves; a central element in what is sometimes called the national conversation. And although we tend to be quite unaware of other countries' heroes and household names, many of them sporting creations, sport is also a means of intertwining national narratives and participating together in the international community. No wonder political entities everywhere strive to exploit these sentiments, and private sponsors pay to be associated with them.

1

The Wolf King

Monteagudo rises 150 metres over the *Huerta de Murcia* on which Spain's seventh largest city sprawls. In ancient times the pointed mountain offered farmers refuge from attack. In the twelfth century, Ibn Mardanīsh, the Wolf King, built a castle there to keep watch over Islamic *Mursiyah*, and found the spot so agreeable that he added a palace and moved his court there. Ibn Mardanīsh had his detractors, one of whom traced his name back to its supposed origins in the Latin word *merda*, but in 1165 one of his civil servants had a son who, as Ibn 'Arabi, became a great Sufi mystic and author, celebrated the Muslim world over. When the great cultural flowering of Al-Andalus was finally snuffed out, the conquering Christian king, Alfonso the Wise, made a present of the castle and palace to his wife, Violant of Aragón, although Ibn 'Arabi remained Monteagudo's most famous son until Alejandro Valverde, born in the Monteagudo hamlet of Las Lumbreras on 25 April 1980.

Today, a gigantic Christian statue uses the outcrop as a plinth. The *Cristo de Monteagudo*'s placid gaze, outstretched arms and commanding, 14-metre height suggest a town united in its faith. Look more closely and something like the opposite emerges. The serene face hides the strain of a long and bitter polemic.

The current incumbent of that eight-metre pedestal is not an ancient construction. Completed in 1951, at the height of the Franco regime, He replaced an even more imposing statue, 30 metres halo to foot, and 28 fingertip to fingertip, erected in the 1920s during Primo de Rivera's Country, Religion and Monarchy dictatorship. The Catholic press described it as 'the work of all the people of Murcia', although this is hard to square with the city's loyalty to the leftist Republic throughout the Civil War a few years later and the city council's decision to have it blown to smithereens in November 1936.

Victory in the Civil War by the Republic's enemies heralded a second coming, and it is the replacement monument that stands there these days, although now, as the old religions wane, camera drones buzz the *Cristo de Monteagudo* in the golden dawn, like wasps around a candy bar, catching the new-age vibe. As recently as 2010, a Murcian lawyer,[1] acting on behalf of the *Asociación Preeminencia del Derecho* (the 'Association for the Primacy of the Law'), demanded the statue's demolition on the grounds that it was incompatible with a non-confessional state. The court rejected his petition, ruling that 'symbols of a religious nature such as crucifixes, monuments or similar are not to be interpreted as representing intolerance towards non-believers'. So the statue remains, less a symbol of unity than a pointed means employed by one part of a divided community to force its convictions down the other half's throats, even if the contentious issue today is not religion but water.

Eight years older than Bala, Javier Moreno, a mathematician and science fiction author, grew up a few hundred yards away from him. As a child, Moreno told me, 'Almost everyone owned one or two small plots where vegetables and citrus fruits are grown, despite the lack of rainfall on the *Huerta de Murcia*, which depended on irrigation from a pipeline carrying water between the Tagus and Segura rivers.

'Water was always a crucial issue,' Moreno continued, 'and it aligned the population with the centre-right Partido Popular, which has always favoured more water pipes. During the Aznar government' – the eight years following 1996 – 'another pipeline from the Ebro river to the Segura was planned, although the Partido Popular lost the national elections in 2004 and the pipe was never built.'

Moreno explained the local geography to me. 'Monteagudo consists of three villages: Las Lumbreras, where Alejandro grew up, La Cueva, where I was born, and Monteagudo proper. They are what are called *pedanías* [peripheral rural dependencies] of Murcia. Although very close to each other, they are separate communities. There were people working outside the villages, but they weren't dormitory towns. Everyone knew each other, and each village had its own social life.

'That said, the villages are not structured around central squares and there are very few common areas. I say this because, outside the village festivals, community feeling left a lot to be desired. This individualism translated into a popular local expression: *Cada perrico se lame su pijico* – every dog licks its own genitals.

This individualism went hand-in-hand with a sort of structural economic corruption in the shape of clothing and shoe manufacturers employing homeworking seamstresses on black market wages. Moreno had relatives in the village who performed such work for local companies. This, in turn, fed an inability to develop a genuine Murcian identity, a common theme of discussion among the local intelligentsia.

'Our identity has been created by default,' says Juan José García Escribano, professor of sociology at the University of Murcia. 'We Murcians have nothing in common except what we don't have. In the early 2000s the things that united us were poverty and feelings of underdevelopment.'

In October 2007, as a new law was progressing through parliament in Spain requiring town councils to remove 'coats of arms, insignia, plaques and other objects or commemorations celebrating the military uprising, Civil War and repression under the Dictatorship', the Murcian authorities named a section of the city's new ring road Avenida ('Avenue') Miguel Indurain. Perhaps there was some relief to be had from the political feuding by honouring the five-time Tour winner from far-away Navarre.

After all, it came into effect in December 2007, the new law was largely ignored in Partido Popular strongholds like Murcia. In 2020, the region's Socialists complained, 'We still have fifty-six streets that celebrate military officers, dates in the Civil War or Franco's dictatorship.' The Civil War may have ended eighty years before but, in the minds of many, taking sides still mattered.

At the end of October 2018, a four-mile section of the N340 Alicante road heading north-east out of Murcia and passing through the three villages of Monteagudo, became Avenida Alejandro Valverde. Take it back into Murcia, bear left at the Homage to the Poets roundabout onto Avenida Miguel Indurain as far as the Alicante road, and you are in the neighbourhood known as Puente Tocinos. There, in 1973, a group of amateur cyclists founded the *Club de Ciclismo Puente Tocinos* and started organising bike events and races. Despite Murcia's unforgiving heat, the project snowballed.

Cycling in Spain was not much more than an amateur sport in those days, with small teams and modest aspirations. True, it had produced Federico Bahamontes in the 1950s, the historic Basque team Kas, founded in 1956, and the remarkable Luís Ocaña in the 1960s, although Ocaña had started cycling in France and his greatest victories, the 1973 Tour de France among them, had been with the French team Bic.

But when Luis Puig, a sports administrator from Valencia, became president of the Royal Spanish Cycling Federation (the *Real Federación Española de Ciclismo* or RFEC) in 1968, cycling had gained a dynamic leader. Mentalities changed and standards rose, although the nation's premier race, the Vuelta a España, with its poor accommodation and limited national resonance, still exhibited the country's underdevelopment. In

1979 its owners, the Bilbao-based, Spanish-language newspaper group *El Correo Español-El Pueblo Vasco*, threatened by the Basque separatist group ETA, abandoned it. Puig convinced a publicity agent and bullring manager called Enrique Franco, whose family owned a small advertising company called Unipublic, to take it on,[2] and the 1979 race went ahead, against all odds. When it reached Murcia, the Puente Tocinos club helped with the logistics. Juan Argudo, a protégé of Luís Ocaña, born, like him, in the village of Priego, near Cuenca, won the stage by eight minutes, twenty-seven seconds, after a 95-kilometre solo breakaway.

Puig and Franco were two of a number of strong characters who contributed to the sport's development. Santiago Revuelta, from Santander in Cantabria, founded the TEKA team in 1976 before becoming the president of the Spanish Association of Professional Cycling Teams; Javier Mínguez, a former domestique from Valladolid, and Víctor Cordero, a sports administrator from Gerona, created the Zor team in 1979. Cordero went on to become president of the International Association of Professional Cycling Teams (AIGCP), general director of the Vuelta a España and president of the International Association of Organisers (AIOCC), where he fought a long battle with the International Cycling Union. In 1980 Diego and José 'Pepe' Quiles, the owners of the shoe manufacturer Kelme, took over the Transmallorca-Flavia team, while Eusebio Unzue and José Miguel Echávarri, from Navarre, took the Reynolds team into the professional ranks. There had never been so many pro teams.

Even so, in a 2007 interview with *El Correo*, Víctor Cordero remembered the low esteem in which cycling was held in the early 1980s. 'Zor was one of the best teams in Spain but hotels didn't want us. After one stay, a hotel in Torremolinos sent us a letter to thank the riders for not stealing anything. Cycling was still very inward-looking. We didn't dare leave Spain.'[3]

Yet world-class riders gradually began to emerge: Marino

Lejarreta (with fifty-two victories in a professional career that started in 1979 and ran until 1992), Vicente Belda (twenty-six wins between 1978 and 1988) and Ángel Arroyo (eighteen wins between 1979 and 1989).

In 1983, Televisión Española decided to show the Vuelta[4] live for the first time, and the sport took a giant leap forward. With the support of a prominent radio journalist named José María García, whose hourly race reports were eagerly awaited every spring, Puig and Franco turned the Vuelta around.

'Then,' Cordero continued, 'Pedro Delgado arrived, and he changed everything.'

Delgado, born in Segovia in 1960, won the Vuelta in 1985 and 1989, and the Tour de France in 1988. Close on his wheel came his Reynolds, then Banesto teammate Miguel Indurain, who won the Tour every year between 1991 and 1995, with Giro d'Italia–Tour de France doubles in 1992 and 1993. Indurain ushered in a period of prosperity in which three big-budget teams, Banesto, ONCE and Kelme, became fixtures in the top races.

However, if Spanish cycling mirrored the country's progress from dictatorship to democracy, which began even before Franco's death on 20 November 1975, it was thanks to community initiatives like the Puente Tocinos club, which, by the end of the 1980s, was one of the best established in Spain. One of its former riders, Jesús Montoya, finished second in the 1992 Vuelta a España.

One of the club's founders was an assistant pharmacist at the Martínez Navarro pharmacy in Puente Tocinos named Antonio Serrano Oliva. He told me, 'Some years we held forty or fifty races a year: we organised the national women's championships and the national amateur championships.'

In 1990, one of the club's amateur members brought his son into the Martínez Navarro pharmacy. Juan Valverde was a truck driver who ran one of the many small packaging and transport firms in Monteagudo and the surrounding hamlets. His staple was distributing locally produced fruit and veg from Murcia's *Huerta*. When he was at home, he rode in the club's social rides. 'He was powerful, physically very strong, and he always did very well, even if they were events for veterans,' Antonio Serrano explained, 'hobby races, not official ones.'

Juan's eldest son, Juan Francisco, was one of the club's best young riders. Now Juan wanted to enrol his third born. Serrano remembers, 'When Juan came in, he said, "Antonio, turn him into a cyclist." Alejandro was quite chubby at the time, and I joked, "He'll have to cut down on his snacking first."'

Every telling of Alejandro's beginnings is different. In one version, as a small child on a tiny bike, he rode up and down the slope outside the house with such insistence that his father's training partners noticed, and commented, 'He never gets tired.' In another, he caught the cycling bug aged six, when his father bought him his first bike. In yet another, it was while watching the 1988 Tour de France on television. A fourth account says it was after Miguel Indurain's first Tour stage win, which makes it 1989, that he made his first outing on a blue MBK bike, aged nine, and rode a hundred kilometres.

Common to every version is the central role played by Juan Senior.

'My father is unique,' Alejandro says. 'I think that my ability to win races of all kinds is genetic, and it all comes from him' – although this cannot be strictly true. The mitochondria that make possible the physiological adaptation to endurance exercise are passed on down the maternal line, so his sporting talent is thanks as least as much to his mother, María Belmonte.

Antonio Serrano recalled, 'When he was starting off, we used to say, "With the restless temperament on his mother's side of the family, and the physical strength on his father's, he's going to be a phenomenon." And so it turned out.'

After leaving school he started vocational training in automotive and administrative studies, and passed his heavy goods vehicle test, so, if Bala had not succeeded in sport, he would probably have followed his father into truck driving.

But that was later.

Serrano took the boy and his father to the offices of the Murcian Cycling Federation that afternoon, helped them fill in the necessary forms, and Alejandro joined his first club. That the club's cycling school, which depended on the availability of volunteers and sponsorship, was dormant in 1990, did not prevent him from starting the inter-club race calendar in March. His first race was in Jumilla, 70 kilometres north of Murcia. Antonio Serrano says, 'I remember it well. His birthday was in April, so it was a month or so before it. He came into the pharmacy on the Monday: "How did you do?" "Second." "Wow, great result." And he says, "No, no, wait until next time. You'll see."'

His second race was around the town of Yecla, not far from Jumilla. Serrano recalls, 'His father came in the following Monday. "How did he do?" "He won." And he won the next one, and the next one, and the next. He was a winner, and he always has been.'

Riding sometimes for Puente Tocinos and sometimes for another local team, Santomera, he won in Cieza, 45 kilometres north-west of Murcia, in Torre Pacheco, the same distance southeast of Murcia, near the coast, and in Las Torres de Cotillas, 20 kilometres west of Murcia. Serrano says he did not lose another race for two years. It might have been three, or four, or five. In the *infantil* ranks, for thirteen- and fourteen-year-olds, the parents of other riders are said to have pleaded with him to let someone else win from time to time.

When he was ready to move up into the next age group, Manolo López, the director of Azulejos J. Ramos, the best local 'cadets' team for fifteen- and sixteen-year-olds, invited him to join.

López told me, 'I knew [his father] Juan because we went out riding together on Sundays. We went to watch Alejandro ride several times.' And, according to Manolo López, 'In his last year of *infantiles*' – as a fourteen-year-old – 'he didn't lose a race.'

Bala became known as *El Imbatido* ('the undefeated'), an epithet more suited to a boxer. He was soon being compared with Mariano Rojas, his predecessor as the best young Murcian rider. Rojas had had a brilliant amateur career, finishing third in the under-23 Circuito Montañés in Cantabria in 1993. There he caught the eye of Manolo Saiz, the director of the ONCE team, with whom he turned professional in 1994. In 1995 he was elected Best Sportsman in the Murcia Region.

Serrano told me, 'Mariano was very different from Alejandro: he would go out, attack – bam! – and win on his own. Alejandro was more conservative, but more of a winner. He'd stay in the group knowing he would win the sprint or, if there was a break-away, he would mark them and then beat them. Either way, he would win. Full stop. He had to win, come what may. That's how he's been all his life.'

Manolo López also worked with Mariano Rojas in the *juveniles* category and they remained close. He told me that Bala, aged fourteen or fifteen, went out to train with Rojas, at the start of his professional career, on the Pantano de Santomera circuit, a regular ride for which López had reference times. Valverde stayed with Rojas, who reported back to López, 'Keep your eye on him, Manolo. There is no one else like him.'

In 1995, at the age of fifteen, Valverde continued his cycling career with Azulejos J. Ramos alongside Mariano Rojas' cousin José Cayetano Juliá Cegarra.

The victories continued in his first year in the cadet category for 16- and 17-year-olds: he won the Murcian championship and the hill climbs at the Cresta del Gallo near Murcia, Montjuic in Barcelona, and, of course, at Monteagudo.[5]

'Azulejos J. Ramos riders won thirty-four of the thirty-six races we disputed,' López recalled. 'Alejandro won nineteen of them and his teammates won the rest.'

While Alejandro shone in the junior ranks, Mariano Rojas showed great potential among the professionals. In February 1995 he finished third in the Vuelta a Andalucía or Ruta del Sol. In May he finished fourth in the Midi Libre. The youngest starter in the Tour de France, he abandoned after a fall on the Tourmalet stage, in which he fractured a collarbone, while nineteenth overall.

In 1996 he broke his collarbone again in the time trial of the Dauphiné Libéré. After an operation to stabilise the fracture, with his second Tour and the Olympics on the horizon, he set off for the national championships. Soon after midday on Friday 22 June 1996, minutes away from home, his car collided head-on with a lorry. It was then sideswiped by another car. Two days later, at 5.30 a.m. on Sunday 24 June, in hospital in Murcia, Mariano Rojas died.

No one understands the dangers of the road like professional cyclists. Every one of them has a friend, relative or rival who lost their life on the road. Their community of the mind comprises the living and the dead. Bala knew that now.

Aged seventeen, riding against stronger opponents from further afield, he was no longer invincible. Still thickset, and with the overhanging thighs of a track sprinter, he could be beaten on the right terrain. One of his rivals, his future masseur Juan Carlos Escámez, recalled, 'He had a fat arse so he could be dropped on the climbs, although you had to attack on the steepest gradients and get rid of him before the sprint. If you finished together, you didn't stand a chance'.

Alejandro's father told him, 'If you don't stand out as a junior, then it's better to start thinking of your future and find something else to do.'

A member of the Spanish national team at the 1997 Donostia-San Sebastián road world championships, he had travelled north with two other future professionals: the tall, powerful Rubén

Plaza,[6] born in Alcoi and raised in Ibi, both in the province of Alicante, 1.91m tall, and the lightweight Xavier Florencio, a climber from Montroig, near Tarragona. In an important pre-world championships race, the Gipuzkoako Klasika 1997,[7] in the San Sebastián district of Egia, Bala took his biggest victory so far.

He reflected later, 'I had always achieved good results in the north, and I was very motivated. It was a supremely important victory, my first giant step. It made a name for me.'

Days later, at the world championship junior road race on 11 October, Italy's Crescenzo D'Amore won the sprint and the title. Benjamín Noval, who had finished third in the Gipuzkoako Klasika, was the best Spaniard, finishing tenth in the same time as the winner. Bala, ninety-sixth, finished 7 minutes 10 seconds down.

Even so, his adaptability was remarkable. He was called up both as a sprinter and as a team pursuiter for the world track championships, which took place in Cuba between 15 and 19 July 1998. Plaza finished fourth in the individual pursuit won by Bradley Wiggins. Bala lined up in the kilometre, where he finished eighth in a time of 1 minute 8.547 seconds. In the team pursuit, with Plaza, Unai Elorriaga and Pablo Fernández, he achieved a time of 4 minutes 31.290 seconds and finished seventh overall. Then, in a poorly drilled Olympic sprint trio, he finished eleventh in a time of one minute 6.741 seconds.[8]

Even so, victory in the 1997 Gipuzkoako Klasika earned him a move to the Banesto amateur team for 1999. Bala later recalled, 'We all wanted to sign up for Basque amateur teams because we felt that it was the only way to move up to the pros.'

He had not noticed that the Banesto team was not Basque at all but proudly Navarran. And, although his stay at Banesto Amateurs was brief, it brought him into contact with the team that would define his career. It lifted him out of schoolboy sport and brought him closer to the political and economic power that surrounded elite sport in Spain. His high-wire walk through the world of corrupt money and power had begun.

2

Two Teams

It was as a Banesto rider that Miguel Indurain had won five consecutive Tours de France between 1991 and 1995, two Giro d'Italias in 1992 and 1993, and time trial gold medals at the 1995 world championships and the 1996 Olympics. His story, and that of the Banesto cycling team, fill 130 pages of David García's official history, *Nuestro ciclismo, por un equipo* ('Spanish cycling as seen through a team'), although the team's proximity to political power is illustrated in just two words: Mariano Rajoy. The prime minister of Spain from 2011 to 2018 provided the introduction, writing, 'Delgado's achievements, like those of Indurain later, were celebrated in our country with the same intensity as football, the most popular sport. Which is to say that this team and its riders have played a major role in Spain's sporting history' – although, if sporting history is allowed to include the wider context, the picture is not so rosy. The word 'sportswashing' – using sport to divert attention away from reputationally damaging behaviour – would not be invented for twenty years, but it could have been coined for Banesto, although only long after the team's amateur beginnings in 1970 at Irurzun, 20 kilometres from Pamplona, the capital city of the Chartered Community of Navarre.

In 1974 the town's main employer, the INASA aluminium factory, owned by the US tin foil giant Reynolds, came in as the main sponsor and the team became Reynolds. So it remained when it joined Spanish cycling's boom by turning professional in 1980, and for the following seventeen years. It was for Reynolds that Ángel Arroyo finished second in the 1983 Tour de France, Pedro Delgado won it in 1988 and added the Vuelta a España in 1989. If the sponsorship lasted so long, it was perhaps because INASA's managing director, Juan García Barberena, had served on the town council at Abárzuza, the home town of one of the team's central figures, José Miguel Echávarri, a former professional rider who had ridden for Bic in 1969 alongside the Tour de France winners Jacques Anquetil and Lucien Aimar, and the future Tour director Jean-Marie Leblanc. In 1977 Echávarri had offered Reynolds the services of a Uruguayan sprinter named Héctor Rondón. Rondón won thirteen races for the team in 1978, and both men ended up staying – in Echávarri's case, until his retirement in 2008.

Echávarri managed the team in tandem with one of its former riders, Eusebio Unzue, who, although limited in physical ability, was said to have a special talent for reading a race. In 1975, at the remarkably young age of eighteen, Unzue took a sports director's licence and assumed the team's direction. Echávarri was creative by temperament and, it is said, progressive in his politics (even if, in one interview, he introduces an anecdote with, 'I remember the fear in Spain in 1982, when the Socialists won the elections . . .').[1] Unzue was rather right wing and of a sceptical disposition. But they made an extremely effective couple, referring to each other as the accelerator (Echávarri) and the brake (Unzue).

In 1980, as they embarked on the adventure of professionalism, they took on a coach named José Luís Pascua Píqueras, and, in 1983, they set off for the Tour de France with Ángel Arroyo and Pedro Delgado. Delgado took second place in three stages. Arroyo finished second overall. Afterwards, Echávarri joked, 'We went to the casino and had some beginner's luck.'

At the end of 1984 he let Pedro Delgado go. It was a terrible mistake. Delgado won the following year's Vuelta a España with his new team Seat-Orbea, which became Caja Rural-Orbea and finished second in the 1987 Tour de France.[2] But in 1988, riding for Reynolds again, Delgado launched Spanish cycling's growth period by winning the Tour de France. Success came at a price: between 1980 and 1989, INASA's sponsorship budget increased from 15 million pesetas (€90,000) to 300 million (€1.8 million), which meant it was spending more than 8 per cent of its entire turnover on publicity. A new sponsor was needed. As Unzue and Echávarri began their search, nearby Pamplona provided a unique network of contacts among the moneyed and the powerful, thanks to its place at the heart of a very Spanish institution.

Opus Dei ('the work of God') was founded in 1930 by an Aragonese priest named Josemaría Escrivá de Balaguer y Albás. Four hundred years after Calvin, Escrivá instructed his followers to serve God in their ordinary, everyday lives. Unlike Calvin, he targeted the political and economic elites, writing in his manifesto, a book of motivational aphorisms called *The Way*: 'You, a follower, like a sheep? You were born to be a leader' (aphorism sixteen).

Foreign translations of *The Way* sought to camouflage Escrivá's pro-Franco militantism. In the original, aphorism 145 makes explicit reference to the Spanish Civil War and Franco's siege of Madrid. It begins, 'The Madrid front. Twenty officers are enjoying noble and happy camaraderie . . .' then quotes one of their songs as heard by *un tenientillo* ('a young, aspiring officer'): 'I have no use for divided hearts. I give mine whole and not in parts.' The various English versions make the officers 'young men', turn the *tenientillo* into 'a boy', and either replace 'The Madrid front' with 'The battle front' or just leave it out.

Unsurprisingly, at the start of the Spanish Civil War in 1936, Escrivá fled Republican Madrid. He settled in Pamplona, and dispatched his followers to Spain's top Catholic universities to recruit students. In 1952 he founded the University of Navarre. Consistently ranked the best private university in Spain, it now has campuses in Pamplona, San Sebastián, Madrid, Barcelona, Munich and New York.

Escrivá's philosophy contains more than an element of ideological control. Aphorism 339 reads:

> Books. Don't buy them without advice from a Catholic of real knowledge and discernment. It's so easy to buy something useless or harmful. How often a man thinks he is carrying a book under his arm, and it turns out to be a load of trash!

Escrivá also recommends secrecy. In aphorism 643, he says, 'Be slow to reveal the intimate details of your apostolate. Don't you see that the world in its selfishness will fail to understand?'

Apostates report being put under unbearable psychological pressure, with harmful consequences for their mental health. There are even claims that the celebrated Clínica Universidad de Navarra, one of the country's best hospitals, inaugurated by Opus Dei in 1962, has, or had, a secret facility for members with mental disorders brought on either by the austerity imposed by the organisation, or by the harassment of waverers. This is setting aside the obvious, that any account about a powerful, clandestine network pursuing its own, covert goals unseen by ordinary people is going to smack of a psychotic episode.

As a result, to investigate Opus Dei's inner workings and methods is to wade through defectors' accounts that sound slightly unhinged. Titles tend to start 'The Truth about' or 'The Criminal Nature of', and end 'Catholicism's Secret Sect' or 'Heaven in a Cage'. One deserter, who also happens to be an expert in the history of science at Linacre College, Oxford, describes 'having my incoming and outgoing letters read, handing over my salary, sleeping on the floor once a week', and, three times a week for thirteen years, administering 'forty lashes of private self-flagellation with a wax-cord whip', during which, he says, 'we were encouraged to "draw a little blood".'

Even so, if talk of Opus Dei can easily sound delusional, its penetration of Spanish society is documented by the best historians. In February 1957 one of its number was appointed Minister of Trade. By the start of the 1970s, the ministries of Finance, Trade, Industry, Foreign Affairs, Education, Information, and the Development Plan were all in Opus Dei's hands. The tutors of the future king, Juan Carlos, were Opus Dei. Franco's successor as head of government in June 1973, and *his* successor, were both Opus Dei. Members rose through the police and armed forces, the judiciary, even the institutions of sport. In cycling, the team Xacobeo-Galicia, active under various names between 2006 and 2010 and sponsored by the Galician regional government, the Xunta de Galicia, whose capital, Santiago de Compostela, is such a magnet for pilgrims, was known in the milieu as 'the team of Opus Dei'.

In 2014, two of Mariano Rajoy's ministers attended the beatification of Escrivá's successor, Álvaro del Portillo. Whether or not they were members was never clarified.

All of which is to say that, when Dan Brown peopled *The Da Vinci Code* with well-connected, self-flagellating Opus Dei fanatics waging a violent campaign to stamp out the theory that Mary Magdalene bore Jesus Christ a child, he had plenty of material.

Echávarri explained, 'We have always been respectful, at least, we have tried to be. Some have interpreted this as if we were men of the cloth. "Here they come, *los curas* – the priests!"'[3]

In the period 1982–1996, when the Socialist leader Felipe González served four consecutive terms as president, Spain moved towards neoliberalism and industrial reconversion. In 1988 the Minister of Economy and Finance, Carlos Solchaga, said, 'Spain is the country where you can make the most money in the short term in the whole of Europe and perhaps one of the countries where you can make the most money in the world.' It marked the start of the *pelotazo* – the 'loadsamoney' era – when greed became good and there were fortunes to be made by risk takers prepared to stretch the bounds of rectitude.

In his enormous book *A People Betrayed: A History of Corruption, Political Incompetence and Social Division in Modern Spain*, the British historian writes:

> The scale of uninterrupted corruption and periodic ineptitude demonstrated by the political class at various levels of society since 1982 has been remarkable. Politicians of both right and left have been unable or unwilling to deal with corruption and the pernicious clash between Spanish centralist nationalism and regional desires for independence . . . [In particular] the boom of the 1990s fostered corruption and witnessed political incompetence on an unprecedented scale . . .

Like the hagiographies of medieval saints, descriptions of the beneficiaries of this corruption are full of the same stock phrases: charismatic, energetic, a brilliant student. So, in 1972, a young meteor from Galicia named Mario Conde passed the State Bar exams with the highest mark in history. He was 24, and, as he told it, it had taken him only two years of preparation, compared with the usual four or five. In 1987, having already made a fortune through financial operations in the pharmaceutical sector, he engineered one of the biggest private business transactions in Spanish history, selling a major antibiotics manufacturer for €300 million. He invested the profits in shares of one of Spain's oldest and largest banks, the Banco Español de Crédito, also known as Banesto, the third-largest financial group in Spain, with around 1,770 high street branches, buying his way onto the board and becoming, at the age of 39, its youngest ever chairman.

Peopling his board with loyal confidants and political appointees, some of them close to the Socialist government of Felipe González, he was idolised by the centre-right, who saw in him a potential Partido Popular leader capable of unseating González, unlike the current incumbent, José María Aznar. And no wonder: at the peak of his power, Conde was said to exercise personal control over 1 per cent of Spain's entire GDP. And, as the owner of a television station, Antena 3, and a newspaper, *El Mundo*, he wielded considerable influence over public opinion.

These developments piqued Echávarri's instincts.

As the official history tells it, INASA's managing director, Juan García Barberena, had an acquaintance on Conde's board, Martín Rivas, who had represented the bank in Pamplona for fifteen years. García Barberena offered Banesto a piece of the team. Rivas took the proposal to Conde's deputy, Arturo Romaní, a well-known cycling fan. On 14 June 1989, two weeks before the Tour de France, the phone call came. Banesto wanted in, not at the end of the year but straight away, in time for the Tour, as Reynolds' co-sponsor.

On 30 June, at the Grand Départ in Luxembourg, Romaní, sitting between Miguel Indurain and Pedro Delgado, presented the deal to the press. As fate would have it, the new venture started with the most notorious cock-up in Tour history, when Delgado, in the *Maillot Jaune* as the defending champion, missed his start time for the prologue by 2 minutes 38 seconds, and lost the Tour before he had even started.

To the team's new sponsor, the debacle was of no great importance. For Conde, Romaní and their accomplices, the cycling project had other ends. Banesto's upbeat, red, yellow and blue logo emblazoned across the jersey of the quixotic Delgado or the prodigious Indurain was the perfect cover for a mass of fraudulent transactions that went undetected until December 1993, when the financial authorities discovered an astonishing €3.636 billion black hole in the bank's accounts.

No one knew it at the time, of course, but the day before his appearance in Luxembourg at the start of the Tour, Romaní, on Banesto's behalf, had entered into a mind-bogglingly complex agreement involving warrants, that is, stock options that give the owner the right to buy ordinary shares in a company on a specified future date at a specified price. According to the contract, a company called Euris undertook to buy warrants worth US$21.5 million in Carburos Metálicos, a Spanish metal carbides company in which Banesto held a stake.[4] Banesto undertook to buy the warrants back at a later date at a guaranteed price. In the course of the operation, €8.4 million of bank funds went missing.

The arrangement came to light only after the discovery of Banesto's monstrous deficit four years later. Hanging on the interpretation of dozens of impenetrable financial documents, and statements from 470 witnesses, the Carburos Metálicos investigation was one of a long series into the illegal financial operations through which Conde, Romaní and their associates used bank funds to enrich themselves.

The second half of 1989 saw the withdrawal of huge quantities of cash, €1.9 million of which were delivered in unmarked duffle bags to Adolfo Suárez, Spain's first democratically elected prime minister after the Franco dictatorship and a key figure in the country's transition to democracy. It was justified as some sort of payback for a favour he had done the Bank of Spain. Meanwhile, Conde and Romaní sold Banesto stocks and bought themselves real estate in Seville and Mallorca with the proceeds.

During the 1990 Tour de France, Banesto's first as the main sponsor, Conde and Romaní issued false invoices amounting to €3.6 million, and gave orders for their payment from a Banesto shell company in the Cayman Islands to a trust account in Saint Vincent.[5] During Miguel Indurain's victorious Giro d'Italia in 1992, they bought shares through their own companies, then sold them on to the bank at inflated prices.

Although the cycling team served primarily as window dressing, it was not entirely aloof from the mendacity. In 1992, Romaní purchased 25,000 copies of an aerobics video by Jeannette Rodríguez, a Venezuelan actress with whom he was romantically linked. The bill for the videos,[6] entitled *Tensión dinámica, ponte en forma* ('Get in shape with dynamic tension'), bounced from desk to desk until it reached the office of the cycling team, which settled the account. The tapes were delivered to a team warehouse. Of no use to professional cyclists, they presumably stayed there until Romaní was safely behind bars.

The bank's auditors, Price Waterhouse (now Pricewater-houseCoopers, or PwC), failed to notice any anomalies in its accounts, and the scandal was only uncovered in an inspection by the national bank in December 1993. Banesto shares went into freefall, leading the Spanish Stock Exchange Commission to suspend trading in them. The Bank of Spain stepped in, removed Conde and his board and refloated the bank with €600 million of state money.

The Banesto banking crisis contributed to the recession that hit Spain hard in 1994, when unemployment reached 3.5 million (24 per cent of the workforce). It prompted the first state intervention of its type in banking history, foreshadowing the 2007 sub-prime mortgage scandal and the global financial crisis, although it was still not enough to cover the missing €3.636 billion. Private banks matched the state contribution, and Banesto's shareholders covered the rest. After injecting over a billion Euros of its own, the Santander Group took over Banesto.

As Banesto's new board began to sell assets, its cycling team, with Indurain and three Tours de France under his belt, was on the point of disappearing. Many years later, Luis Abril, one of the executives who helped refloat the bank, remembered why they decided to continue. 'It would look very bad,' he explained, 'if we sent the message to Spanish society that we couldn't even afford Indurain's wages.'[7]

The Bank of Spain's investigation concluded in February 1996. It revealed six years of continuous accounting fraud by Conde, Romaní and their confederates. The trial lasted from 1 December 1997 to 3 December 1999. On 31 March 2000, the Audiencia Nacional sentenced Mario Conde to ten years two months in prison, and Romaní to thirteen years eight months. In addition, Romaní was ordered to pay back the €8.4 million misappropriated in the Carburos Metálicos operation. In 2002, on appeal, the Supreme Court increased Conde's sentence from ten to twenty years. By then, a lawsuit filed by Banesto share-holders against Price Waterhouse for failing to notice anything wrong with Banesto's accounts, had been dismissed because the statute of limitations had expired. Romaní and Conde started their prison sentences on 29 July 2002, the day after the Champs-Élysées stage of the Tour de France. At least they had been able to watch it at home.

Santander completed its takeover of Banesto's share capital in February 1998, and, from 1999, Banesto focused on strength-ening its service of buying and selling securities via the internet, thanks to an agreement with Telefónica. In 2001 the cycling team was rebranded iBanesto, which it remained until the end of 2003.

But in 1999, when Alejandro Valverde joined, the team was still Banesto, and Toni Cerdá, the national track coach, still had high hopes for him and Rubén Plaza as track riders. He called them up for a couple of training camps at the start of the year, in Hotel San Diego, El Arenal, Mallorca with Carlos Torrent, a future individual pursuit bronze medallist at the Athens Olym-pics in 2004, who recalled, 'Plaza and Valverde had just signed for Banesto's amateur team. They were very serious and obses-sive about their training, and they took more care of themselves than the rest of us, who were a bit more relaxed because the season had not started yet. You could see that they were both very focused.'[8]

Any plans Bala may have had to rival Chris Hoy ended when his new team put him on a rigorous diet.

'My first memory at Banesto Amateur was a strength test, after which they told me I had to lose weight. That was my first transformation, seventy-three to sixty-four kilos in a year. The diet was strict, but I followed it to the letter. Since then I've fluctuated between sixty-two kilos during the season and sixty-six kilos out of competition.'

The team used the same equipment as the professional team: the same Pinarello bikes, the same accessories, helmets and sunglasses. Adidas casual wear. A Russian rider, Denis Menchov, had joined Banesto in January 1999 and moved into a residence in Pamplona. Within weeks he had won the Vuelta a Albacete and finished second in the Vuelta al Bidasoa. Bala grew weary of the 500-mile journey from Murcia to races in the north, so, when the Kelme-Costa Blanca team, based at Elche, 60 kilometres north-east of Murcia, promised him a five-year contract with two seasons at under-23 level followed by a guaranteed move to professionalism in 2002 – an extraordinary offer for a nineteen-year-old – he took it.

In 2000, another year older and free of the endless travelling, Bala came into his own. On 11 May, in Hondarribia in the Basque Country, the new Kelme-Costa Blanca under-23 rider won the sprint from a group of seventeen including four riders from Banesto Amateur, now called Banco de Vitoria. Valverde insisted he still had plenty of friends at his old team, although the sports daily *Mundo Deportivo* entitled its race report 'Revenge is a dish best served cold'.

In 2001 he won the two most important amateur cups, the Porvenir Cup and the Spanish Cup, as well as the under-23 national championships around León. He added a bronze medal at the 2001 Mediterranean Games in Tunisia, riding for the national team.

His national team pursuit colleague Unai Elorriaga remembered the 2001 European U23 road race at Apremont in Savoy. 'There were courtesy bikes at the hotel and I think we did more kilometres on these bikes than on our racing bikes, because in the afternoons or evenings we would take them to go to the village, doing cyclo-cross through the fields. I have great memories of him, very cheerful, always joking.'

Kelme's local roots were as profound as his own. The town of Elche, 50 kilometres north-east of Murcia, on the way to Alicante, had specialised in footwear manufacture for generations. By the 1890s it already had eighty *espadrille* factories turning out six million pairs a year. When the First World War interrupted shoe production elsewhere in Europe, orders poured in. At one point Elche supplied the French army with 40,000 pairs of boots.

Then came the Spanish Civil War. Elche was a major supplier for the Republican side, with whom the immense majority of the workers are said to have sympathised although the war, and the purges that followed took a heavy toll.[9] Even so, the post-war demand for civilian footwear led to a boom, and Elche reaped the benefit.

In the 1970s two long-serving distributors, the brothers Diego and José 'Pepe' Quiles, who had achieved financial success in the export trade, bought out the biggest of Elche's shoe manufacturers, Kelme, and entered the sports sector with a range of football boots aimed at the international market. Cycling came knocking at Kelme's door in 1978, when Basque nationalist violence was at its peak. Between 1978 and 1980, ETA committed 242 assassinations. Although the murderous cruelty never touched cycling, the threat of sabotage hung heavy over the Vuelta a España. The penultimate stage in 1978, from Bilbao to San Sebastián, had been stopped at the town of Durango by barricades and tacks. The riders had boarded team cars and resumed racing after a 64-kilometre transfer at Zárauz. The following day, more debris was dumped in the road and sand was thrown in the face of some of the riders, ruining the final time trial.

In January 1979 the race organiser, the newspaper group *El Correo Español-El Pueblo Vasco*, pulled out. With fewer than five months to go, the president of the Spanish Cycling Federation, Luis Puig, asked Enrique Franco to step in. Looking for a sponsor for the mountains competition, Franco called Kelme.

Pepe Quiles said, 'For four million pesetas' – about €24,000 – 'they gave us a minute of television advertising a day.'

After the Vuelta, a cycling team director named Rafael Carrasco visited the Quiles brothers and asked them to take over his team, Transmallorca-Flavia, whose best rider, Vicente Belda, had taken a stage at the 1978 Vuelta a España. It made sense. Pepe Quiles continued, 'For ten or twelve million pesetas' – about €72,000 – 'we could ride the Vuelta, the Giro, the Tour and everything else.'

Kelme grew and grew. At the 1992 Olympic Games they sponsored the Spanish athletics team. Two years later it hit the big time with a five-year contract to supply Real Madrid with its kit, for one billion pesetas (€6 million) over five years, or 200 million pesetas – €1.2 million – per season.

In 1997 the cycling team became Kelme-Costa Blanca-Eurosport. Costa Blanca – literally, white coast, referring to the 120 miles of Mediterranean coastline either side of Alicante – was a brand name owned by the Generalitat Valenciana, the institution of self-government in the region of Valencia. The Generalitat's goal was to establish itself as Spain's pre-eminent beach destination, driven by its leader, another tanned, charismatic variation on Mario Conde called Eduardo Zaplana. Zaplana had been the mayor of Benidorm from 1991 to 1994, and the following year he had led his party to victory in the regional elections, initially in a coalition with the right-wing *Unió Valenciana* (the Valencian Union, the 'defender of Valencian identity'). As president of the Generalitat from 1995 to 2002, Zaplana gave his megalomaniac tendencies full rein.[10] One of his pet projects was a massive theme park whose roots lay in the region's old ambition to host the European version of the greatest theme park of all.

Visions of talking animals presumably date back to the dawn of humanity. Even so, Walt Disney's creation of Mickey Mouse in 1928 was a modern milestone. When Disneyland opened in

1955, it was a success from the start. The Florida version, Walt Disney World, opened in 1971, by which time plans were already afoot for a European franchise, even if Japan got there first with Tokyo Disneyland in 1983.

Late the following year, Disney drew up a longlist of 1,200 potential European locations. By March 1985, it had whittled them down to four, all of them in either France or Spain. The town of Pego-Oliva, an hour and twenty minutes south of Valencia, was the front runner until December 1985, when Disney announced that they had chosen the Marne-la-Vallée region, 35 kilometres from Paris.[11] It should not have come as a surprise: the selected site was far wealthier than Spain, with infrastructure and communications, and 40 million people living within 300 kilometres. Euro Disney opened in 1992.

The selection process had left some Spanish politicians with theme parks on the brain. PortAventura, in Salou and Vila-seca, south of Barcelona, opened in 1995.[12] In Seville, Isla Mágica opened on the Expo '92 site in 1996, in the presence of King Juan Carlos I. Zaplana wanted to outdo both with a park near Benidorm. Exactly where was undecided until 1992, when convenient forest fires cleared a strategic area of protected pine forest.

Four years after the suspected arson, the Generalitat Valenciana created the Sociedad Parque Temático de Alicante SA (the Alicante Theme Park Company), which drew up plans for a hotel area, two golf courses, and a theme park called Terra Mítica, based on the ancient civilisations of the Mediterranean basin. It was calculated that three million visitors per year were needed to justify the €270 million construction costs. A Canadian consultancy called Economic Research Associates (ERA), who had previously worked for Disneyland Paris, PortAventura, Warner Bros and Legoland, warned that it could only expect 1.3 million.[13] Zaplana turned to the US-based Baker Leisure Group, but their forecast did not exceed two million. It was the obliging

PricewaterhouseCoopers who came up with the magic figure of three million visitors a year in January 1999,[14] although, by then, construction was well under way.

By the time Prince Felipe, the future king, attended Terra Mítica's official opening on 27 July 2000, its logo had already achieved global visibility. It first appeared on the shirts of Valencia FC in summer 1998. Valencia then won the 1999–2000 Spanish Super Cup and finished third in La Liga, before going down 3-0 to Real Madrid at Paris in May 2000, in the final of the UEFA Champions League, all the while wearing the Terra Mítica logo. In 1999 it appeared on the jerseys of the Kelme-Costa Blanca cycling team, supplanting the Eurosport logo, and was seen around the world on stage fifteen of the Tour de France, won by Kelme's leader, Fernando Escartín, and on the final podium, where he stood on the bottom step below Lance Armstrong and Alex Zülle.

Despite all this well-placed advertising, Terra Mítica's year-one attendance was a million short of PricewaterhouseCooper's three million forecast, and 1.4 million short in year two.[15] From 2003 to 2008, the park averaged only 1.1 million visitors each year. Four years after opening, with €220 million in liabilities, it went into temporary receivership. In 2009 and 2010, attendance slumped to 0.7 million and 0.54 million. From the initial clearance of protected woodland by fire to the construction costs that eventually ballooned to €425 million, €155 million over budget, Terra Mítica provided the national press with corruption stories for years to come.

Accused of money laundering and bribery, Eduardo Zaplana was arrested in May 2018 and remanded in pre-trial detention. After eight and a half months, he was released in view of the leukaemia he had been suffering since 2015. In October 2022, according to a charge sheet seen by the newspaper *El Diario*, the Anti-Corruption Prosecutor's Office in Madrid alleged that Zaplana led 'a criminal organisation with a perfectly structured distribution of roles that moved up to 20.6 million euros in bribes scattered in tax havens. According to prosecutor Pablo Ponce, who was requesting a 19-year prison sentence for the alleged crimes of criminal group, money laundering, bribery, forgery and administrative malfeasance, "The total amount of criminal money obtained through corruption operations by Eduardo Zaplana and his criminal organisation amounts to 20,606,364 euros."[16]

The case is still pending.

3

Spain's Most Endorsable

In 2002 Spanish cycling was simultaneously on top of the world and in meltdown. A Spaniard, Óscar Freire, had been world champion in 1999 and again in 2001. He had been riding for Mapei–Quick-Step, the world's number one team, since 2000, but Mapei had announced that it would be leaving the sport at the end of 2002, meaning that the market would be flooded with top riders and support staff. In Spain, ONCE had let it be known that its cycling sponsorship would not be continuing beyond the end of 2003. Smaller teams like Euskaltel, Relax and Jazztel stayed afloat only thanks to public funding from the Euskadi (or Basque Country) government, the city of Fuenlabrada, south-west of Madrid, and the group of seaside towns around Almería on the Andalusian coast. Jazztel was already looking for a new sponsor, and the sponsorship deal sustaining Euskaltel was due to end in December 2004.

The solvency crisis extended across borders. The two Belgian teams Lotto and Domo had decided to merge for 2003, making another team's worth of riders and staff unemployed. The German outfit Team Coast was limping on, unable to pay its wages, while the Danish team CSC, run by the 1996 Tour de France champion Bjarne Riis, wanted to sign Jan Ullrich but needed a second sponsor to pay his wages. In Italy, Mario Cipollini's Acqua & Sapone team was staking its survival on an injection of funds from Renault, which never materialised.

In February 2002 Banesto had announced the election of a new chair: Ana Patricia Botín, the eldest child of the chairman of Banco Santander, and the great-granddaughter of Banco Santander's first chairman.[1] Soon after that summer's Tour de France, where Francisco Mancebo finished seventh and the team had won no stages, the new board informed Echávarri and Unzue that its sponsorship would be ending in December 2003.

In 1998, Kelme, which had a turnover of approximately ten billion pesetas (something over €60 million), was spending 3 per cent of this on its cycling project, with the rest of the team budget coming from the sale of advertising space on the uniform. Kelme had redesigned its logo, spent €9 million on an industrial estate halfway between Elche and Alicante and made investments of €18 million in Russia and Eastern Europe. Then, out of the blue, Real Madrid rescinded its contract with Kelme, allowing Adidas to take over. It left Kelme in freefall. From 1999 to 2002, its turnover plummeted from €55 million to €38 million, and its debts grew to €40 million. Propped up by the Generalitat Valenciana, under Partido Popular rule, the company limped on. So Bala turned professional with a team in deep financial crisis.

He was not an immediate success. After eighth place in the Clásica de Almería sprint, he headed to his home race, the Vuelta a Murcia, and, on 7 March, he joined a three-man breakaway on stage one, attacking after five kilometres. They led by 5 minutes 30 seconds by kilometre 40 and were caught at kilometre 89. During the race, perhaps even the same day, encouraged by his father, he treated himself to a brand-new Mercedes. His girlfriend picked it up at the dealership and drove it to the team hotel. Kelme was less sure of its finances. As early as May's Tour of Catalunya, Bala was telling other cyclists that Kelme was having problems paying its riders.

Stage nine of the Vuelta a España, the shortest of the race

barring time trials, was an anodyne, 130-kilometre loop starting and finishing in Cordoba, much of it along multi-lane, high-speed roads.[2] After 20 kilometres of frantic racing, the peloton split. Francisco Mancebo, the leader of iBanesto.com, missed the split, as did seven of his teammates. After 88 kilometres, he pulled over to the side of the road and abandoned.

The only iBanesto.com rider in the decisive break was Pablo Lastras. He bided his time as the leading group fragmented, attacked on the final climb, crossed to the leading pair, descended like a man possessed, and, with something under ten kilometres to go, opened a gap. He held off the chase to the finish line, where he celebrated more in relief than joy, and dedicated his victory 'to the Banesto family'.[3] Everyone understood it for what it was: a plea for clemency.

Twenty-one seconds behind Lastras, Alejandro Valverde, riding for Kelme, outsprinted Erik Zabel for fourth place, his best stage finish in his first Grand Tour. He completed fourteen stages before stepping off after a crash on the stage to Angliru. In sixty-one days of racing in 2002, he had taken no wins.

In February 2003 five consistent performances in the Challenge de Mallorca allowed Bala to take the series overall, even if, strictly speaking, it was not a stage race but five independent one-day races, and the general classification was unofficial. Meanwhile, in Elche, Kelme announced a wave of redundancies. Through the Valencian Institute of Finance, the Generalitat Valenciana guaranteed Kelme a €9 million loan and appointed two executives to manage the company.

Stage three of April's Vuelta al País Vasco, from Palencia to Vitoria, ended with a steep 2.2-kilometre climb at a gradient of 11 or 12 per cent. Gerolsteiner's Davide Rebellin, led out by his teammate Fabian Wegmann, seemed to have the sprint won. Wegmann even gave Rebellin a celebratory pat on the back as he came past. Then Valverde appeared, darting past Wegmann at speed and beating Rebellin with a perfect throw of the bike. It was Bala's first professional win.

Four days later, at the Klasika Primavera at Amorebieta, 25 kilometres east of Bilbao, he won again, and five days after that, in stage three of the Vuelta a Aragón at the top of a one-kilometre climb. The newspaper *Mundo Deportivo* spoke of him as 'the future star' of 'the generation born out of the unexpected and surprising rainbow successes of Óscar Freire'.[4]

Absent from Kelme's nine-man Tour de France team, he took two stage wins at Torres Vedras, just outside Lisbon, in the Troféu Joaquim Agostinho on 12 and 13 July. The first of them coincided with the longest and one of the toughest days of the Tour, stage seven, from Lyon to Morzine in the Alps. Despite Bala's absence, it was a stage that would come back to haunt him. A breakaway of four riders formed soon after flag drop. Behind them, after 41 kilometres, low down on the category-two Col de Portes, Kelme's Jesús Manzano attacked, chased by Quick-Step–Davitamon's Richard Virenque. Virenque caught him and continued his attack, bridging to the leaders and ending the day with the stage win, the race lead overall, and also the lead in the mountains competition.

Manzano left the race in an ambulance after fainting ten kilometres into his attack. He ended the day in hospital at Belley. 'That morning I was given a substance I had never used before,' Manzano explained, seven months later. 'It was supposed to keep your haematocrit low and your haemoglobin high.' While he was attacking, he said, 'I became sluggish and lightheaded, the way you feel when you've been riding for two hundred kilometres. After half a kilometre of climbing my hands fell asleep and I couldn't change gear. I had no strength left in my arms. The gear levers felt soft. After three kilometres I started to feel very hot. Then the cold sweats started. I can't remember falling or being moved or anything else. My vision went. I came to in an ambulance. My jersey had been cut off and they were giving me an injection, electrocardiograms and so on. My tongue felt swollen and I couldn't breathe. If they had made a hole in my throat I would have appreciated it.'

He added, 'It was because of . . . the poor state of conservation of those products.'[5]

Five days later, another Kelme rider, Javier Pascual Llorente, the winner, earlier in the season, of the Vuelta a Murcia and the Vuelta a Andalucía, tested positive for EPO after the stage twelve time trial. He declared himself 'totally innocent' and blamed the result on 'the French method of detection, which is not reliable'. It was, he said, part of 'a French campaign of persecution against Spanish cycling'.[6]

Bala was well off out of it. On the twenty-fifth of the month he added to his successes at the GP Villafranca de Ordizia in the Basque Country, then prepared for the main goal of his season, the Vuelta a España. José Miguel Echávarri and Manolo Saiz, his counterpart at ONCE-Würth, spent the race presenting dossiers to potential sponsors.

In the time trial around Zaragoza on stage six, Bala moved into the top ten in the general classification. The following day, at Cauterets, he rose to eighth place. A buzz began around him. On stage nine, with 20 kilometres to go to the mountain finish line at Port d'Envalira, Andorra, Belda told him, 'Alejandro, there are a lot of tired riders around. Have a go.' He duly attacked. 'Straight away I could see that the other riders in the group were finding it hard to go with me,' he recalled. 'I opened a gap. A group containing strong riders like Dario Frigo and Aitor González came up from behind, but, going into the final sprint, I said, "No one's going to beat me here."'

He danced easily away to take his first Grand Tour stage win and burst into tears as he dismounted.

Sixth the next day at Sabadell, he moved into the top seven overall. After the next time trial in stage thirteen, he entered the top six.

Then, at La Pandera, the highest point of the Sierra mountains south of Jaén, the race leader Roberto Heras launched his attack four kilometres from the finish. Félix Cárdenas, the Colombian leader of Labarca-2-Café Baqué, joined him, with Valverde and his teammate Óscar Sevilla giving chase. Inside the last kilometre, on a final descent, Valverde darted past Heras and Cárdenas to win his second stage.

He was now fifth overall.

The following day, with the riders Santos González, Jorge Ferrio, Aitor González, Enrique Gutiérrez, Joan Horrach, Miguel Ángel Martín Perdiguero and Óscar Sevilla, Bala appeared nude in the pages of the magazine *Interviú*.

Martín Perdiguero explained the scrawny spectacle. 'We have to put some glamour into the sport or we are dead.'

Later that day, ten kilometres from the finish line on the Sierra Nevada, Sevilla went on the attack with Cárdenas on his wheel. Belda called him back to work for Valverde. Sevilla pulled out his earpiece in frustration. Cárdenas continued the move alone, caught the solo leader Juan Miguel Mercado inside the final kilometre and rode to victory, to the humiliation of the two Kelme riders. A month later, Sevilla announced that he was leaving the team.

The Vuelta culminated in an 11.2-kilometre mountain time trial final from the monastery at San Lorenzo de El Escorial to Mount Abantos. Bala finished the stage second, 14 seconds behind the winner, Roberto Heras. It lifted him into third place overall. In only his second Grand Tour, he had made the podium. Competitive on all terrains, and with his whole career ahead of him, Spain had a new stage race hero.

After the 2003 Vuelta, Echávarri had announced that he was close to agreeing terms with the autonomous community of the Illes Balears or Balearic Islands, the archipelago that includes Mallorca, Menorca, Ibiza and Formentera. Given the import-ance of German tourism (ten years earlier, a German MP had announced, not entirely in jest, 'Mallorca has almost become an island with a German population. The federal government should make contact with Spain and try to buy it'), the islands wanted Jan Ullrich on the team.

Three weeks later, on 12 October, Spain's world championships went badly wrong three laps from the end. With Italy forcing the pace, Óscar Freire was held up by a mechanical problem and four teammates waited for him. Minutes later, Igor Astarloa slipped over on a left-hand bend as Paolo Bettini and Michael Boogerd made a testing acceleration.

Then, with just eight kilometres of the race to go, Óscar Sevilla abandoned, although by then the decisive move had been made. With 11 kilometres to go, the Belgian classics specialist Peter Van Petegem had dragged away a group of seven, including the 1998 world champion Oscar Camenzind, Bo Hamburger, Boogerd, Bettini – and Astarloa. They extended their lead to 25 seconds, but then the peloton closed them down to ten seconds. On the Claremont climb, with 3.5 kilometres to go, the catch was imminent. Astarloa chose that moment to attack.

Moments later, two riders bridged across from the peloton to the Bettini group: Canada's Michael Barry, and Bala. Barry moved to the front and piloted the chasers to within eight seconds of Astarloa. Valverde waited at the back. On the last descent, the chasers stopped cooperating with each other and, on the final corner, Astarloa knew his ten-second lead would be enough. Behind him, Valverde powered past Van Petegem to take the silver medal. Spain's new stage race hopeful was a one-day racer too – and the best Spaniard in the world rankings, second place in the world championships lifting him up to seventh.

Mundo Deportivo proclaimed, 'Closely supervised by Dr Eufemiano Fuentes, his development has been spectacular, and in his second pro season he has achieved lift-off. His current salary is €60,000 but during his brilliant Vuelta a España he signed a much-improved contract for four more years.'

It was true: the day of his second stage win at the Vuelta a España, Bala had signed an agreement tying him to Kelme until 2007. But his third place in the Vuelta and second in the world championships followed that contract signing and changed everything. Valverde's agent, Gorka Arrinda, revealed that he had been able to build into the contract a number of sporting conditions: for instance, Valverde's status as team leader, his race calendar for the following season, and so on. The sheer amount of detail allowed Arrinda any number of pretexts for tearing up the contract. Sevilla's departure, disclosed three days after the world championships, was one. The decision of the tax authorities to freeze Kelme's accounts was another.

On 29 October the insurance company Liberty Seguros announced that it was coming in to replace ONCE with a five-year commitment. Still at the helm, Manolo Saiz contacted Valverde, and reported back to Liberty Seguros's new chairman, Manuel Piñera. Despite his new contract, Bala saw his future more at Liberty than at Kelme. Piñera was soon on the phone to Pepe Quiles telling him that he wanted Valverde on his team. The sticking point was Bala's €2.5 million escape clause.

Towards the end of November, Kelme announced a new agreement with the Generalitat Valenciana, although the Partido Popular-run government had one condition: the team had to sign the 2001 Vuelta winner Ángel Casero. If *Mundo Deportivo* was right, Casero's wife and manager had offered him to Euskaltel and Saunier Duval a few weeks earlier for €60,000 per annum. With Kelme he secured a two-year contract for €300,000 a year. He was, after all, a Partido Popular militant who had joined the party's first pre-campaign rally in March 2003 with the tennis player Juan Carlos Ferrero, the ex-footballer Fernando Giner, and the former long and triple jumper (and future secretary of sport for Valencia) Niurka Montalvo.

Arrinda tried to make Casero's signing a contract breaker. 'Casero's signing makes Valverde's future with the team more difficult. Imagine you are Beckham and they sign you to play in the Champions League with all the team's star players, and then they send you to small games with other players. It's a different project.'

At a meeting on 27 November, things seemed to have sorted themselves when the team, the rider and his agent agreed that Valverde would stay for €1 million per year and an escape clause reduced from €2.5 million, with the details to be worked out. Vicente Belda even came out of the meeting talking about signing up Aleksandr Vinokurov for the team's twenty-fifth season.

However, the situation unsorted itself on 17 December 2003, the day of the Vuelta a España route presentation, when it emerged that Kelme was two months behind in its wage payments, and had missed two deadlines for submitting the compulsory bank guarantee, equal to three months' salary for all riders and staff members, to the International Cycling Union (UCI). It had until midday on Friday 19 December to meet its obligations, but, when the UCI published the names of twenty-nine of the thirty so-called GS1 or first division teams that Friday evening, Kelme's was missing.

The crisis rumbled on. On 8 January Vicente Belda confirmed that, after 'the day of our lives', all the requirements demanded by the UCI had been met to guarantee the team's continued existence 'at least for another year'. The following day, Friday 9 January, 'sources linked to the UCI and the team' assured *Mundo Ciclístico* that Kelme had submitted neither the guarantees nor its bank details.

The bombshell came on 10 January: due to financial problems, Kelme, the international peloton's oldest team, had been relegated to the second division (GS2). A new scramble for Bala began. His signature on a contract seemed to be the only guarantee of survival for any domestic team. Vicente Belda, his team manager at Kelme-Costa Blanca, called him 'a genius like Cruyff, Di Stéfano or Induráin', and *'el hombre más publicitario de España*' – the most endorsable man in Spain, Rafael Nadal before his time.[7] It would barely be exaggerating to say that, at that moment, Alejandro Valverde *was* Spanish cycling. The only problem was that neither Manolo Saiz nor José Miguel Echávarri had the cash.

4

The Only Story

On 30 August 2003, Bogdan 'Bob' Madejak, a Cofidis team soigneur, had discussed blood transfusions in a telephone conversation with a rider, Marek Rutkiewicz. The police were listening in, and, on 22 January 2004, the French current affairs magazine *Le Point* published the transcript. It suggested that autologous blood transfusion, that is, the collection and reinfusion of the athlete's own blood, had been widespread during the 2003 Tour de France. Commonplace in sport during the 1970s, autologous blood transfusion had been banned in 1985 after the Los Angeles Olympic Games, then effectively replaced by the banned red blood cell booster erythropoietin (EPO), which achieved essentially the same effects.[1] But now, it seemed, it was back.

On 13 January 2004, Rutkiewicz had flown from Warsaw to Paris's Roissy-Charles de Gaulle airport with seven vials of EPO in his luggage. More were found at his home in Hyères, between Marseilles and Saint-Tropez.

The Cofidis Affair was under way.

In raids all over France, amphetamines, EPO, growth hormones, testosterone and corticoids, plus transfusion equipment and quantities of cocaine, were seized. A war of words started between Dick Pound, president of the World Anti-Doping Agency (WADA), and Hein Verbruggen, president of the UCI. Pound observed, 'The public is not stupid. They know that Tour de France cyclists and other athletes take forbidden substances. It's the same thing in the US with American football. Even the president of the UCI will have to admit that there is a problem in cycling and it's been going on for a hundred years.'[2]

His case was reinforced when Cofidis rider Philippe Gaumont, an Olympic bronze medallist in the 100-kilometre team time trial in 1992, and the winner of Gent–Wevelgem in 1997, admitted to taking EPO.

Days later, on Tuesday 27 January, Belgian prosecutors announced that Franck Vandenbroucke, once tipped to emulate Eddy Merckx, would be tried for possession of nine different drugs including EPO, clenbuterol and morphine. In December 2003, Banesto's climber José María Jiménez had died in a psychiatric hospital in Madrid, aged 32. Then, on St Valentine's Day 2004, the 1998 Giro d'Italia and Tour de France winner Marco Pantani was found dead in a Rimini hotel.

Much later, in the Cofidis trial, the judge asked Madejak, 'You thought of these young people as sons, yet you fed them products that cause physical harm, madness and death. What do you have to say?'

And what was there to say? As Dick Pound insisted, cycling and doping had a long history together. But only in 2004 did it become impossible to write about the one without mentioning the other. Doping became the only story.

Not that any of this affected Alejandro Valverde. His year started with Spanish sport's awards season. Unable to attend *Mundo Deportivo*'s Gran Gala at Catalonia's Palau de Congressos on Friday 30 January 2004, he was represented by the former Barcelona footballer Hristo Stoichkov, who collected the Best New Sportsman trophy on his behalf. Four days later, Bala went to Burgos for the Spanish Sports Press Association's National Sports Gala, where the main award winners were the world champion cyclist Igor Astarloa, the French Open tennis champion Juan Carlos

Ferrero, and the 5,000 metres silver medallist from the world athletics championships, Marta Domínguez.

Valverde flew the same evening from Burgos to Palma de Mallorca where, the following day, he won the third and hardest race of the Challenge de Mallorca, 150 kilometres to Port de Sóller, over two second-category cols. Three days later he finished fourth in the final race. On 22 January he was second to Óscar Freire in the Luis Puig Trophy.

In mid-January, the Generalitat Valenciana had assumed the larger part of the team budget and Kelme-Comunitat Valenciana became Comunitat Valenciana-Kelme, so February's Volta a la Comunitat Valenciana was a kind of homecoming. Bala finished seventh in stage one, first in stages two and three, when he took the race lead overall, and fourth in stage four, the big mountain stage, the day the wildcards for the Tour de France were announced.

The top fourteen teams in the UCI ranking on 1 January 2004 qualified by right. The remaining eight teams were invited by the race organisers. Domina Vacanze, excluded in 2003 despite having the reigning world champion, Mario Cipollini, in its ranks, was in. So were the French teams, AG2R, La Boulangère, Crédit Agricole and RAGT, the Swiss team, Phonak, and the Belgian team, Lotto. That made seven. Of Kelme's chances, race director Jean-Marie Leblanc said, 'They only have sixteen riders and they are hoping to ride the Giro and Vuelta. But we also hear that they are reinforcing their squad and expecting additional finance. With Ángel Casero, they could have twenty-three riders. We are patient but sceptical.'[3]

Belda said that the Tour organisers had called him promising him a place if he would only take Valverde.

'I told them no. I said he was already at his first peak of the season, and that at twenty-three years of age I wasn't going to make him try to peak three times in one season. He'll peak again at the end of the season for the Olympics, the Vuelta and the world championships. If everything goes well, he will make his Tour debut in 2005.'[4]

But this was merely repeating the terms in Arrinda's contract.

In stage five of the Volta a la Comunitat Valenciana, Valverde started his sprint too early and finished third. He still won the race overall by nine seconds. Before he raced again, the Tour de France and the Giro d'Italia issued invitations to Kelme.

Belda rejoiced. 'One minute, we're half dead, the next, we're the only Spanish team in the big three.'

With a stage finish at altitude and a time trial, the Vuelta a Murcia, at the start of March attracted the two big favourites for the Tour de France, Lance Armstrong and Jan Ullrich, although Valverde won it overall without a stage victory.

Meanwhile, the war between WADA and the UCI intensified. In an open letter released during the Vuelta a Murcia, Lance Armstrong said that Dick Pound's 'forbidden substances' comments had left him 'stunned and saddened'.

'I believe that I am the most tested athlete on this planet, I have never had a single positive doping test, and I do not take performance-enhancing drugs.'

A WADA spokesman responded, 'Mr Pound insists that no one would be happier than he would be if cycling were a doping-free sport, but recent events have suggested that there is work to be done.'[5]

Just how much work emerged between Wednesday 24 and Sunday 28 March 2004, when the Spanish sports daily *As* serialised a long interview with Valverde's former Kelme teammate Jesús Manzano. In page after page, he revealed in staggering detail the doping system he had taken part in for his three years with the team, listing practices, substances, dates and doses. To *As*'s rival, the sports paper *Marca*, he admitted, 'I'm not doing this for money, I'm doing it for revenge.'

The morning after the first instalment, at the start of stage three of the Setmana Catalana in Castelló d'Empuries, Kelme director Vicente Belda tried to explain away Manzano's revelations.

'We were looking for a pretext to terminate our relationship,' he said. 'During the Vuelta, at the team hotel the night before the Abantos time trial, we found him with a girl in his bed. It was not his wife. It was the opportunity we had been waiting for. His contract ran until the end of 2004. We suggested ending it then and there, and he agreed. I imagine that he has run out of money, so he has resorted to this.'

He added, 'The matter is with the Spanish Federation, who are considering legal action. I don't know who they are going to sue: the rider, the journalist or the newspaper.'[6]

Yet, given that Manzano had no degree in medicine or pharmacology, or, indeed, veterinary science (in the third instalment of his interview, he says, 'Haemoglobin comes in several brands, but I only know Oxyglobin, an animal product for dogs with anaemia'), it was hard to see how he could have made it all up and, before the serialisation was over, the Tour de France had withdrawn its invitation to the Kelme team.

'I'm accusing myself and no one else,' Manzano wrote. But he could hardly have helped implicating the Kelme team doctor, Eufemiano Fuentes.[7] Well known in cycling circles, Fuentes had been identified by the newspaper *El Mundo* as the doctor of the winner of the 1988 Tour de France, Pedro Delgado, who had tested positive for Probenecid, a masking agent banned by Olympic doping rules but not yet listed by the UCI.

Born into a powerful Canary Island family, Fuentes' grandfather had made his fortune importing Cuban tobacco leaves to Gran Canaria's freeport, and exporting them as cigars.[8] An uncle inherited the business, founded the Unión Deportiva Las Palmas football team and built their first ground, the Estadio Insular, before being kidnapped and murdered in 1976.[9] A cousin became world lifeguard champion in 1974 and, twenty years later, was convicted of the murder and dismemberment of a prostitute whose remains were found in a bin in 1994.[10] All three were called Eufemiano.

The fourth Eufemiano, Eufemiano Claudio Fuentes Rodríguez, was born in 1955 at Las Palmas, Gran Canaria. A millionaire from birth, he was said to live for strong emotions.[11] The cyclist Jörg Jaksche said, 'There's something brilliant about him, even if he sometimes goes a bit crazy. He's the kind of guy who will drive through a red traffic light just to see what happens.'[12]

Others, who preferred anonymity, observed, 'He only knows how to live on a razor's edge, half outside the law. He will never change. It is in his genes.'

Another colleague, who had seen him at work in a team context, described a man with 'an immoderate taste for thrills, a dose of vanity, a dose of impunity and a dose of conceit . . . Plus absolute contempt for cyclists and their lives.'[13]

It was the usual story: energetic, charismatic, a brilliant student, in his case, of medicine at the Public University of Navarre in the mid-1970s, Fuentes was also a 400 metres hurdler, mediocre in some accounts, 1976 national university champion in others, trained by one of Spain's foremost athletics coaches, Manuel Pascua Piqueras, whose brother, José Luís Pascua Piqueras, was the coach chosen by Echávarri and Unzue in 1980 when the Reynolds team turned professional. Manuel Pascua Piqueras' stable was said to include prominent riders like Jorge Ruiz Cabestany, a professional between 1980 and 1982, and Jokin Mujika, eleventh in the 1987 Giro d'Italia. Two years later, after graduating, Fuentes used his residential internship to specialise in gynaecology, only switching to sports medicine later, at his coach's bidding. He finished his degree in sport sciences at Madrid's Complutense University in 1983 and joined the Spanish Athletics Federation as doctor of the Blume Residence attached to the Higher Sports Council's elite training facilities in Madrid.

José Luís Pascua Piqueras provided the introduction that brought Fuentes into cycling. In 1985 he worked for Pedro

Delgado's team Seat-Orbea, which became Caja Rural-Orbea and went to the Tour de France in 1987, although he continued his work with athletes, marrying one of them, the sprinter Cristina Pérez, who, in her best year, 1988, broke seven Spanish records, and ran 55.23 seconds in the 400 metres hurdles, a mark which stood for thirty-three years.

In 1987 the national Higher Sports Council appointed a new director of sport, Rafael Cortés Elvira. Moving into his office, he found a sheet of athletics federation notepaper lying in a drawer. Headed 'Sterane project', it was signed Eufemiano Fuentes. Cortés, a chemist, understood immediately: steroid molecules are built around a sterane nucleus. Fuentes was removed from the Blume Residence and his federal positions.

Yet, although his name, and that of Manuel Pascua Piqueras, disappeared from the organigram of the athletics federation, they quietly continued what they called 'biological preparation' in the margins. Pascua returned to the federation officially in 2003.

EPO entered cycling soon after Fuentes, although Eufemiano continued to trust in blood transfusions. In 1989 he began to work with the ONCE team, managed by Manolo Saiz. At the 1991 Vuelta a España, on the eve of the stage eight time trial around Cala d'Or, Mallorca, he flew to the island with a cool box on the next seat. To journalists on the same flight, he boasted, 'This box contains the key to the Vuelta'. A ONCE rider, Melchor Mauri, won the time trial and the Vuelta overall.[14]

In 1995, after a stint with Javier Mínguez's Amaya team, Fuentes joined Kelme. More than the team doctor, he became its main strategist, although he was also involved with the football teams Elche CF and, for the 2001–02 season, Unión Deportiva Las Palmas. After an important game against Rayo Vallecano in Madrid, syringes were found in the Las Palmas dressing room. Fuentes claimed to have received an offer to work at FC Barcelona under Josep Lluís Núñez, club president until 2000. In his account, he accepted the invitation, then turned it down 'to avoid envy and controversy'.

Fuentes had been linked to another Canary Islander, Estefania Godoy, three times the Spanish champion in the high jump, who tested positive for steroids in April 1996. In 1999 another of Fuentes' athletes, the Kelme rider Santiago Botero, tested positive for high testosterone levels, although Fuentes claimed they were natural.

He was thought of as a man whose principal loyalty was to his own financial interests. Kelme permitted him to work with other athletes, although even they might have been surprised to learn that he would collaborate with their greatest rivals. After the Festina rider Ángel Casero had won the 2001 Vuelta a España, with Kelme's Óscar Sevilla second, the cycling weekly *Meta Dos Mil* released the transcript of a voice message Fuentes had left for Casero before stage fifteen, when Sevilla, Fuentes' own athlete, was leading the race:

Hi, Angel, good morning. Eufemiano. No, just calling to see if everything's okay. The vampires [the anti-doping inspectors who take blood] came yesterday but I see it's all fine. So, today is the key day, big boy. Today you have to suffer like a dog, eh? Don't forget that from today until Saturday is the key to the Vuelta, okay? I hope everything goes well. I'm in the car right now, it's ten to nine, I'm heading for Madrid, to . . . well, to be ready with you-know-what, just in case. I'll call this afternoon after the stage, okay? But remember, today is the day. Today is the day to go through the pain barrier, okay? So, good luck, champ. See you later.

It was a curious message to send your team leader's closest rival. Fuentes explained, 'I was only passing on a message from his doctor, the Italian Luigi Cecchini'. He explained that 'you-know-what' was a set of extra-long, 180-millimetre cranks for the final time trial, even if Casero won the Vuelta in the final time trial without extra-long cranks.[15] The national daily *El Mundo* called Fuentes a 'witch doctor under permanent suspicion'.

Yet, despite all that was common knowledge about Fuentes, the institutions of Spanish sport – the athletes, the federations, the overarching bodies and the sports ministry – reacted to Jesús Manzano's revelations with mutism. The association of Spanish cycling doctors observed collective silence. Spain's cycling federation, the RFEC, urged the public not to generalise, and announced a fast-track investigation more into Manzano than his allegations. In a text message, the president of the Spanish branch of the riders' association advised the entire Spanish peloton to say nothing.

Ninety-three riders at the one-week Setmana Catalana signed a petition calling on the Professional Cyclists Association to take legal action against Manzano. Before the start of the last stage, the peloton held a two-minute protest.

The cycling correspondent of the daily newspaper *El País*, Carlos Arribas, wrote a scathing attack on this zombie-like acquiescence:

> In France, Italy, Belgium and elsewhere, conscience-stricken confessions followed action by the police and the justice system, and led to self-criticism, corrective programmes, shows of concern in wider society. In Spain, Manzano's confessions were made against a background of *omertà* and rumour, of 'everyone knows but nothing can be done.' If the reactions to the serialisation are anything to go by, they will be followed by more of the same, to re-establish an environment in which the cheats feel protected . . .[16]

In a three-hour hearing on Monday 5 April 2004, Manzano repeated to the cycling federation the allegations printed in the papers. Only two other riders[17] – Darío Gadeo[18] and Pedro Díaz

Lobato,[19] both with the Costa Almería-Paternina team – were even prepared to admit that doping existed. For their honesty, they were shunned by their colleagues.

None of this affected Bala. On 4 April, at the GP Indurain, he was part of a late, five-man attack that was caught at the last gasp by the peloton, and finished tenth. Two days later, he won the first stage of the Vuelta al País Vasco with, to quote *Mundo Deportivo*, 'insulting ease', getting the difficult final corner right as those around him misjudged it.

After pulling on the leader's jersey, he said, 'I am amazed by everything I've read in the press. It is not at all true. These have been difficult times for us and I hope that this victory will restore some happiness.'

He surrendered the race lead on stage three, regained it on stage four, lost it on the final day to Denis Menchov, then, on 11 April, two days after the race, won the Klasika Primavera.

Meanwhile, the Manzano case was moving fast. On Tuesday the thirteenth, he delivered handwritten prescriptions and doping schedules for the years 2001, 2002 and 2003 to the Cycling Federation, with packaging for prohibited substances including EPO, human growth hormone, insulin, cortisone and testosterone. It is hard to imagine what more they could have asked for.

The commission of the Royal Spanish Cycling Federation (RFEC) took statements from eight witnesses, drafted a report and sent it to the Antidoping Committee of Spain's national sports council (CSD). Yet, even six years after the 1998 Tour de France, the notorious Festina Tour, Spain's sporting authorities still lacked the institutions, authority, legislation and desire to take on doping themselves. So the CSD passed it on to the police, accompanied by a formal complaint by the RFEC arising from the publication of Manzano's allegations.

On Friday the sixteenth, the Madrid Investigating Magistrate's

Court No. Ten contacted the RFEC. It was looking into whether the doping practices that Manzano was alleging might constitute an offence against public health law. Meanwhile, cycling gradually returned to its uncertain equilibrium, and business carried on as usual, with Valverde winning stages three, four and five of the Vuelta a Castilla y León, which gave him ten victories in thirty-one days of racing, despite Bala and his teammates not being paid in April, and seven riders being prevented from competing because of incomplete paperwork.

The press described Valverde, who had turned 24 on 25 April, as having one and a half feet in Liberty Seguros.[20] Arrinda asked the UCI to terminate his contract, opening the way for the move to Liberty Seguros without paying the massive escape clause, although nothing came of it.

While all this was going on, a major reorganisation of elite cycling was looming. Called the UCI ProTour, the idea was to gather the thirty most important races into a single series, and oblige the top twenty teams to enter them. The races to be included were the three Grand Tours (Tour, Giro and Vuelta), the top one-day races, and the other 'Hors Categorie' stage races, of which Spain had two: the Volta a Catalunya and the Vuelta al País Vasco, both of which had been losing ground in recent years. June's Volta a Catalunya attracted criticism for attracting a poor field. Bala's presence secured it some sense of being top tier, while at the same time raising his own value and status.

Even so, at the Vuelta, an opening 28-kilometre team time trial ensured that he was never in the hunt. After losing 33 seconds there, he rode out the race as preparation for the national championships the following week. At Cabárceno, 17 kilometres from Santander, he finished second to Francisco Mancebo after 228 kilometres in soaring temperatures.

The Tour de France was due to start in Liège on Saturday 3 July with Lance Armstrong as the hot favourite, and Jan Ullrich, Tyler Hamilton and Iban Mayo expected to be his three main rivals. But, on Monday 14 June, extracts of a new book, *L.A. Confidentiel: Les secrets de Lance Armstrong* ('L.A. Confidential, the secrets of Lance Armstrong'), co-authored by Pierre Ballester and David Walsh, appeared in the French news magazine *L'Express*. It was full of doping allegations. French Minister of Youth and Sport, Jean-François Lamour, responded with the announcement that he had no confidence in the anti-doping procedures and would not be going to the Tour.

Valverde, still judged too young for the world's leading stage race, missed it too. He resumed racing in August at the Vuelta a Burgos, where he won three stages out of four and the race overall.

'I feel great,' he said afterwards. 'The Olympic Games are not far away, and this was an important test. My intention is to be at my best although, in a one-day race, luck counts a lot.' He added, 'I have to thank my teammates, not to mention my *grupeta* in Murcia, for helping me in training.'

As Valverde went from strength to strength, the season's doping stories kept coming. On the final day of the Vuelta a Burgos, the British Cycling Federation suspended David Millar for two years. After police had raided his home in Biarritz as part of the Cofidis investigation, and found two used syringes, Millar, 27, had confessed in a French court to three counts of doping with EPO, one in 2001 and two in 2003. The federation said it no longer considered him the world time trial champion, a title he had won in 2003, although the cancellation of his gold medal had yet to be ratified by the UCI.

Bala's last pre-Olympic race was the Clásica San Sebastián. He punctured at the very moment Paolo Bettini attacked at the foot of the Jaizkibel climb, and finished sixty-first, more than five minutes down.

After three of the 224 kilometres in the Olympic road race in Athens the following week, Igor Astarloa crashed out and headed to hospital. Of the Spanish quintet, only Bala finished the race, forty-seventh, 2 minutes 29 seconds behind the winner, Paolo Bettini.

Bala refocused. He went to the 2004 Vuelta a España intending to build on the previous year's shining performance.

In his pre-race press conference he was still talking about the team's finances, 'I will only know halfway through the Vuelta if the Comunitat Valenciana will be in the ProTour. I'm very happy with this team and I'm indebted to them, but if they don't make it into the elite, I'll probably have to change team next year.'[21]

With great fanfare, the Vuelta organisers had flown in the Sysmex XT-2000i Automated Hematology Analyzer used at the 2004 Tour de France. It reached León in a private plane, like a rock star. The newspapers reported that it could detect variations in blood values, synthetic haemoglobin, high haematocrit, autotransfusions, plasma and synthetic products. Every day the stage winner, the overall leader and two or more riders drawn by lot, were tested. In addition, there were morning blood tests, and surprise tests conducted by WADA. In stage three, finishing in Soria, south-east of Burgos, the race hit the final series of steep climbs as rain began to fall. Valverde exploded out of an elite group of eleven and finished ahead of fast finishers like O'Grady, second, and Freire, fourth.

Two days later, on the short, vicious climb up to the walled city of Morella, he took third place behind Menchov and Aitor González. It left him nine seconds off the race lead.

The same day, the UCI announced the names of seventeen of the eighteen ProTour teams. Comunitat Valenciana-Kelme was not among them.

In stage ten, won by his teammate Eladio Jiménez over a saw edge of a route that ended on the Xorret de Catí climb outside Valencia, Bala leapfrogged into second place overall behind US Postal's Floyd Landis.

As the racing approached the monastery town of Caravaca de la Cruz, whose cross Valverde wore around his neck, the scene was set for a coup. A win at an intermediate sprint would have been enough for him to take the race lead. Instead, seven kilometres into the stage, with the peloton at high speed, his chain jumped as he forced power down into the pedal, and he lost balance. After banging the back of his head on the road surface, he scraped along the ground, bloodying his knees, elbows, hips, back and ribs. Helped by his teammates, he regained his feet, jersey in tatters. No one else had fallen.

With one knee already swelling up, he changed his jersey and was borne off by his teammates. Out of solidarity, the peloton slowed as Valverde rejoined them, allowing the sole attacker, David Zabriskie, to build a twenty-minute lead. Only halfway through the stage was normal service restored as the sprinters' teams set about bringing back the breakaway.

After a post-stage check in the team bus, he went to hospital in Almería for X-rays, which showed no fractures. The stage was followed by a rest day, when an MRI scan confirmed the result.

The next day, Roberto Heras won stage twelve and took the leader's jersey. Bala, fourth in the stage at 1 minute 27 seconds, was not discouraged. The race doctor Juan Mari Irigoyen had told him the story of the 1992 Vuelta, won by the Swiss-Danish rider Tony Rominger after a serious crash in Gandía on stage five and another fall in the Pyrenees.

Valverde said, 'I surprised myself. Heras was the strongest and the Vuelta route suits him. But the race is not over. Quitting? No way, after going through all this.'

In stage fourteen, Bala attacked a kilometre from the summit of the main climb, the Monachil, then plummeted down the descent, forcing the race leader Heras to respond in person. They finished together, 46 seconds behind Santiago Pérez, who won again the following day, in the 29.6-kilometre Granada–Sierra

74

Nevada mountain time trial. Bala put in a memorable performance that day, passing Isidro Nozal, fourth overall, after 21 kilometres, and gaining 44 seconds on Heras. He ended the day five
seconds behind Heras in the general classification, on the eve of
the second rest day.

The next race day was stage sixteen to Cáceres. It was won
by Valverde's room-mate José Cayetano Juliá. The following
morning's sports pages shared the stage reports with yet more
doping stories:[22] it turned out that Tyler Hamilton had tested
positive for blood doping on 19 August in Sydney, after winning
the Olympic time trial, and again on 11 September, after winning
in stage eight of the Vuelta. Now 33, Hamilton faced a two-year
suspension and the loss of his Olympic medal. In a press conference, he said, 'I am 100 per cent innocent and I will spend every
last Euro proving it.'

The same day, the prosecution in the case involving the Italian
doctor Michele Ferrari, whose most prominent client was Lance
Armstrong, formally requested a fourteen-month prison sentence for administering doping substances to cyclists. The case
dated back to 2001.

The day after that the headline in *Mundo Deportivo* was
'Adios Valverde'.[23] Under relentless attack by the Liberty Seguros teammates of the race leader Roberto Heras, Bala held on
until the final climb where, with his jersey open, his casquette
reversed and his mouth gaping, he clung to Heras until the gradient reached 10.5 per cent with seven kilometres to go. There
Heras sped away.

Bala finished the 2004 Vuelta a España fourth. Second overall
with three stage wins was Santiago Pérez, until the end of October 2004, when news emerged that he had tested positive for a
homologous blood transfusion.

At the world championship road race on 3 October, Óscar
Freire found Bala's wheel. Germany's Erik Zabel and the Italian
Luca Paolini struggled to pass, but Valverde led his teammate

into the final 200 metres and Freire did the rest. Bala was sixth.

After the race, Freire admitted, 'I won thanks to Valverde.'

5

Sporting Royalty

In 2004, Menorca Bàsquet, the island's basketball team, was battling for promotion to the top division of the Spanish basketball league and the Balearic government announced that, to support it, it would be reducing its commitment to cycling. The team was saved by a call from the French former rider Yvon Ledanois offering the sponsorship of the French savings bank Caisse d'Épargne, which contributed €6 million over the following two years.

On Thursday 3 February 2005, when the Illes Balears-Caisse d'Épargne team was presented at the Pueblo Español in the capital of the Balearic Islands, in the presence of the Minister of the Presidency and Sports, María Rosa Puig, and the Director General of Sports, José Luis Ballester, the Banesto logo was missing from the team jerseys for the first time in fifteen years.

The stars of the show were the Spanish road-race champion Francisco Mancebo, sixth in the 2004 Tour de France and third in the Vuelta a España; Russia's Vladimir Karpets, best young rider at the 2004 Tour de France; the Spanish time trial champion José Iván Gutiérrez; and Alejandro Valverde, whose plan was to ride the Tour de France as a support rider for Mancebo, to learn the ropes, then lead the team at the Vuelta a España.

Preventing one of Spain's sporting jewels from leaving the country had been a political triumph for the Partido Popular. The press reported that the escape clause in his contract had been reduced and that Illes Balears had paid Kelme something between €600,000 and €720,000. Despite the fact that the two teams concerned, Comunitat Valenciana-Kelme and Illes Balears, were funded, wholly or in part, by public money, the financial arrangements were never disclosed.

Information imparted at a press conference days after the team presentation suggested that at least one of the administrations involved did not regard financial probity as its primary concern. Summoning the media was Antoni Diéguez, a Socialist Member of the Balearic Parliament who, in November 2005, had attended a lavish convention in Palma de Mallorca called the Illes Balears Forum, in which celebrity guests like Rafael Nadal and Samuel Eto'o espoused the benefits of using sport to generate tourism on the islands. Given that, in 2003, golf in the Balearics had generated €198 million for the regional economy, and cycle tourism €71 million, supported by the annual Challenge de Mallorca bike race which dated back to 1992, it struck Diéguez as an expensive way of promoting what was happening anyway.

In a written parliamentary question, Diéguez requested the forum's budget and invoices. He eventually received the former, although not the latter, and announced to the press that the four-day congress, which only really had two days of activities, had cost the staggering sum of €1.2 million.

It was not just the potential misuse of public funds that was newsworthy. The entity which had organised the forum, something called the Nóos Institute for Applied Research, turned out to belong to a household name. A former professional handball player, Ignacio 'Iñaki' Urdangarin Liebaert enjoyed enormous visibility, and not only because of his six-foot-six-inch frame. As a sportsman, he was a national figure. After joining Barcelona's handball team as an eighteen-year-old in 1986, he had won six European Cups and represented Spain at three Olympic Games. At Sydney 2000 he had captained the Spanish handball team and won his second Olympic bronze medal. He had joined the Spanish Olympic Committee in 2001 and become its vice-president in 2004, although it was his marriage to the Infanta Cristina Federica de Borbón y Grecia,[1] a former Olympic yachtswoman but also the third child of Juan Carlos I, King of Spain, and, as such, sixth in line to the throne, that placed him squarely in the public eye. On his last day as a professional sportsman, he had scored Spain's final goal of the Sydney Olympics, watched in the stands by Queen Sofia, her son, the future monarch Prince Felipe, and her daughter, Urdangarin's wife, the Infanta Cristina, holding little Juan Valentín de Todos los Santos, their first child. Aged thirty-two, Urdangarin now faced the transition to normality that awaits every professional sportsperson.

By coincidence, Valverde's team, Illes Balears, owed Urdangarin its existence, for it was at his suggestion, made during a friendly game of padel in September 2003 with the president of the Balearic government, that the islands should replace Banesto as the team's sponsor. When the deal came about, Urdangarin took a hefty commission, while his company, Nóos Strategic Consultancy, was soon charging the Balearic government €300,000 a year to monitor the value of the sponsorship deal.

Studying the accounts of the Illes Balears Forum, Antoni Diéguez noticed an incongruity in Urdangarin's involvement. 'When I saw that he was being paid, despite the Nóos Institute being theoretically non-profit, alarm bells went off.'

However, Spain was not ready for the national scandal that would explode some years later as the Nóos Case, and Antoni Diéguez's complaint slipped silently out of the news, not to resurface for four years. When it did, it dragged the sponsorship deal that created the Illes Balears team into the mud, not that it mattered. By then the team had moved on to other sponsors.

Had the Partido Popular's Jaume Matas won the Balearic Islands elections in July 2007 and stayed in power, the Nóos Case might never have come to light. He had held his main campaign rally in the Palma Arena, the impressive indoor velodrome he had commissioned to host the track cycling world championships in 2007. It was only after he had lost the vote and the presidency had changed hands that an €83 million overrun in the Arena's construction costs was discovered. Initially budgeted at €27 million, it had eventually devoured €110 million.

An anti-corruption investigation got under way in August 2008. It branched into dozens of separate cases. In July 2010 the investigating magistrate's eye was drawn to a handful of papers that mentioned the Illes Balears Forum, the subject of Antoni Diéguez's complaint four and a half years before.

The Nóos Case soon came to centre on the royal couple, the image of a modernising royal family. Cristina was the first woman in the Spanish royal family with a university degree, and had a public-service career at the charitable foundation. She and Urdangarin had a reputation for simplicity,[2] although this was not the full story. It came out much later that, to get out of his military service, Urdangarin had claimed, falsely, to be profoundly deaf. During his playing career, he had racked up debts of thousands of Euros in unpaid parking fines and other taxes.

He too sought an education on which to build his post-sporting career. In September 1999, still competing professionally, he had enrolled at Barcelona's *Escola Superior d'Administració i Direcció d'Empreses* (Higher School of Business Administration and Management) or ESADE. A prestigious Jesuit business school attached to Barcelona's Ramon Llull University, the school counted among its alumni the prime minister of Andorra, the president of the Parliament of Catalonia, and the CEOs of PepsiCo, HP Inc., Diageo (the owners of Guinness) and Manchester City FC.

Most students took five years to gain their Bachelor's and Master's degrees in business administration. Urdangarin did it in two. He was hard to miss even without his two bodyguards, yet the investigative newspaper *ARA* spoke to ten ESADE students who read the same subject at the same time as him but could find no one who had ever seen him at a lecture. It emerged much later that his thesis was written by an ESADE lecturer, Pedro Parada, who later held the position of treasurer at one of Urdangarin's companies.[3]

Newly graduated, Urdangarin retired from professional sport into the new field of strategic sports consultancy. He was soon listed as an 'academic collaborator' with ESADE's Department of Company Policy, and later shared a platform with International Monetary Fund president Rodrigo Rato at another business school, IESE, the *Instituto de Estudios Superiores de la Empresa*, attached to the Opus Dei-run University of Navarre. Urdangarin spoke about corporate social responsibility, a subject, it soon emerged, he was not best qualified to address.

The director of ESADE's Strategy Innovation Lab, Associate Professor Diego Torres, an expert in competitive strategy, patronage, sponsorship and, again, social responsibility, divined in the towering, royally connected Olympian a door opening on wide corporate vistas. Together, they began to assemble a complex network of apparently independent companies that would be connected only later by a full-sclae corruption investigation.

In April 1999, Torres's wife, her brother, and another ESADE graduate had founded a not-for-profit market research organisation, the Nóos Institute for Applied Research (*Nóos* being the classical Greek word for mind or intelligence), the declared aim of which was 'to carry out research on the role of market intelligence in the competitiveness of companies.' Aspiring to bring together professionals in the field, while promoting the dissemination of research carried out through courses, conferences, seminars and publications, it chimed with the life of public service that Urdangarin professed. In September 2003 he and Torres joined the Nóos Institute as president and vice-president. An institute brochure listed Cristina de Borbón and her secretary, Carlos García Revenga (described as 'advisor to the household of H.M. the King'), as board members. Torres designed the projects and managed the structure and the human and material resources. Urdangarin used his privileged position to give clients the impression that they were buying into a well-connected network of influence.

In January 2003, Torres and Urdangarin took over a colleague's real estate company, extended its corporate purpose to include 'consulting related to the implementation of strategic plans, business plans and project management', and renamed it Nóos Consultoria Estratégica, SL, (Noos Strategic Consultancy Ltd, or NCE for short). There were now two companies called Nóos, one not-for-profit, the other very much for commercial gain. One of the small team of Nóos employees later said that he considered the consultancy and the research institute to be 'one and the same,' and he was sure his colleagues felt likewise.

Corporate clients contributed handsomely to their coffers. In three years, Volkswagen-Audi paid the Instituto Nóos more than €430,000, Telefónica €406,000 and the oil company Repsol €275,856, with other international clients including Adecco, Air Europa, Europcar, Iberia, Sol Meliá hotels and Toyota.

Urdangarin chaired the Nóos Institute for Applied Research in 2004 and 2005, during which he and Torres issued the two Nóos companies invoices for a total of €3.6 million, billing them through other companies. Urdangarin's was called Aizoon SL. Created in 2003 and jointly owned by Urdangarin and his wife, it potentially implicated the Infanta in the wrongdoing.

Although in 2006 the press had quickly dropped the Illes Balears Forum story raised by Antoni Diéguez, it had caused alarm bells to sound in the Zarzuela Palace, the private residence and working offices of the King, who sent a legal advisor to give Urdangarin a very clear order.

Urdangarin later recalled before a judge: 'He told me not to hold any position of presidency, not to lead any project, not to have any long-term business or corporate relations with Mr

Diego Torres, and to stay away from contracts with any public administration.'

Urdangarin left the Nóos Institute for Applied Research on 20 March 2006. Three months later he was appointed director of Telefónica Latinoamérica, a subsidiary of the telecommunications giant Telefónica. In April 2009 – Bala was winning the Vuelta a Catalunya at the time[4] – the Royal Household announced that the Duke and Duchess of Palma would be moving to Washington DC, where Urdangarin would continue to work for Telefónica.

It was not until 7 November 2011 that police raided the Barcelona headquarters of the theoretically non-profit foundation Nóos Institute for Applied Research.[5]

On 15 November the newspaper *El Periódico* informed its readers that investigating magistrate José Castro and the Anti-Corruption Prosecutor's Office of the Balearic Islands were looking into Urdangarin's corporate network for alleged embezzlement and had extended their enquiries to the Matas government's cycling sponsorship. They had documents suggesting that Urdangarin may have received at least €300,000 of public funds for his part in sealing the sponsorship deal between the Balearic Islands government and José Miguel Echávarri's cycling team.

The idea for the team sponsorship deal originated with another recent ESADE graduate, Juan Pablo Molinero. In 2002, fresh out of college, and after a temporary job as a venue information officer at the FIFA World Cup in Korea and Japan, Molinero had joined the auditors PricewaterhouseCoopers and played some part in setting up a sports department in Barcelona and Madrid. As we have seen, soon after the 2002 Tour de France, Banesto informed the team that its sponsorship would cease in December 2003. Sometime after receiving the news, the team management entered into agreement with PwC to find a new sponsor.

Molinero's contact with Urdangarin was presumably part of the search, although Torres told police investigators: 'Molinero had been wanting to collaborate with Iñaki for some time . . . From the moment Nóos was constituted, he started bombarding Iñaki with cycling ideas.' According to Diego Torres, Molinero emailed Urdangarin from his PwC email account as early as February 2003, to tell him that he had a cycling team in need of a sponsor. Was Urdangarin interested?

Urdangarin had a Balearic connection. When he had married the Infanta Cristina in October 1997, he had taken the courtesy title The Most Excellent The Duke of Palma de Mallorca, although they lived in Barcelona. A close friend of his, José Luis Ballester, an Olympic sailing champion in 1996, was now the island's Director General of Sports.

In May 2003, elections in the Illes Balears had returned the Partido Popular to power under Jaume Matas. With his party leader José María Aznar heading the government in Madrid until April 2004, Matas was sure of his power base. An autocratic spirit, he treated the islands as his own fiefdom, with sport at its heart.

In July 2003, Matas put Ballester, who was also close to the future King Felipe, in charge of sport. That summer, Urdangarin contacted Ballester eight or nine times, repeatedly mentioning the idea of taking over Banesto's cycling sponsorship, and claiming to represent or have influence over Unzue and Echávarri.

Ballester raised the sponsorship project with Matas at the end of August 2003. Matas told him to arrange a meeting with Urdangarin. The three met at the Marivent Palace, the summer residence of the Spanish royal family in Palma de Mallorca, in September 2003, and played padel. This was when Urdangarin made his pitch. As well as the sponsorship deal, Urdangarin insisted on the need for what he called a 'project office' to promote and monitor the team. He would take personal charge of this through his company Nóos Consultoría Estratégica. It would cost €300,000, to be paid independently of the team sponsorship.[6]

According to Ballester, Matas verbally approved the sponsorship deal and the project office at the end of September. In court in February 2016, Ballester explained, 'There was never any doubt that the contractor had to be Iñaki Urdangarin . . . the price was never questioned . . . there was no discussion.'[7] In a television interview, Matas made light of it. 'The Duke of Palma and his non-profit organisation comes to the President of a Community with what we genuinely believe to be a worthwhile project. Does anyone imagine we are going to say to the Duke of Palma, "Okay, hold on, I'll put it out to public tender and we'll see if you are lucky"?'

But that was precisely what the law demanded. Strict rules governed public procurement, placing definite limits on the exercise of power. They required professional contracting bodies, transparent procedures, thorough consultation, competitive tender mechanisms and clear, exhaustive documentation. The whole point was to rein in rogue administrations like that of Matas.

Yet the Illes Balears sponsorship deal circumvented the entire process.

The following month, Matas, Ballester and Echávarri reached a verbal agreement. Matas ordered the Balearic Tourism Institute ('Ibatur') and the Foundation for the Support and Promotion of Balearic Sport ('Illesport') to arrange the finance and, on 10 November, Echávarri, Unzue and their partners incorporated Abarca Sports, the company that would manage the team.

Matas had his functionaries fill a procurement file with false documents to give the deal a veneer of legality. According to the minutes of an Illesport trustees board dated 24 November 2003, 'the actions stipulated by the executive committee necessary to support the contracts for the cycling team sponsorship arrangements for 2004, 2005 and 2006 [were] unanimously approved.' But, questioned by the police, those mentioned in the minutes – councillors, directors and secretaries of relevant organs of government – said that no such meeting had ever taken place.

On 21 November 2003 the Consell de Govern approved the sponsorship deal, and the contract was signed six days later to the value of €6.96m for 2004, €6m for 2005 and €7m for 2006. The invoices were authorised by the manager of the Illesport Foundation, who had already received verbal orders from Matas to this effect. Urdangarin took a commission of 1.7 per cent.[8]

Torres and Urdangarin hired Molinero in December 2003 to work mainly on the sponsorship project for the Banesto cycling team, although Molinero's version of events diverges from that of Diego Torres.[9] 'A friend of mine, Iñaki Urdangarin, called me and insisted on the Nóos thing that was being set up at the time,' Molinero explained. 'And for me, friends are important. He told me that I had to help him out, so that's where I went.'

What PricewaterhouseCooper thought about Molinero taking the Banesto dossier with him is unclear.

Molinero busied himself with the spurious procurement dossier. Illesport's statutes required a contracting process and an administrative file, so he invented the false traces of a competitive tender for the project office. For media monitoring inside Spain and internationally, Illesport received a quotation dated 10 January 2004 from Virtual Strategies Ltd for €58,000 plus VAT, an undated quote from Aizoon Ltd for €50,000 plus VAT, and a third from Sofres-TNS Intelligence for €47,000 for monitoring in Spain and €21,500 for international monitoring. Molinero sent all three quotes from the same fax number. The Sofres-TNS Intelligence offer was sent on 16 January 2004. It had been accepted four days before. Urdangarin's signature on the Illesport–Sofres-TNS Intelligence agreement, finalised on 20 January 2004, was a forgery.

The minutes of another non-existent meeting, of the Illesport Foundation Executive Committee, dated 12 January 2004, which also went in the file, read: 'It is unanimously agreed to approve the contracting of an entity to carry out the coordination of the cycling team.'

The interim charge sheet issued on 30 January 2013 dedicated 18 of its 540 pages to describing and debunking the bogus documents.

Within the broad torrent of illegality, smaller eddies of deceit formed. Urdangarin and Torres concealed an agreement they had reached with Abarca Sports making it responsible for 25 per cent of the costs of the project office, for which they would receive an extra €200,000 in 2005.

When the time came to settle, Nóos Consultoría Estratégica was instructed to invoice the Illesport Foundation, although it was the Director General of Sports, José Luis Ballester, who authorised payment. Illesport duly received quarterly invoices for 'Professional collaboration according to agreement' on headed paper just marked 'Nóos', making no distinction between the not-for-profit Nóos and the commercial one. Ballester explained before the justice system that Matas authorised payment of anything Urdangarin invoiced.

Given the operation's success, Urdangarin and his confederates embarked on other projects, using the same methodology to outflank the official public procurement procedures. After preliminary contact late in 2003, Urdangarin met the president of the Generalitat, Francisco Camps, and the mayor of Valencia, Rita Barberá, on 29 January 2004 at the Zarzuela Palace. As well as concluding a €382,203 contract with the Generalitat for promoting Valencia as the venue for what would have been the inaugural European Games, if they had taken place, Urdangarin proposed an annual Valencia Summit on Sport and Tourism, which duly took place in 2004, 2005 and 2006 at a cost of €3.1 million to the public purse. More than €2 million of this went into the pockets of Urdangarin and his business partner. Add finance from private sponsors, which lay outside the police investigation, and their profits must have been astronomical. This was on top of the €2.5 million that the Nóos group of companies received from the Matas government.

Urdangarin's last official act as a member of the royal family was on 12 October 2011, Spain's national day. He was formally charged in December of that year, during which his wife was removed from the official life of the royal family. Weeks later, in his Christmas Eve speech, her father Juan Carlos I commented, 'Justice is equal for all', making it clear that the head of state was not going to try to protect his youngest daughter and son-in-law. In January 2012, the former head of the King's Household, Fernando Almansa, sent the Infanta Cristina a message from her father: divorce or renounce your place in the succession. She did neither. Once considered the most highly valued institution in Spain, the monarchy saw its public approval plummet.

Then, in April 2012, as the economic crisis bit, Juan Carlos suffered a catastrophic lapse of judgement. Soon after making a speech demanding discipline and sacrifice from his subjects, he flew to Botswana for a private elephant hunting trip. It was organised by his secret Danish mistress, Corinna zu Sayn-Wittgenstein-Sayn. Even setting aside the King's position as honorary president of the Spanish branch of the World Wildlife Fund, the trip was a disaster. After falling and fracturing a hip, he had to be repatriated, exposing the hunting trip and his secret affair. A leading Socialist suggested Juan Carlos should choose either to fulfil his public responsibilities or abdicate.

Days later, newspapers published emails sent in 2007 which suggested that the King and the Infanta Cristina had used their influence to try to secure the involvement of Urdangarin and Torres in a new sailing team to target the America's Cup. This was after the King's order not to work on any project with Torres. The hunting trip and the emails only added to the crisis. By 2013, there was open talk of the King's abdication. It came in June 2014.

It would, of course, be folly to attribute the abdication to the Illes Balears cycling team. Even so, its creation amounted to far more than the random flapping of a butterfly's wings.

*

However far-reaching, the Illes Balears investigation had its limits. Valverde's transfer from Comunitat Valenciana-Kelme to Illes Balears was never scrutinised. As for the alleged reduction of the escape clause payment by two-thirds, nowhere was it asked whether the operation had been subjected to proper institutional oversight, or whether the relevant competition law allowed state-owned enterprises operating in the open market to agree contractual changes in this way. When Jaume Matas was questioned about the use of counterfeit documentation, he replied, 'It was a system.'[10] The judgment agreed that it was long-standing, habitual practice.[11] Since many of the same people and institutions arranged Valverde's transfer, why would they not have used the same methods?

6

The First Tour

In the first two races of the 2005 Challenge de Mallorca, the triple world champion Óscar Freire was unbeatable. Then Illes Balears took over, riding the rest of its home race like politicians. On a rainy 8 February, after a race of many breakaways, Valverde attacked with his Mallorcan teammate Toni Tauler and two Rabobank riders in tow. He dropped his companions at the foot of the final climb, and rode away alone to the Mirador d'es Colomer, the first altitude finish in the history of the Challenge de Mallorca, replacing Freire at the head of the general classification.

The following day, Bala joined an eight-rider attack with another Mallorcan teammate, Toni Colom. Again, he powered away to take a second consecutive stage win.

In the last stage, Colom himself attacked on the last pass and sped away to a third stage victory for the Illes Balears team. Valverde, fourth on the day, was proclaimed overall winner. And there was more good news that day when Madrid Investigating Magistrate's Court No. Ten informed the Spanish Cycling Federation that the facts alleged by Jesús Manzano did not constitute a crime.

Overinterpreting the decision, Vicente Belda told reporters, 'It has been demonstrated that there is no guilt on the part of any of the people who had been accused, although the damage that has been done to us can never be repaired.'

Jesús Manzano saw things rather differently. 'I knew this

would happen,' he announced, 'but it is not going to stay like this. My witnesses have not been called to testify. I will continue to fight for them to be heard. The Secretary of State, Jaime Lissavetzky, promised to act and has done nothing. There is no justice in Spain.'[1]

The first race of the new ProTour was Paris–Nice. In the difficult final stage, having already ascended the Col de la Porte and the Col de la Turbie, Bala posted two accelerations on the Col d'Eze to reduce the group of the race leader Bobby Julich to about twenty riders. In front, Liberty Seguros-Würth's 22-year-old Alberto Contador escaped from a breakaway of seven. Vinokurov joined him, but they were caught with 300 metres to go. Bala won the sprint to take his first stage victory outside Spain. Second overall, he missed out on the GC by ten seconds.

At Milano–Sanremo on 19 March, he attacked on the Poggio with five other riders. 'I gambled everything on the climb and failed,' he said. 'But it was a good learning experience.'

Doping stories continued to dog the sport. In the days before the Vuelta al País Vasco, the German sprinter Danilo Hondo, the winner of two stages at the Vuelta a Murcia and second in Milano–Sanremo, had returned a positive anti-doping test for an undisclosed stimulant. Then a former mechanic for Lance Armstrong named Mike Anderson revealed that he had found a box of a banned drug in the rider's home.

Unaffected, Bala took two consecutive stage victories in the Basque Country. They brought his total to five wins in nineteen days of racing.

Then he faced his first ever week in the Ardennes. It ended with thirteenth place in the Amstel Gold Race, thirty-ninth in Flèche Wallonne, and thirty-third in Liège–Bastogne–Liège. He did not compete again until the Volta a Catalunya on 16 May, where he started a block of races that led to his first Tour de France.

Stage seven slipped over the German border to Karlsruhe, where Robbie McEwen took the win. Stage eight started in Pforzheim and headed back into France, crossing the Col de la Schlucht on the way to the finish line in Gérardmer. An early, seven-man breakaway grew smaller and smaller until Rabobank's Pieter Weening was alone at the head of the race. T-Mobile's Andreas Klöden broke across to him, and they disputed the stage together. The photo-finish showed Weening's front wheel on the finish line, seven millimetres ahead of Klöden's. Bala won the sprint for third place, 27 seconds too late for his first Tour de France stage win.

Three days later, stage ten took the riders 181 kilometres over the 20-kilometre Cormet de Roselend, and up the 22-kilometre climb to Courchevel-Altiport. So hot was the pace set by Armstrong's teammates that all three T-Mobile leaders, Vinokurov, Ullrich and Klöden, dropped off the pace on the lowest slopes of the final climb. With eight kilometres to go, Armstrong moved to the front and accelerated, and another of the favourites, CSC's Ivan Basso, lost contact. That left four out front: Armstrong, Michael Rasmussen, and the Illes Balears pair of Mancebo and Valverde. It was Bala who led them under the flamme rouge.

Rasmussen was the first to attack. Bala darted across the gap with Armstrong on his wheel. With 450 metres to go, the American squeezed between Rasmussen and the barrier and launched his sprint. Bala followed, biding his time, then, in the final 75 metres, eased past to take the win.

After the stage, he said, 'No words could describe my happiness. It is the most important day of my life on a bike. It was very fast from the foot of the climb. I was flat out, close to throwing in the towel. Only the thought of victory in a monster stage like this gave me the strength to carry on.'

Armstrong admitted, 'Valverde was impressive. I was surprised to see him there. He's a difficult rider to classify, very fast and also very strong. A guy like him – and I'm not blowing smoke – could be the future of cycling, because he's a complete rider and he's always been good. Valverde was good from the first day he showed up and he's proven it here. The only thing he would have to work on for this race is his time trial, but I suspect he'll do it [in the future].'

The next morning, a rest day, Bala revealed that he was struggling with a knee injury. 'The pain is worse during the first few kilometres of the stages, although when the joint warms up, I feel better.'

He spoke of anti-inflammatory drugs and ultrasound sessions in the hotels, but not of leaving the Tour. But the following afternoon, 80 kilometres into stage thirteen, he slipped out of the back of the group, stopped at the roadside and abandoned.

'It's the saddest moment of my sporting life,' he said. 'I love this race. One day I will come back with even greater ambitions.'

He tested his knee three weeks later, on a training ride in the mountains near Murcia, but the results were not good. The doctors prescribed ten more days of complete rest, which meant no Vuelta a España.

He tested the joint again at the Clásica de los Puertos de Guadarrama on 21 August. The race had six climbs. If all went well, he would target the world championship road race around Madrid on 25 September. He finished the Clásica de los Puertos tenth. 'There's very little pain when I'm climbing,' he explained, 'but descending, it is bad. I feel great in terms of strength, but when I lift my foot, the knee hurts.'

Even so, his place in Spain's nine-man world championship team was confirmed on 13 September. On 24 September, the day before the thirteen-lap, 273-kilometre race, he reported, 'I'm as good as or even better than I was at the Tour. I've done a lot of training, although, after 273 kilometres, I don't know how I'll be at the end. It's a sprinter's race. Our job is to find a breakaway group that doesn't have [the sprinters Alessandro] Petacchi or [Robbie] McEwen in it.'

The first five hours saw a four-man breakaway build a lead of 11 minutes 40 seconds. They stayed away for 210 kilometres. The monotony was broken by a puncture on lap five: five teammates shepherded Bala back to the group. On lap nine, Paolo Bettini lost patience and attacked on a climb. Germany's Fabian Wegmann made it across to him, and they were joined by two Belgians – Stijn Devolder and Philippe Gilbert – a Dane (Jakob Piil) and two Spaniards (Martín Perdiguero and Bala). There was little cohesion in the group, and Valverde worked hard, closing down attacks and keeping the pace high for his teammate Perdiguero.

At the start of the final 21-kilometre lap, the peloton was just 15 seconds behind them. Perdiguero, then Bettini, alone, then Piil and Gilbert together, soon joined by Wegmann, persisted in their attacks, but the Australian team, working for Robbie McEwen, brought the race back together.

On the final climb, Vinokurov, Bettini and two Dutchmen, Koos Moerenhout and Michael Boogerd, led a string of riders attempting to ride clear. Bala joined a second group containing Tom Boonen and three of his Belgian teammates. The two groups came together 550 metres from the finish line, on the slight climb to the finish. With 250 metres to go, the turnover of riders at the front churned Bala into the lead, giving him little choice but to start his sprint too early. Boonen then came powering past.

After the race, he said, 'If I had let Boonen go first and sprinted from his slipstream, maybe I could have won, but I might also have got myself boxed in. In any case, this silver medal tastes good to me after my injury in the Tour.'

It was Spain's eleventh elite men's world championship medal in the nine years of Valencian coach Francisco Antequera's tenure. The same day, in Brazil, Fernando Alonso became Spain's first Formula 1 champion, and, at 24 years, one month and 27 days, the youngest in history. With two nineteen-year-olds, Rafa Nadal, second in the world tennis rankings, and Dani Pedrosa, already motorbike world champion in the 125 and 250cc categories, the 21-year-old footballer Fernando Torres, the 25-year-old golfer Sergio García, number six in the world, and the 26-year-old triathlete Iván Raña, already a world and European champion, Spanish sport was on a high – and Bala was at the heart of it.

But such sporting success had a flipside. On 27 October, the UCI notified Liberty Seguros-Würth that its Vuelta a España champion, Roberto Heras, had tested positive for EPO in a control on stage twenty, the Guadalajara–Alcalá de Henares time trial.

Early in August, Francisco Mancebo, who had finished the Tour de France fourth, 3 minutes 38 seconds off the podium, signed a contract for the French team AG2R, who, he said, pointedly, had promised him 'a team that works only for me in the Tour'. He added, 'Between what Echávarri can pay and what others are offering, the difference is massive.'

Echávarri retorted, 'In France, cycling means the Tour and every French team wants to beat the other French teams. Since Armstrong's retirement, the value of everyone who has finished in the top five in recent years has multiplied.'[2] But he was forgetting that his team was turning French in 2006. On 24 January 2006, the team, Caisse d'Épargne-Illes Balears (which would continue as Illes Balears-Caisse d'Épargne in the Spanish races) was presented in Paris.

Then, just before Christmas 2005, the best Spanish sportsmen and women voted Lance Armstrong world sportsman of the year for the fourth time in five years. This was in spite of the August 2005 story, broken by the French newspaper *L'Équipe*, that samples of Armstrong's urine, collected and frozen during the 1999 Tour de France had been thawed, analysed and found to contain traces of EPO.

The International Association of Cycling Teams proposed that their riders should give their DNA at the request of the sport's authorities, until it was pointed out that Portugal, Spain and Italy considered mandatory DNA testing a criminal offence.

7

The Fifty-eight

Euphoric after the 2005 world championships, Bala declared, 'Next year I'm going to base my whole season around the Tour. Instead of starting in Mallorca, I will go to the Basque Country and have a one-month peak instead of the three-month peak I had this season. To win the Tour I have to improve against the clock. There are a few muscles in my legs that I need to strengthen.'

To this end, and to reduce wear and tear on his knees, he lowered his saddle by a centimetre, shortened his cranks from 175 to 171.5 millimetres, changed the position of his shoes in the pedals, and increased his cadence from 90 turns per minute to 105.

However, even as he professed to have a single-minded focus on the Tour, he was preoccupied with other goals, as he revealed in an interview with Carlos Arribas in *El País*:

Q. Of the spring classics, which one do you like the most?
A. Liège. I've already learned that it's about doing as little as possible and getting to the end in one piece.
Q. But for all your ability in the classics, and for all your track record, for the fans, and perhaps for yourself, the most admired image of Valverde is his victory in Courchevel at the Tour, ahead of Armstrong. The fans want a Tour man. Can it be you?
A. I loved the Tour and the fans also loved me in the Tour, and

they already see me more as a Tour rider than a Classics rider. And that's how I see it too.[1]

As it turned out, he did start his season in Mallorca, albeit to test his new pedal stroke at race speed, not to try to win. His first victory of the 2006 season came at the start of March, in stage two of the Vuelta a Murcia. A month later, he won the first stage of the Vuelta al País Vasco, emerging out of Óscar Freire's slipstream and throwing his bike, like the former track sprinter he was, to win by fifty-three thousandths of a second. He was third the following day, twelfth in stage three, fourth and tenth in stages four and five, then, significantly, second in the final time trial, which secured him second place overall.

Then came Ardennes Week.

In the Amstel Gold Race, on Sunday 16 April, the Luxembourger Fränk Schleck attacked midway through the third ascent of the Cauberg, with its 12 per cent slopes, to win in Valkenburg. Bala finished twenty-third, one place behind his teammate Constantino Zaballa, both of them at 1 minute 34 seconds. In Flèche Wallonne the following Wednesday, on the gruelling ramps of Huy, Igor Astarloa attacked early. Bala wisely waited near the front of the peloton. On the steepest part of the climb, the Liberty Seguros-Würth rider David Etxebarria stormed past Astarloa, as Valverde still held back. For a moment, he lowered himself into the saddle. Then, as Samuel Sánchez, to his right, and Karsten Kroon, to his left, threatened to overwhelm him, he rose again and started his sprint. It was unanswerable. He had time to look over both shoulders and raise his arms in celebration before the finish line.

Then, Sunday's Liège–Bastogne–Liège, on a 262-kilometre route between Liège and Ans. Boogerd and Bala's brilliant teammate, Joaquim 'Purito' Rodríguez, led on the Saint-Nicolas, with its 11 per cent gradient. Perdiguero (Phonak), then Patrick Sinkewitz (T-Mobile) crossed to them. Moments later, Bala

98

appeared, with Fränk Schleck, Michael Boogerd, Chris Horner, Damiano Cunego, Ivan Basso, Paolo Bettini, Danilo Di Luca and Andrey Kashechkin close by.

Five kilometres to go, Valverde sent Purito to the front to keep the pace high.

With 3.4 kilometres to go, Bala appeared at the front, showing signs of impatience. At that moment, Schleck darted away, with Horner and Kashechkin on his wheel. Purito ensured they did not escape.

With two kilometres to go, Purito set the pace at the front again, as Bettini moved onto Bala's wheel. Bala slowed and, with 1.5 kilometres to go, on the Côte de l'Ans, where the gradient hit 9 per cent, Purito attacked. Perdiguero sprang across the gap, chased by Boogerd and Bala.

Under the flamme rouge, Sinkewitz shot past Purito. Basso quickly bridged to him, but Boogerd closed them down, with Bala and the rest of the group on his wheel.

Schleck was the next to attack. Boogerd darted across to him, but Sinkewitz led the file of riders up to them. Then Basso accelerated. Sinkewitz surged past, with Bala on his wheel, and Bettini in third place. The German led around the final, left-hand bend with 250 metres to go. At 100 metres, Valverde eased out of Sinkewitz's wake. No one could match his speed.

He lifted his left hand from the bars in celebration. A new era had started. The win elevated him to first place in the ProTour rankings for the first time. Winning Flèche Wallonne and Liège–Bastogne–Liège in the same week, he joined the likes of Ferdinand Kübler, Stan Ockers, Eddy Merckx, Moreno Argentin and Davide Rebellin. The first four all became world champions.

Eusebio Unzue led the hype while pretending to distance himself from it: 'Valverde can do everything. Even he doesn't know where his real talent lies. But you are exaggerating a bit with him. Everything in due time.'

Two days after Liège, he started the Tour de Romandie, in

Switzerland, with a new saddle embroidered *Eres como una bala verde* ('You're like a green bullet').[2] Completing the skillset he would need to win the Tour de France, he finished second, 0.64 of a second behind Paolo Savoldelli in the 3.4-kilometre prologue. Second in stage three to the new race leader, Alberto Contador, Bala won the next day, in a stage over three category-one climbs, to move within six seconds of his compatriot. But, in the closing 20.4-kilometre time trial, Cadel Evans left him trailing at 1 minute 2 seconds. Bala finished the race seventh overall, with uncertainty again hanging over his time trial abilities, although he had done enough to retain his position as number one in the world rankings.

He would not race again until the Critérium du Dauphiné Libéré on 11 June.

February 2006 had seen two events whose shockwaves would resonate through Spanish national life for the next decade or more – both, in their way, connected to Bala. The first was the press conference where Antoni Diéguez revealed the exorbitant sums squandered on the Illes Balears Forum, leading to the investigation into the Illes Balears team sponsorship contract. The second involved an investigation by a 28-year-old lieutenant with the Consumption and Environment Section of the Guardia Civil (SECOMA) named Enrique Gómez Bastida. Investigating the bulk distribution of anabolic steroids, Bastida had discovered a clandestine printing press turning out cartons for fake medicines manufactured in a bathtub by a gang of conmen. That revelation led him to a nutritional supplement shop in central Madrid whose owner, one Bartolomé Cobo, had lived in Australia, whence he was importing Insulin-like Growth Factor-1, or IGF-1, from a veterinary products lab.

To get through customs checks, Cobo relied on the signature of a helpful neurologist at Spain's prestigious National Research Council, who was investigating IGF-1's potential in the treatment of cerebellar ataxia, Parkinson's disease and Alzheimer's. Some of the imported product went into the researcher's laboratory rats. The rest went onto the black market as a doping product, reaching sportspeople directly through online sales or via intermediaries, some of them well known like the athletics coach Manuel Pascua Piqueras (later investigated in Operación Galgo, which was then annulled) or the cycling coach Eufemiano Fuentes. Looking into Fuentes, Bastida stumbled upon a clinical laboratory in central Madrid owned by José Luis Merino Batres, a haematologist at the University Hospital 'La Princesa' two kilometres away. In March 2006, Bastida began a surveillance operation. Since it involved cycling, he gave it the codename Operación Puerto ('Operation Mountain Pass').

If Fuentes, Merino and their accomplices became the investigation's main target, it also uncovered a huge network of professional athletes who paid them for their services. On 4 May, two active riders, both well-known former Kelme riders, were seen entering and leaving various properties with Dr Fuentes: one was the 2002 world time trial champion Santiago Botero, now with the Swiss team Phonak. The other was the 2005 Clásica de San Sebastián winner Constantino Zaballa, now Valverde's teammate at Illes Balears. On 13 May, another ex-Kelme rider, Óscar Sevilla, the best young rider at the 2001 Tour de France, now riding for T-Mobile, was seen entering the flat with Fuentes and Labarta, Kelme's assistant sports director. The following day, the German rider Jörg Jaksche, winner of the Tour Mediterranean and Paris–Nice for Team CSC in 2004, but now riding for Liberty Seguros, met Fuentes in room 605 of the Hotel Puerta de Madrid. In the conduct of all these persons of interest, the Guardia Civil's Central Operational Unit (UCO) discerned patterns of behaviour characteristic of organised criminal groups: constant changes of mobile phone numbers, the use of nicknames and codenames, extreme vigilance in their movements.[3]

With a warrant to intercept three telephone numbers, two

belonging to Fuentes and one to the lab owner Merino, the investigators found themselves listening at all hours to bizarre conversations filled with ludicrous riddles. At 1.40 a.m. on 19 May, Fuentes spoke to his sister Yolanda, a medical doctor specialising in allergy treatments who had taken over as Comunitat Valenciana-Kelme team doctor at the start of 2004. Santiago Botero had called, she said, asking for 'what Vicente lacks and Ignacio has too much of'. Given that Vicente Belda measured 1.54 metres (five feet, half an inch), and Ignacio Labarta little more, police hypothesised that this reference was possibly to Belda's small stature and the reputed size of Labarta's virile member.

To help them decipher the references in the telephone conversations, the Guardia Civil eavesdroppers hung the general classification of the Giro d'Italia, which was drawing to its conclusion, in their office and put a dot against the names of the riders they recognised.[4]

Destined to finish second overall was 32-year-old José Enrique Gutiérrez, known, it became public knowledge during the race, by the nickname *El Búfalo*. A dot stood next to his name on the Guardia Civil's Giro table. One of the conversations tapped by the Guardia Civil with Fuentes contained the phrase, 'Take food to the buffalo in Italy', which the investigators interpreted as 'Take a bag of blood to Gutiérrez at the Giro'. At the time of his arrest, Alberto León was carrying a ticket stub for a plane ticket to Milan dated 22 May, during the Giro.[5]

But it was all inspired guesswork.

Their enquiries led them to other properties, some belonging to Fuentes and his family, and to three other individuals connected to Fuentes: the laboratory owner Merino; José Ignacio Labarta Barrera, the team's 48-year-old assistant sports director and physical trainer since the mid-1990s; and a former mountain biker fallen on hard times named Alberto León Herranz, who acted as driver, delivery man and cleaner.

By 23 May the Guardia Civil were ready to move in. Enrique

Gómez Bastida approached Fuentes in the street outside the Pio XII Hotel in north Madrid, and told him: 'You are under arrest, Dr Fuentes.' Merino and Manolo Saiz, the director of the Liberty Seguros team, were with him. The hotel was a two-minute walk from one of Fuentes' apartments. Labarta was arrested in Zaragoza and León in El Escorial in coordinated raids.

The same afternoon, six properties were searched: four in Madrid, and one each in Zaragoza and San Lorenzo de El Escorial. As well as blood transfusion equipment, medical products and documentation, they found fridges and freezers containing hundreds of chilled and frozen blood bags, dated and identified in marker pen using a variety of numbers and codenames.

At the time of his arrest, Fuentes had three mobile phones and eight SIM cards on him. Interviewed for the first time on the afternoon of 23 May, he explained that, since his voicemail had been hacked in 2001, he had a phobia about journalists and regularly changed numbers and phones. It had never occurred to him, he claimed, that the police might have any interest in him.[6]

It soon emerged that Fuentes and Merino had been performing secretive blood transfusions in hotel rooms the length and breadth of Spain for many years. If Fuentes appeared to dope mainly cyclists, Merino, in coordination with other doctors, was in charge of the blood transfusions of several athletes whom he called 'his own' and Fuentes called 'the atletix'.[7] Other investigations established that most of the 'atletix' were trained by Manuel Pascua Piqueras.

In addition, Fuentes had been prescribing drugs off-label, while Merino had been duping hospitals into releasing medical supplies under the pretence that they were for his legitimate business. Fuentes claimed that he sent medical waste to be incinerated at the laboratory, although the surveillance team had witnessed the suspects depositing medical waste in ordinary urban litter bins.

Then there was the money: actual cash, including €60,000 in Manolo Saiz's briefcase, and substantial payments flitting between bank accounts. In 2002 and 2003 the disgraced Tyler Hamilton paid him €25,000 to €30,000 a year, plus extra for 'the other performance enhancing substances'. In 2004 Fuentes had raised his fee for transfusions to €50,000 after buying a new freezer which permitted longer storage. If the police had not turned up, 2006 would have cost Ivan Basso €70,000. That was wholesale: for the 2005 Tour, Jörg Jaksche went retail, paying €4,000 a transfusion, or €6,000 for two.

On 26 May, the Guardia Civil delivered a report to the investigating magistrate. It described the actions they believed were criminal, and the names of about ten cyclists.

The arrests put Fuentes' clients in a complicated position. There being no law against doping in Spain, they knew they would not face criminal prosecution. But, if unmasked, they faced being banned from the ProTour, rejected by the three-week tours, and shunned by the sporting public.

With the benefit of hindsight, getting caught might have been the best option. Consider Ivan Basso, who was leading the 2006 Giro d'Italia as it entered its final week. When news of the arrests broke, Giro director Angelo Zomegnan summoned the race leader and told him, 'If you have anything to do with this, I'll strangle you with my own hands.'

On 29 May Basso won the Giro by more than nine minutes, the biggest winning margin since 1965. He eventually served a two-year ban ending on 24 October 2008. In May 2009 he made the podium of the Giro d'Italia, aged 31. In May 2010, he won it. Or Michele Scarponi: suspended from racing between May 2007 and November 2008, he won Tirreno–Adriatico in March 2009 and finished second in the Giro d'Italia two years later, becoming the winner when Alberto Contador's results from the 2010 Tour de France to the end of January 2012 were expunged. Until his tragic death in a road traffic accident in 2017, Scarponi was one of the most loved figures in Italian sport.

A confession, full or partial, followed by a suspension, then the resumption of life and racing, was surely preferable to years in limbo. Lacking insight into the future, some opted to retire, others attempted to race out the storm in Portugal, the USA or Colombia, spending years on the breadline and presumably regarding the tiny handful of riders who were publicly unmasked and prosecuted with pity: 'There but for the grace of God.'

In short, although these are things we cannot know in advance, limbo was a poor choice. The word, from the medieval Latin *in limbo*, means 'on Hell's border'. Its most sublime depiction is that of the medieval Florentine genius Dante Alighieri, in whose magnificent vision limbo fills the uppermost of the many circles of Hell carved into the rock beneath Jerusalem and descending towards the centre of the earth.

Cycling's limbo was crammed inside a Taper ULT 790 Elite chest freezer kept at a fourth-floor flat at 20, Calle Caídos de la División Azul, in the Chamartín area of northern Madrid.[8] Dr Fuentes had bought the freezer at a department store in December 2005 for €7,495. Keeping it at a constant minus-35 degrees Celsius, its owner called it Siberia, one of many in-jokes among his collaborators that also served as a kind of code.

Dante's Inferno had nine concentric circles. Fuentes' Siberia had five horizontal layers, crammed with cardboard boxes containing not the souls of the dead, but body fluids belonging to the living, one to four bags per box, making fifty-seven bags of frozen blood or red blood cells, and ten of plasma. In Dante's account, the demon Minos heard the confessions of the dead at the entry to Hell, and coiled his snake-like tail into loops, the quantity of which corresponded to the number of the circle of Hell where they would spend eternity. Fuentes did not need his clients' confessions. He already knew their sins and guaranteed them proximity to the realm of the dead by using a freezer with no running temperature log or back-up generator. In the event of a power cut, the blood could thaw and the cell membranes rupture. If it was then infused, it could have been lethal. There were no printed adhesive labels with barcodes corresponding to a central database, just a bag number and either initials or some sort of nickname handwritten with a marker pen. Infuse the wrong blood, and, again, the outcome could have been deadly. As Bastida learned, both of these errors may have taken place although, by luck more than judgement, there were no actual fatalities. The freezer and bags were kept secret. Fuentes made no explicit mention of them on his many mobile phones.

The poet Virgil guided Dante through limbo at Easter 1300. Bastida's men discovered cycling's limbo on the afternoon of 23 May 2006, the day of Fuentes' arrest. As well as the freezer, they found hundreds of pages of documents, in no obvious order. To make them manageable, they added page numbers at the top of each sheet. Page 114, headed 'ARCÓN' – chest freezer – '4/05/04', contained a list of numbers and codes which corresponded to the blood bags:

Layer one: 1 – JAN; 2 – BIRILLO; 3 – SANSONE;
Layer two: 4 – NICOLAS; 5 – SEVILLANO;
Layer three: 6 – SANTI-P; 7 – 1AI: 8 – ATR;
Layer four: 9 – URCO; 10 – ROSA; 11 – 4142; 12 – GUTI;
Layer five: 13 – ALCALDE; 14 – RH; 15 – CÉSAR; 16 –
VCS; 17 – GOKU; 18 – VALV. (Piti); 20 – VAINS.

In some cases, little or no effort had been made to disguise the rider's identity. Who could Jan be if not 1997 Tour de France champion Jan Ullrich, or Sevillano if not Óscar Sevilla, seventh and best young rider in the 2001 Tour, or, again, Santi-P if not Santiago Pérez, second in the 2004 Vuelta a España? And so they proved to be.

Others required more digging.

There was no key connecting code with real names, or explaining the symbols, and, with Fuentes and Merino citing medical secrecy, the police had to make circumstantial connections. They referred to the symbols and abbreviations in Fuentes' notes as 'Eufemiano's Sanskrit'.[9] The investigators believed 'vino' (wine) to mean blood, 'niño' (child) to mean human growth hormone, 'Ignacio' or 'IG' to refer to IGF-1, PCH to testosterone patches.[10] An E in a circle appeared to mean extraction and an R in a circle, reinfusion.[11] A small coloured circle meant EPO: the colour indicated the quantity.[12] Fuentes said the Guardia Civil had made lots of errors in their interpretations, but he refused to correct them.[13] He said that he could only say to whom the nicknames of the blood donors corresponded by consulting notes he had at his home in Las Palmas.

It was Jörg Jaksche who first admitted that his codename, Bella, was a beloved Labrador which had died two years before. Italian observers noticed that Birillo was the name of Sylvester Stallone's bullmastiff in the Italian version of the *Rocky* movies. It was also the name of Ivan Basso's Chihuahua. The brilliant Fuentes was using the names of his clients' pets!

Sansone turned out to be a Belgian sheepdog-German shepherd cross belonging to the classics champion Michele Bartoli; Urco, a Rottweiler cherished by the 2002 European 5,000m champion Marta Domínguez. There were exceptions: Francisco Mancebo, fourth in the 2005 Tour and Vuelta, was Goku, not a dog but a character in the *Dragon Ball* manga series, whom he was said to resemble.

What about VALV. (Piti)? In the 23 June 2006 edition of the sports paper *As*, a clue appeared. As Alejandro Valverde prepared for the Tour de France, journalist Enrique Iglesias joined him to gather material for a day-in-the-life piece. After a training ride, Iglesias followed the rider home, where, he wrote, 'Piti, a German shepherd dog, welcomes us, and from the living room window it is Figura, a very friendly parrot, who greets us.' The same bird who repeated 'champion' and 'handsome' at him.[14] Blood bag eighteen was ready to give up its secrets, or so the Guardia Civil must have thought.

The lawyer acting for Fuentes, Labarta and León played down the gravity of the allegations. 'There is no crime against public or private health. [My clients] have not put anyone's life in danger.'[15]

Jesús Manzano and Tyler Hamilton would have disagreed. On 6 April 2004, a few days after he signed a short-lived contract with the Amore e Vita team, Manzano had given a statement to an Italian investigating magistrate describing the aftermath of his terrifying experience at the 2003 Tour de France.

> Doctor Virú [another of the Kelme doctors] summoned me to his clinic in Valencia to give me my last bag of blood which he had taken several weeks before, and finish the autotransfusion treatment started with other teammates. There, Virú's assistants gave me just under half a unit of blood (about 175cc). I immediately felt sick and fainted. When I came to, I asked them to get me to a hospital, but they refused. Instead they injected Urbason [methylprednisolone, a corticosteroid used to stop anaphylactic shock] into my buttock. When I recovered I walked to the railway station to go home. On the train I felt sick again. My girlfriend called my mother, who called my team manager, who called Dr Virú. As the train had not yet left, Virú arrived and took me back to his clinic, stopping first at a pharmacy to buy more Urbason. I don't know what happened to me, but I can tell you that the bags of the Kelme riders' blood, which had been taken previously and stored, were not individually labelled for each athlete.

Tyler Hamilton spoke of reinfusion carried out in a French hotel during the Tour de France in 2004 by a German doctor with the Phonak team, who assisted only because there were many journalists around and they did not want anyone from Fuentes' circle in the hotel. In any case, thirty-five to forty minutes after the blood was reinfused, his urine was black. He was sure that it was one of the bags that Dr Fuentes had previously extracted from him because it had his code, 4142. He believed the blood may have deteriorated.

Hamilton's relationship with Fuentes had ended in mid-September 2004, after he tested positive at the Vuelta a España. Told he had someone else's blood in his system, he believed, on that occasion, that either his sample had been tampered with, or that the test had been badly executed, or that he had simply been given the wrong bag by mistake.

One of the few decisive, principled stands was taken by Thomas C. Ramey, chairman and president of Liberty International, a subsidiary of the Liberty Mutual Group of Insurance Companies in Boston, USA. Their team, Liberty Seguros, had already been affected by three scandals in 2005: Nuno Ribeiro's exclusion from the Giro d'Italia due to high haematocrit; Isidro Nozal's exclusion from the Dauphiné Libéré for the same reason, and the EPO positive that cost Roberto Heras his fourth Vuelta, which led to a redrafting of the sponsorship contract with more demanding clauses. Manolo Saiz's arrest was the last straw. Liberty's €8 million a year contract with the team's management company, Active Bay, was due to expire at the end of 2008. On 25 May 2006, Liberty International terminated the deal. Active Bay had already received a large part of its 2006 sponsorship from Liberty, and its riders started the Bicicleta Vasca race on 31 March in white jerseys adorned with the logo of its second sponsor, the German building supplies company Würth.

The Liberty Seguros leader, Aleksandr Vinokurov, looked for a replacement sponsor among the oil producers in his native Kazakhstan, through a former professional cyclist, his friend Daniyal Akhmetov, prime minister from June 2003 to January 2007, and, at the same time, president of the Kazakh cycling federation. First reports were that the state railway company of Kazakhstan, Temir Zholy, had agreed to finance the team for the next two and a half years. Then, it transpired that five Kazakh petroleum companies were picking up the €8 million a year contract.

On 2 June, Phonak announced that Colombian Santiago Botero and Valencian José Enrique Gutiérrez would not race again until the situation had been clarified. The same day, Manolo Saiz announced that the team was now called Astana-Würth. On the thirteenth the Tour de France withdrew Comunitat Valenciana-Kelme's invitation. The same day, the former Liberty Seguros, now Astana-Würth rider Ángel Vicioso, who, according to Guardia Civil recordings, used Fuentes' services, won a stage of the Tour of Switzerland. (In March 2013, Vicioso's team, Katusha, provisionally suspended him due to his appearance as a witness in Operación Puerto, in which he denied any doping plan with Eufemiano Fuentes and assured that the relationship with the doctor during his years riding for Liberty Seguros in 2004–06 was limited to 'sporadic and free medical consultations in Madrid'. The suspension lasted six days.)[16]

The licensing commission of the UCI ProTour approved Astana-Würth's documentation on 22 June. The following day Alberto Contador, Isidro Nozal and Luis León Sánchez wore Astana-Würth jerseys at the Spanish time trial championships – and Pablo Antón, the team's general manager, received a fax from Christian Prudhomme to say that they would not be welcome at the Tour de France. Antón appealed to the Court of Arbitration for Sport (CAS).

On 25 June, on the starting line of the Spanish road championships, the Spanish peloton refused to take part as a protest against the 'generalised accusations that put everyone under suspicion of doping' following the publication of page 114, the document listing the numbers and codes of the blood bags, in *El País*.

On 27 June 2006, SECOMA detailed their findings in a document labelled 'Summary Report 116'. The document showed some progress deciphering the various codenames: '1 – Jan' was Jan Ullrich; '2 – Birillo' was Ivan Basso; '3 – Sansone' was originally Michele Bartoli, but when he retired, it was reassigned to Santiago Botero; '5 – Sevillano' was Óscar Sevilla, and so on. There were other names too: fourteen members of Liberty Seguros; eleven Comunitat Valenciana riders; six individual riders apparently last treated by Fuentes and his group in 2004, and six current clients: Basso, Botero, Sevilla, Gutiérrez, Mancebo and Ullrich. 'Summary Report 116' did not name Valverde, although it did mention bag eighteen containing plasma, and the code '18 VALV. (Piti)'.

On Wednesday 28 June, three days before the Grand Départ of the Tour de France in Strasbourg, the public prosecutor asked the investigating magistrate to send a copy of the summary report to the CSD, the Spanish sports council, for disciplinary proceedings. It arrived the following day. The CSD then forwarded it to the national governing body of cycling (RFEC) with instructions to send copies to the World Anti-Doping Agency (WADA) and the UCI. The covering letter referred to 'official information and documentation suggesting possible doping offences by Spanish and/or foreign athletes holding licences issued by the Real Federación Española de Ciclismo and/or the Union Cycliste Internationale'. It called on the CNCDD, the competent body for doping matters within the RFEC, 'to identify the possible disciplinary responsibilities and inform the UCI of any cases which might fall under its jurisdiction'.[17]

The RFEC then sent a copy of the report to the UCI with (according to the later CAS judgment) 'most of its appendices', presumably meaning that it held back some of the supporting documents.

On Thursday 29 June, CAS ruled that Astana-Würth could take part in the Tour de France. This was before 'Summary

Report 116' reached ASO that evening. After studying it all night, the Tour de France organisers announced that, of the twenty-two teams and 198 riders expected, only twenty teams and 176 riders would start. T-Mobile started with seven riders, instead of the nine allowed, CSC and AG2R started with eight. With five implicated riders, Astana were left with a team of four (Vinokurov, Kashechkin, Luis León Sánchez and Carlos Barredo), below the minimum allowed, which conveniently kept them out of the race. The Tour started without the second (Ivan Basso), third (Jan Ullrich), fourth (Francisco Mancebo) and fifth (Aleksandr Vinokurov) riders in the 2005 edition.

Alejandro Valverde's was not among the fifty-eight names listed in the Summary Report. The press had made little or no mention of him, although there had never been any question that he knew Fuentes. They had coincided at Kelme-Costa Blanca. After two years with Kelme's under-23 set-up, Valverde had joined its professional team at the start of 2002, when Fuentes was the main team doctor that season. He left for family reasons at the end of the year, only to return for the 2003 Vuelta a España, when Valverde took two stage wins and a podium place before winning the silver medal at the world championship road race at Hamilton, Ontario. In a throwaway line, the daily sports paper *Mundo Deportivo* had commented, 'Closely supervised by Dr Eufemiano Fuentes, [Valverde's] development has been spectacular, and in his second pro season he has achieved lift-off.'

More than a year later, in November 2007, a Dutch journalist, Sander Vaan, asked Valverde, 'Do you have a dog called Piti?' He answered, 'I have two dogs: Dana and Sarita. Their names can be checked in the registry of their birth. In 2004, I didn't even have a dog, let alone one called Piti.' Piti may not have been a name but a term of endearment, unique to Valverde.

Missing, admittedly, was any mention of Valverde in the telephone conversations of Fuentes and associates during the two weeks from 9 May until the arrests. Nor did he meet Fuentes in

Madrid during the period of intense surveillance, although that was hardly surprising: Valverde had finished the Tour de Romandie on 30 April and would not race again until the Dauphiné Libéré on 4 June.

During their searches, the Guardia Civil had found cards with the words European Championships and two dates, 8 and 13 August, which correspond precisely to the men's 10,000 metres and marathon.[18] Officials were aware of close relations between some Spanish athletics coaches and agents with Fuentes and Merino. However, the police did not find any files on the athletes. The winter season ended in March, just when the investigations were beginning, and May, when intense surveillance began, was still too early for athletes looking to reach their maximum performance in August.

The warrant authorising telephone interceptions was issued on 10 May for a period of a month. The investigators ceased their interceptions on 1 June. They could have continued for nine more days, and perhaps discovered more of Fuentes' clients.[19]

A report published on 25 May, two days after the arrests, suggests that the *El País* journalists Jorge A. Rodríguez and José Antonio Hernández had already been briefed by police that Bala was not involved in the blood doping ring. They wrote:

> During the searches, the Guardia Civil found files and lists containing the names [. . .] of cyclists 'from the main Spanish teams'. According to the same sources, 'We can say that most of the known riders are there, with the exception of Alejandro Valverde.'[20]

Yet his Tour de France lasted just five days. Nineteen kilometres before a finish at Valkenburg that suited him perfectly, the peloton hit the brakes. Someone hit Bala's handlebars. His front wheel touched the rear wheel of the rider in front, who happened to be Óscar Freire, and Bala went down, breaking his right collarbone.

Vladimir Karpets took over team leadership, while Óscar Pereiro was given licence to hunt for stages. On stage thirteen, the longest of the Tour, he joined the breakaway, went with Jens Voigt's winning attack, and finished second at Montélimar. The peloton arrived 29 minutes 57 seconds later. Pereiro, who had started the day 28 minutes 50 seconds behind in the general standings, now led the Tour de France with a 1 minute 29 second advantage over the former yellow jersey Floyd Landis. On Alpe d'Huez two days later, Landis, fourth, took the jersey back, as expected, although Pereiro, thirteenth in the stage, was only ten seconds behind him.

Twenty-four hours later, on the way to La Toussuire-Les Sybelles, Landis's form collapsed and he conceded over eight minutes to Pereiro. The huge favourite suddenly needed a miracle. On 20 July, the day of stage seventeen from Saint-Jean-de-Maurienne to Morzine, he got it. At the start of the Col des Saisies, with the finish line still 140 kilometres away, Landis burst out of the group. He reached the finish line 5 minutes 42 seconds ahead of second-placed Carlos Sastre and 7 minutes 8 seconds ahead of Pereiro, who retained the Maillot Jaune, just, with Sastre second at 12 seconds and Landis third at 30 seconds. On the final Saturday, in the 57-kilometre time trial, Landis, third, gained 1 minute 29 seconds on Pereiro, fourth, giving the American the jersey by 59 seconds. The following day, he won the Tour de France.

Victory lasted four days. The following Thursday, he became the first Tour winner to test positive for doping in the edition of his victory in the race's 103-year history, and in the forty-year history of anti-doping controls. The affair put the Tour on a par with the Vuelta and the Giro, whose winners, Roberto Heras and Ivan Basso, were also implicated in doping cases.

Not until 20 September 2007 would Landis be found guilty of doping with synthetic testosterone in the 2006 Tour de France by a US court of arbitration, officially forfeiting overall victory. The 2006 Tour had no yellow jersey until 15 October 2007 when

Óscar Pereiro received it in a ceremony at the CSD headquarters in Madrid.[21]

In the scramble to compile a list of names in time for the 2006 Tour de France, legal shortcuts had been taken. The many contradictions between the various different levels of justice, criminal, administrative and sporting, it turned out, could each be used to neutralise the others. So, in August, Manolo Saiz sued the CSD's director general, Rafael Blanco, for forwarding Puerto documents to the Tour de France, while nine riders from Saiz's team started proceedings against the secretary general of the RFEC, Eugenio Bermúdez, for abuse of secrecy after he sent blood and urine test results, and training plans from the Puerto investigation, to the organisers of the Vuelta a España. Another group of cyclists filed a lawsuit denouncing the UCI ProTour's Code of Ethics, which stipulated the teams agreed to suspend from racing any rider suspected of doping, and not to sign up any riders with past doping offences.

Even so, evidence confirming the identities of Fuentes' clients was emerging all the time. On 17 August 2006, *Süddeutsche Zeitung* published a fax sent by Fuentes to a Colombian soigneur named Nelson Giraldo just before the 2006 Giro d'Italia:

> Nelson, as agreed, I am sending herewith the list of collaborators in the festival taking place in May, without further ado, hoping to count on your help and collaboration. Best regards. 1, Alessandro Kalc [a coach from Trieste thought to be a courier in Fuentes' network]; 2, Alberto León; 3, Ivan Basso; 4, Marcos Serrano, 5, Michele Scarponi; 6, José Enrique Gutiérrez and 7, Jan Ullrich. Thank you, Eufemiano.[22]

Bala returned to racing on the weekend of 12 and 13 August when, still experiencing pain from his collarbone injury, he finished eighth in the Clásica San Sebastián and fifteenth in the

Subida a Urkiola. On 26 August, he started the Vuelta a España in Málaga as favourite. On stage seven, from León to the Alto de El Morredero above Ponferrada, where he had won in the 2004 Vuelta a Castilla y León, Bala took the stage win and moved to within five seconds of the race lead. In the next two stages, both won by Vinokurov, Bala was twelfth and second. He took the yellow-gold leader's jersey on the second of them and led the race for the next eight stages.

In stage sixteen from Almería to Calar Alto, he finished second to Euskaltel-Euskadi's Igor Antón. With just five days to go, victory looked certain.

'Madrid is closer and I'm a little bit further away from my pursuers,' he said. 'It's something to be satisfied with.'

The following day all that changed.

Stage seventeen, from Adra, on the Andalusian coast, near Almería, to Granada, ascended the forbidding Alto de Monachil, one of the hardest climbs of the race, before dropping 20.5 kilometres to the stage finish. Vinokurov started the day second overall at 1 minute 42 seconds. Three kilometres from the summit of the Alto de Monachil, he attacked. Valverde could not follow. Shirt unzipped, Sastre on his wheel, he could only watch as his rival rode away. Vinokurov bridged across to his teammate and compatriot Andrey Kashechkin, who lay fourth at just over two minutes in the GC, and they worked together.

Risking everything for the first six kilometres of the descent, his shirt flapping behind him, Valverde had Vinokurov's group in sight when the Kazakh darted away again. Valverde bridged to Kashechkin and José Ángel Gómez Marchante, but it was too late.

Afterwards, he would say, 'For a few seconds, I wasn't sure what to do, and I was on a fifty-two-tooth chainring. He had a fifty-three, which allowed him to get away.'[23]

But the truth was, after his long pursuit, Bala was running on empty.

Inside the final five kilometres of the stage, Vinokurov bridged across to the stage leader, Tom Danielson, and they worked together. They led Valverde by 59 seconds with seven kilometres to go, 1 minute 3 seconds with four kilometres to go and 1 minute 24 seconds with two kilometres to go.

Vinokurov did not challenge Danielson for the stage win, bagging the 12-second bonus for second place. Then he waited. Valverde finished 1 minute 39 seconds later. Vinokurov had wiped out Bala's lead and added nine seconds.

The following day, with fewer than six kilometres left to ride on the ascent of La Pandera, near the Andalusian town of Jaén, Vinokurov darted away alone. Again, Valverde was unable to follow. Kashechkin crossed to his leader, who rewarded him with the stage win and took 12 more bonus seconds for finishing second. Valverde came in fourth, 32 seconds down. He now trailed the Kazakh by 53 seconds. The Vuelta was slipping away.

Vinokurov added 19 seconds to his lead while winning stage twenty, a 27.5-kilometre time trial. Valverde finished third. At the end of the final stage, the two Kazakhs occupied the top and bottom steps of the podium, with Valverde in second place.

The next morning, following the Spanish daily *ABC*, the Munich newspaper *Süddeutsche Zeitung* (SZ) assured its readers that 18 – VALV. (Piti) was Valverde. With the world championships in Salzburg in mid-September, SZ's assertion circulated widely in the German-speaking countries.

Fulgencio Sánchez, president of the RFEC, leapt to Valverde's defence. He declared, categorically, 'Valverde is not involved in Operación Puerto,' adding, 'It is my duty to deny it.' Then, he claimed: 'It is clear that the intention of those who have written this information is to break the unity of the national team that has obtained such good results [at the world championships] in recent years.'

Ángel Luis de la Fuente, deputy director general of high

competition of Spain's national sports council, the CSD, agreed: 'I think that there are interests from other countries to break up the unity of the [Spanish] team. This is the conclusion I draw from everything that has appeared in some of the media.' He added, 'I have no doubt that the representatives of the national team are clean of all suspicions related to doping.'

Outside Spain, these comments seemed hopelessly out of tune. In Germany, Ullrich, Sevilla and Olaf Ludwig had been fired from T-Mobile, while the Bonn prosecutor had resolved to compare the contents of blood bag number one with Jan Ullrich's DNA. In Italy, on 20 September, on the basis of Operación Puerto, the Bergamo Prosecutor's Office ordered searches in thirty-six private homes and gyms. One of them belonged to the Liquigas rider Luca Paolini who had won stage twelve of the recent Vuelta. Paolini was in Varese with the Italian national team, preparing for the world championship road race the following Sunday.

On 22 September, *ABC* backtracked to the 2005 Tour de France and asked, why did Bala really abandon the race? Where was the bruise from the blow to his knee that nobody saw? The suspicion was that he had abandoned due to an abnormally high red blood cell count, associated with EPO or transfusion. It was never proven.

Bala's ability to remain focused in the fog of incredulity was extraordinary. Two kilometres from the end of a largely flat world championship course on 24 September, he was in second place, on the wheel of Italy's Filippo Pozzato. Under the flamme rouge, Bala's teammate Samuel Sánchez sped past them both, and Bala darted onto his wheel. Quick to see the danger, Erik Zabel and Paolo Bettini powered across to join them. With 500 metres to go, their advantage was enough to be sure that the next world champion would be one of the four.

With 250 metres to go, as Bala followed Sánchez to the right-hand side of the road, Zabel darted left and launched his sprint.

Bala rose out of the saddle, but he was stranded on the wrong side of the road. He sprinted into the wind while Bettini, easing out of Zabel's wake, took the win. Bala coasted in third. Valverde and Zabel both now had two silvers and a bronze world championship medal.

In spite of his disappointment, the result made Bala the UCI ProTour winner 2006 – in other words, the world's number one rider.

As the racing season ended, Operación Puerto resumed.

On 3 October 2006, the investigating magistrate Antonio Serrano issued an order prohibiting any evidence arising from the criminal proceedings from being used in sporting proceedings. He explained that this was 'due to the impossibility of determining the nature and degree of the involvement of the accused persons at a preliminary stage of the criminal proceedings'. The prohibition was reiterated many times over the coming years, although the legal reasoning behind it evolved out of all recognition. The Public Prosecutor and the RFEC both lodged appeals.

In the meantime, applications arrived from foreign jurisdictions for access to the blood bags. On 9 October, under the European Convention on Mutual Assistance in Criminal Matters, Serrano authorised a request from the Office of the anti-doping prosecutor at the Italian Olympic Committee, the national anti-doping organisation recognised by WADA, making samples available from the bag marked number two, believed to belong to Ivan Basso. On the sixteenth he approved a request from the prosecutor in Bonn for the collection of samples from the blood bag identified as 'Jan' or number one, believed to belong to Jan Ullrich.

The ninety-nine blood bags seized during the investigation had been sent to the laboratory of the Institut Municipal d'Investigació Mèdica (IMIM), part of the Hospital del Mar in Barcelona, for analysis. Their contents were analysed using a new technique pioneered at the Barcelona lab and later published in the scientific journal *Haematologica*.[24] The results were laid out in a report completed in late November. It emphasised that the new method could detect EPO with any certainty only if it had been injected in the three days prior to analysis, so the results reflected the limits of the available science. Either way, follicle-stimulating hormone (FSH) had been found in three bags identified as number twenty-four, thought to be female, while definite traces of EPO were found in eight bags. Three corresponded to number five, Sevillano, also known as Óscar Sevilla. The other positives belonged to aliases Klaus, Falla, Mari, Gemma and blood bag eighteen.

By then, the appeals by the Public Prosecutor and the RFEC against Serrano's order prohibiting criminal evidence from being used in sporting proceedings had been dismissed. UCI president Pat McQuaid complained that the decision made the sporting authorities look ridiculous. The decision led to long-running, vitriolic exchanges with jurisdictions abroad. After all, by signing the UNESCO International Convention Against Doping in Sport in October 2005, Spain had committed itself to supporting 'the World Anti-Doping Agency in the international fight against doping' and encouraging 'cooperation between anti-doping organisations, public authorities and sports organisations within their jurisdiction and those within the jurisdiction of other States Parties in order to achieve, at the international level, the purpose of this Convention'. But the UNESCO Convention would not be ratified until 16 February 2007.

As the end of 2006 approached, a draft law making doping a crime in Spain, the so-called Lissavetzky Law on Health Protection and Anti-Doping, named after the Secretary of State for Sport, Jaime Lissavetzky, went to a vote in Congress. The debate allowed several party spokespersons to question the actions of the CSD in relation to 'Operación Puerto'. On behalf of the Partido Popular, Francisco Antonio González expressed his group's support for the law, but accused the Sports Council of being in 'too much of a hurry' in relation to Operación Puerto. 'Fifty-eight athletes have had their fundamental rights trampled on as a result of such haste, without having the slightest possibility of defending themselves against something that has not been sentenced or included in an investigation.'

The Socialist Group's Agustín Jiménez defended the government. 'Neither the government nor the Consejo Superior de Deportes [Sports Council] have suspended anyone. It is the teams who have done so, as a precautionary measure. With this law, sport, athletes and public health win and the cheats lose,' he concluded.

With the 'unanimity of all the groups', the law received 302 votes in favour, with one against and seven abstentions. However, the timing of the new law may inadvertently have aided Fuentes and the other Operación Puerto defendants. As the 2013 judgment of Fuentes noted, '[I]f the legislature has introduced a specific new type into the Criminal Code intended to suppress and punish doping, it is because these behaviours were not previously covered by Spanish criminal law.'[25] Until the new law came into force on 23 January 2007, doping was not a crime in Spain.

Judge Serrano's investigation entered a new phase as he began to collect the first statements by witnesses. Alberto Contador and Jesús Hernández denied having any relationship with Fuentes. Jan Ullrich was summoned. At the same time, Serrano prepared to dispatch letters to more than a dozen Spanish cities and to ten different countries, requesting judicial assistance in questioning the riders implicated in Operación Puerto. He wanted the responses to three questions: 'What relationship do you have or have you had with the accused, what type of treatment have you received from them, if any, and have you had serious health problems as a result of the treatments administered by the accused?'

The prosecution asked the judge to offer the cyclists the opportunity to agree to a voluntary DNA test to rule out whether or not any of the more than 200 bags of blood seized by the Guardia Civil belonged to them. Serrano refused their request.

8

Complacent and Evasive

Presumably reasoning that the courts had done their due diligence for them, T-Mobile, who had lost Jan Ullrich and Óscar Sevilla, made Bala an offer. His contract with Caisse d'Épargne, worth €1.4 million annually, still had a year to run. The German team was ready to buy it out for what was rumoured to be €3 million, then pay him €10 million over three years.

It brought José Miguel Echávarri bad memories of letting Pedro Delgado go at the end of 1984. 'We were left with no leader and an orphaned team. It was a difficult year. Worse, Perico [Delgado] won the Vuelta [the following year] with his new team. We can't make the same mistake with Valverde.'[1]

In summer 2006, Echávarri had met Alberto Contador and discussed him joining Illes Balears. Contador made it clear that he and Valverde were not compatible. Now Valverde's future was in doubt. While Echávarri spoke to Caisse d'Épargne, Unzue travelled to Murcia to meet Valverde's people. On Wednesday 10 January, six days before the team was due to be presented in Paris, Caisse d'Épargne gave the green light and Valverde accepted a new, improved deal, matching, or nearly, T-Mobile's offer and making him the world's highest paid cyclist. It had the advantage of requiring no adaptation to a new foreign team.

The following day, *ABC* leaked another document found in the searches which showed that Fuentes, as well as receiving €70,000 a year from both Jan Ullrich and Ivan Basso, €50,000 a year from Sevilla, Botero, Mancebo and Heras, and €25,000 from José Enrique Gutiérrez and Aitor Osa, was charging performance bonuses of fifty, thirty and €20,000 for each step on the Tour de France podium, thirty, twenty and €10,000 for the Giro and Vuelta, €30,000 for gold in the road race at the world championships and €15,000 for the time trial.[2]

The page mentioned another amount, €110,000, in anticipated bonuses from '18; *azules*; *checo*; Ivan May'. Eighteen, said *ABC*, was Alejandro Valverde. In other words, the Spanish press was beginning to accept his involvement as fact.

By signing up Luis León Sánchez and José Joaquín Rojas, Caisse d'Épargne had become a kind of Murcian national team. Yet, while T-Mobile, CSC and AG2R had fired their Operación Puerto riders, Caisse d'Épargne opted to keep Constantino Zaballa, despite the police having filmed him visiting Fuentes on 4 May 2006. Zaballa missed the team presentation on 16 January. He revealed to his local newspaper, 'José Miguel [Echávarri] told me that it was not judicious to have me in Paris.'[3]

More unwelcome news broke on 18 January, when the AFLD, France's national anti-doping agency, announced that in two doping controls during the Tour, the Paris laboratory had detected the asthma drug salbutamol in Óscar Pereiro's urine, in quantities of 158 and 159 nanograms per millilitre.[4] For the World Anti-Doping Agency (WADA), salbutamol was legal as long as it did not exceed 1,000 nanograms per millilitre and the athlete had a Therapeutic Use Exemption (TUE) issued by his international federation and approved by a WADA medical board. Pereiro met both conditions. Even so, the AFLD considered that, since neither the UCI nor the rider had sent it the medical reports, his TUE was not valid. It demanded access to the medical report Pereiro had submitted in his TUE application, despite the World Anti-Doping Code stating only WADA's specialised commission was permitted to see it.

This was not even the most glaring disconnect between

cycling's institutions. The ProTour's governing council inside the UCI was talking about establishing a body to manage the television rights of all the ProTour and world championship races, and giving the teams a cut of the revenues. The project was well known to be the brainchild of former UCI president Hein Verbruggen and the recently arrested Manolo Saiz. The race organisers ASO were having none of it. They announced that only eighteen of the twenty ProTour teams were invited to Paris–Nice in March.[5] The UCI responded with a threat to ban the race and, at the start of February, Pat McQuaid sent a letter to all the riders on ProTour teams asking them for their support against the organisers of the Giro, Tour and Vuelta.

On 22 January, *El País* published a rare interview in which Carlos Arribas coaxed Valverde into addressing the situation, and his own involvement in Operación Puerto. His responses vacillated between mystified:

> We have to keep training and just hope it all gets sorted out. I don't know what I can say . . . If I had the secret and I could say 'This is how you fix it', I would, but I can't.

– complacent:

> I can see the fans suspect us, but I think, in the end, they like cycling and they are beginning to set all the other issues aside. Change habits? But we work and train the same as ever, that's all I know.

– nostalgic:

> As Perico [Delgado] used to say: in his day, they trained, looked after themselves and gave the best of themselves. Of course, in those days, the Guardia Civil didn't intervene and the winner

of the Tour didn't test positive, but . . . It's a pity, it's true. But let's see if this can change for the better . . .

– irritated:

Lately they've been making it sound like I'm involved in Operación Puerto. It's the same thing over and again. So what if Eufemiano [Fuentes] wrote 'Valverde' on a business card, with a bunch of other names?

and evasive:

I knew Eufemiano when I was at Comunitat Valenciana and he was the team doctor. That's it. In 2005, when I came to Caisse d'Épargne, I stopped seeing him. It's crystal clear.[6]

Quite what exactly knowing and seeing Eufemiano entailed was not quite so plain.

On 25 January 2007, Pereiro's positive test was recognised as an administrative error and lifted.

In the last week of January, the Balearic government announced that it was terminating its secondary-sponsorship of the Caisse d'Épargne team. José Luis Ballester attributed the decision to 'problems with the UCI . . . such as the number of times a rider had to wear the jersey of a certain sponsor, so we decided to bring forward the end of our collaboration.'[7]

Bala started the season quietly, with anonymous rides in three of the Challenge de Mallorca races in late February. His next race was the Volta a la Comunitat Valenciana on Tuesday 27 March. The day before it started, a former T-Mobile soigneur named Jef D'hondt told a Belgian TV programme, *Panorama*, that the team doctors Andreas Schmid and Lothar Heinrich, attached to the University of Freiburg, oversaw systematic doping in the team, and that both of its Tour de France winners, Bjarne

Riis in 1996 and Jan Ullrich in 1997, had used EPO.[8] The same day, Jan Ullrich announced his retirement, no doubt apprised of the imminent announcement, which came a week later, on 2 March, that the DNA of his saliva samples taken by the German police matched the blood in one of Fuentes' bags. As everyone had suspected, 'Jan' was Jan.

The following day, after finishing fourth and second in the last two stages, Bala emerged with overall victory at the Volta a la Comunitat Valenciana, 'a race', he said, 'I didn't even come here to win.'

Two weeks later, on 8 March, investigating magistrate Serrano closed the Operación Puerto criminal proceedings on the grounds that doping, at the time of the incriminating facts, did not constitute an offence. The ongoing requests for national and international judicial assistance in interviewing the riders were set aside. Serrano explained that, given the information already available, the interviews would not change the fact that no offence against public health existed. It was odd that he had not noticed this before.

No doubt powered by euphoria, Bala celebrated with the first time trial win of his professional career, a 23.3-kilometre effort in stage four of the Vuelta a Murcia.

At the same time, *El Mundo* published a document showing that Fuentes expected to receive €500,000 in 2006 from his private clients. He and Merino could surely have been pursued for tax avoidance, Al Capone-style. But investigating magistrate Serrano elected to close the case with a *sobreseimiento libre* or free dismissal, which prohibited any future investigation *even if new evidence were discovered*.[9] The legal effect was to acquit Fuentes and his seven co-defendants.

Venting his frustration in a brilliant piece of writing, Carlos Arribas revealed that Serrano had refused the investigators access to Fuentes' computers, meaning, among many other things, that the suspected involvement of other cyclists, athletes, footballers and tennis players, some of whom Fuentes had mentioned himself, could not be checked against his computer files.[10]

On 21 March the State Prosecutor's Office joined the appeal initiated by the Madrid Public Prosecutor's Office against the closure of Operación Puerto. Four days later, the State Prosecutor's Office and Jesús Manzano both appealed against the decision, and the UCI became a civil party to the appeal. Days later, WADA and the UCI condemned the closure and requested access to the findings of the investigation.

Serrano was paradoxically helpful to foreign jurisdictions. On 13 April, CONI requested information relating to Michele Scarponi, who eventually admitted to giving blood for an autotransfusion, and was found guilty of a doping offence. Then, on 18 April, six bags of blood and two of plasma, all labelled number two, were defrosted so that samples could be taken by Italian police, in connection with a doping investigation opened months before by the public prosecutor of Bergamo.

Before the anti-doping office of Italy's Olympic Committee (CONI), Ivan Basso admitted his involvement in Fuentes' doping ring. He was Birillo, and had used blood autotransfusions, EPO, growth hormone, testosterone.[11] He also announced his 'total willingness to collaborate', a course of action which might have led to a reduced sanction of less than two years. No fewer than fourteen public prosecutors' offices in different parts of Italy had opened investigations relating to doping. After Basso's confession, the authorities in his home town of Busto Arsizio, in Lombardy, opened an investigation into him, which made it fifteen. Basso's confession overshadowed two third places by Bala, in the Critérium International and the GP Miguel Indurain.

Even so, after finishing fifth overall in the Vuelta al País Vasco on 13 April, and second again in the Klasika Primavera de Amorebieta two days later, Bala started his second Amstel Gold Race a week later. It ended in disappointment. The German Gerolsteiner team had two riders in the final selection, Stefan

Schumacher and Davide Rebellin. When Schumacher attacked three kilometres from the finish, no one would take up the chase.

'And then I saw that everyone would rather lose the race than take me with them,' Bala said later.

Schumacher cruised to victory, with Rebellin second. Bala, sixth, did not even bother sprinting.

His bid to win a second successive Flèche Wallonne on the day of his twenty-seventh birthday was overshadowed by the publication of an open letter from UCI president Pat McQuaid to Jaime Lissavetzky. Copying in the presidents of the IOC and WADA, McQuaid urged Lissavetzky to take action. Lissavetzky's reply, also open, reminded him that Operación Puerto was in the criminal investigation phase, and that the blood was in the custody of the judge until the appeal against its closure was resolved.

'As in all European Union countries,' he wrote, 'the principle of the separation of powers exists.' The executive, meaning the government, through the CSD, could not interfere with the judiciary. But it was disingenuous. Serrano's erratic decision-making hardly inspired confidence, and, anyway, the way a case is framed – the procedure used, the charges prosecuted – goes a long way towards determining its final outcome, and both are amenable to political pressure, and it was not hard to imagine political pressure behind the decision to prosecute solely under public health law, or to use the *sobreseimiento libre* or free dismissal procedure.[12]

While Bala was out reconnoitring the Côtes de Thon and Bonneville, both of them new to the Flèche Wallonne route, Tour director Christian Prudhomme insisted at a meeting with Pro-Tour teams that riders suspected of involvement in the Fuentes case would not be allowed to take part in the Tour, which started in London on 7 July.

Meanwhile, out of the public eye, Italian police visited the anti-doping laboratory in Barcelona to take samples from four blood bags, two of them marked number two and dated 12 January 2006 and 11 November 2005, the others marked 'Birillo' and dated 8 August and 15 December 2005. On their return, CONI's anti-doping office announced that the Public Prosecutor's Office in Rome was starting proceedings in connection with the Operación Puerto investigation, initially with respect to athletes affiliated with the Italian Cycling Federation. While the investigation continued, Basso's team, Discovery Channel, decided that Flèche Wallonne, and Liège–Bastogne–Liège the following Sunday, would take place without him.

At Flèche Wallonne, Danilo Di Luca blinked first. With 14 kilometres to go, he forced the pace, taking Kim Kirchen and Bala's teammate Purito Rodríguez with him. The trio crossed to the two leaders, Sergei Ivanov and the Vuelta al País Vasco winner Juan José Cobo.

Then Bala blinked too. With only 20 seconds separating the leaders from the main group, he joined Thomas Dekker, Cristian Moreni and Yaroslav Popovych in an attempt to bridge across. By the time they reached the leading group, Purito and Kirchen had attacked. The move allowed Bala to recover at the back of the chasing group. Just inside ten kilometres, as the chasers caught them, Purito attacked again, alone this time. Same tactic, although Bala had already made powerful accelerations that he might have saved for the final climb.

With 1.4 kilometres to go, Rodríguez and all the chase groups were absorbed by the main group. Davide Rebellin, in the white jersey of the ProTour leader, climbed behind Matthias Kessler and alongside the Italian revelation Riccardo Riccò, the winner of two stages in Tirreno–Adriatico. Rinaldo Nocentini joined them, with Bala just behind. On the steepest section, those five began to ride away.

Kessler and Rebellin opened a gap, Rebellin waited before launching his sprint and winning the race with ease. On the final corner, as the German faded, Bala inched past Di Luca to take second place, six seconds behind Rebellin. But the race had been a tactical examination, and Bala had failed.

Liège–Bastogne–Liège ended much as Flèche Wallonne had. Paolo Bettini tried to get away before the wall of San Nicolas, but Valverde chased him down. Four kilometres from the finish, Fränk Schleck attacked on the descent after San Nicolas. Danilo Di Luca joined him, and they worked together to reach the last kilometre with a big enough margin to dispute the win. Di Luca's finishing speed made him untouchable. Valverde sprinted past the Luxembourger to take second place.

In May 2007, Jaume Matas, the team's champion in the Balearic government, was voted out. The islands' new socialist cabinet froze its payments to the cycling team, although Echávarri sued and the courts upheld his claim. It cost the administration €800,000 to buy its way out.[13]

On 13 May, Bala won the 7.3-kilometre time trial at the two-day, three-stage Clásica de Alcobendas. He would not race again until the Critérium du Dauphiné Libéré and the Tour de France. By then, cycling would have gone through yet more convulsions.

The same day as Flèche Wallonne, it had become public knowledge that blood bags belonging to Ivan Basso were in the Italian Olympic Committee's possession. Ettore Torri, the committee's anti-doping prosecutor, had scheduled a DNA analysis for 2 May, with or without Basso's cooperation. The blood from a surprise test carried out on Basso a few weeks earlier was enough. An implacable anti-doping campaigner, Torri had investigated the Brazilian footballer Ronaldo, in his Milan years, for using 'growth factor therapy', which involved drawing thirty to forty cubic centimetres of blood which is then centrifuged to obtain a concentrate that is then injected into the damaged muscle, although nothing illegal came out of his enquiries.[14] He had also pursued the consumers of Continuous Erythropoiesis Receptor Activator or CERA, known as third-generation EPO, and caught, among others, the cyclists Emanuele Sella (in an out-of-competition test in July 2008 after winning three stages of the 2008 Giro d'Italia, and suspended for a year), Riccardo Riccò (suspended for two years in October 2008 after admitting doping during the Tour de France) and Leonardo Piepoli (suspended for two years in January 2009 after two failed tests during the 2008 Tour de France).

On 6 May, Basso went to the offices of the Italian Olympic Committee's anti-doping office to go into greater detail about his doping. Yet, at a press conference in a Milan hotel the following day, his story changed. He had gone to Fuentes in a moment of weakness, he said. The blood had been in the freezer since the winter of 2005. It was to be used in the 2006 Tour, but he did not take part, so it was, at worst, a case of unconsummated doping. His change of story made complete sense. A public confession of doping would have meant an automatic two-year ban, the loss of the 2006 Giro, and criminal prosecution. The World Anti-Doping Code may not have differentiated between attempted and actual doping, but Italian criminal law did.

After his CONI hearing, he added, 'They didn't ask me for the names of other people, other riders, and I couldn't have given them to them either because I don't know them.'

Basso's cooperation was eventually judged insufficient, and on 15 June he was suspended for twenty-four months, three more than requested by the Olympic Committee.[15] Michele Scarponi, codename Zapatero, had already accepted his involvement in Operación Puerto, although, with no blood bags labelled with his number or codename, he too was taken to be an unconsummated doper.

In a meeting at the CSD headquarters in Madrid, the Spanish riders' union, representing the thirty or so Spanish cyclists implicated by the Guardia Civil in Operación Puerto, attempted to follow suit. They wanted to negotiate a reduced sanction with the Spanish Federation, ideally a one-year suspension in exchange for their confession and cooperation.[16] The talks represented a U-turn from their position of total denial at the Spanish championships. They demanded that the Federation ask the ProTour to waive the code of ethics that extended any doping sanction imposed by any federation by two further years, putting the best races, including the Grand Tours, out of reach.

Fulgencio Sánchez, the president of the Spanish Federation, referred them directly to the ProTour. 'It is out of our hands.'

Meanwhile, at a meeting in Liège at the end of April, the ProTour Teams Association agreed that none of the riders on any of the various Operación Puerto lists would start the Giro d'Italia. So, while Mancebo, Vicioso and Sevilla, riding with the second division team Relax-Gam, prepared to take part in the Volta a Catalunya, Tinkoff and Caisse d'Épargne removed Tyler Hamilton, Jörg Jaksche, Constantino Zaballa and Rubén Plaza from their Giro teams.

Against this background, on 14 May 2007, the French sports daily *L'Équipe* published a front-page story under the title 'A shadow over Valverde', reporting that José Miguel Echávarri had been convened to a meeting at the Caisse d'Épargne headquarters to explain the gravity of the evidence against Valverde, as well as Zaballa's return to racing and the hiring of Rubén Plaza, named in Summary Report 116 but signed up by Caisse d'Epargne in April 2007.

The following morning, a Caisse d'Épargne spokesperson made light of the meeting: 'True, there was a meeting this morning, but it was a normal meeting, nothing to do with press speculation about doping. We are a bank, we don't understand cycling, we have a sponsorship contract with the cycling team, and relations with the riders are the team's responsibility. We have no contractual relationship with the riders.'

But Echávarri had already spoken to Carlos Arribas of *El País*. 'I asked them [Caisse d'Épargne] what I could do. As his employer, I can't ask for his DNA, because labour law prevents me from doing so, to compare it with a plasma bag from 2004, when Valverde was riding for Kelme. And, even if I had his DNA, the bag is evidence in a case that has been closed by the judge. How could we have access to it? We are in a state of complete helplessness.'[17]

On 1 June, a substitute judge seconded to Operación Puerto dismissed a complaint by Jesús Manzano that the case had been closed while the responses to Serrano's letters were still pending.[18] The locum was categorical: he was under no obligation to carry out tests requested by the parties if he considered them inconsequential. Doping had not been a crime in Spain until the new law. In any case, there could be no talk of crimes against public health because the EPO in some of the blood bags was due to 'prior administration' by doctors, whose decisions were justified in advance by their professional status.

The judge was saying, in effect, that doctors can administer whatever they want to anyone they choose simply because they are doctors. Six parties – UCI, WADA, the international teams' association, the RFEC, the Spanish public prosecutor and state lawyer – lodged appeals.

As one scenario closed, another opened.

In Germany, where the world championships were due to be held in October, the magazine *Der Spiegel* published excerpts of a book in which Jef D'hondt expanded on his claims about doping at T-Mobile. On Monday 21 May, Bert Dietz, a Vuelta a España stage winner in 1995 for the same team, then known as Team Deutsche Telekom, also confessed to doping, and confirmed that the team doctors Heinrich and Schmid had been administering EPO since the mid-1990s.

The team's sponsor, Deutsche Telekom, by revenue the largest telecommunications provider in Europe, had succeeded the state-owned monopoly Deutsche Bundespost on privatisation in 1995. The historical link to the German state created a sense that the country as a whole was somehow implicated. In Spain, doping had friends in high places. In Germany it brought back distressing memories of the Democratic Republic, where state-sanctioned doping had extended to pre-pubescent children. The nation's politicians felt they had to be seen to act.

As Spain's cyclists and institutions closed ranks and rode out the storm, Germany's riders began making confessions and its politicians began taking a stand. By the end of the week, eight former Team Deutsche Telekom employees – six riders, one of them, Erik Zabel, still active, and two doctors – had come forward.

Two retired Danish riders soon joined them: the Dane, Brian Holm, a directeur sportif with T-Mobile, used the pages of *Politiken* to expand on a passage about his own doping from his 2002 autobiography *Smerten, Glæden* ('The Pain, the Joy'). Then, on Friday the twenty-fifth, the 1996 Tour de France winner Bjarne Riis held a press conference and admitted to his EPO use. After Riis's confession, the German Chancellor Angela Merkel weighed in. 'After the doping confessions of prominent cyclists, an abyss is opening. In cycling, there has obviously been systematic, long-term manipulation to a degree that could never have been imagined. The confessions and investigations so far are not enough to clear the air. It is time to get to the bottom of things. All doping offenders now have the chance to come clean and break the cartel of silence if they want to give their sport the chance for a clean, manipulation-free new start.'

On 30 May, the International Olympic Committee (IOC) announced the creation of a commission of enquiry into possible doping in cycling during the Olympic Games, in particular at Sydney in 2000, where three Telekom riders, Ullrich, Vinokurov and Klöden, topped the podium in the road race.[19]

L'Équipe's spread about the meeting at Caisse d'Épargne had given Valverde an intimation of what lay ahead for him at the

Tour de France. Before the Dauphiné Libéré, he told *El País*, 'The press, especially the French press, will be all over us all day long, but if there's nothing to report, there's nothing to report.

'What do you want me to do? If I ask the judge to let me give my DNA, he'll laugh in my face. He'll say, "But why, if I'm not investigating you?"

'How many more controls can there be?' he asked. 'Are we going to be pissing all day?'

His solution was simple. 'It's time to say: "Enough. Let's talk about what we used to talk about: the mountains, the races. That's what cycling has to sell, not all this bullshit."'[20]

He started the Dauphiné Libéré promisingly enough. Fifth in the prologue on 10 June, third at the head of the group of sprinters in stage two, and ninth in the 40.7-kilometre time trial. But on the 197-kilometre stage from Hauterives to Mont Ventoux, his race fell apart. Finishing 128th and second-last after a day of vomiting and being unable to eat, he conceded 28 minutes 54 seconds to the winner, Christophe Moreau, and abandoned the following day.

On its own, mere suspicion of involvement in Operación Puerto was not enough for the Tour de France to turn cyclists away, so an alternative strategy was required. On 19 June, the UCI announced what it called a 'Rider's Commitment to a New Cycling', also known as the Geneva Oath. It consisted of a letter that began:

> I swear to my team, my colleagues, the UCI, the cycling world and the fans that I have not cheated and I have not been involved in the Fuentes affair or in any other doping case. I am willing to give a sample of my DNA to the Spanish justice system so that it can be compared with the blood bags of the Operación Puerto and I commit myself to paying one year of my salary to the UCI's anti-doping fund if it is found that I have violated the anti-doping regulations.[21]

Anne Gripper, the UCI's chief of anti-doping, explained, 'The document has no legal validity, only a moral value, but I'm sure everyone will sign it, not for legal reasons, but because of the social pressure it will generate.'

Even so, Christian Prudhomme said, 'We will oppose the presence at the start in London of riders who do not sign the oath. At the present time, when the principle of guilt is more important than the principle of innocence, the precautionary principle must be applied.'

The first to sign were Britain's Mark Cavendish (T-Mobile) and France's Sandy Casar (La Française des Jeux) in the presence of Pat McQuaid. By the end of June, more than 220 cyclists had signed it, even if many considered it abusive and unenforceable.[22] Alejandro Valverde was one of them – and, however insincere, his signed agreement to cooperate with a DNA test would come back to haunt him.

Meanwhile, the search for doping stories provoked a Europe-wide media frenzy. On 23 June, the German current affairs magazine *Stern* published an interview with Jesús Manzano. Asked whether, when he was Valverde's teammate at Kelme, he knew that Bala was doping, he replied, 'They gave him the same stuff they gave me. I remember one evening after a Vuelta stage in 2002, Valverde came to dinner with a testosterone patch. After an hour he tore it off, otherwise he would have tested positive.'

On 30 June, Jörg Jaksche repeated to the competition, *Der Spiegel*, the confession he had already made to the Guardia Civil: that he was Bella in Fuentes' papers. Meanwhile, in *L'Équipe*, Aleksandr Vinokurov confirmed that he had been working with Michele Ferrari for a year, athough he denied doping. 'Ferrari is my physical trainer, not my doctor. I have nothing to hide.'

McQuaid commented: 'The relationship with Ferrari would make a Vinokurov victory in Paris less credible.' Even so, Vinokurov had signed the UCI's ethics charter, and he was allowed to start the Tour.

On 1 July, at the Spanish national road championship, Bala refrained from sprinting to allow his teammate Purito Rodríguez to take the title. He contented himself with second place.

In the days before the Tour, the six leading French teams (Credit Agricole, Française des Jeux, Bouygues Telecom, Agritubel, Cofidis and AG2R) and the two German teams (T-Mobile and Gerolsteiner) attempted to have Caisse d'Épargne, Saunier Duval, Relax, Karpin Galicia, Lampre and Discovery Channel expelled from the International Association of Cycling Teams for failing to remove the Operación Puerto riders from their teams.[23] Not having enough votes to do so, they founded their own association, which they called the Movement for Credible Cycling.

A few days before the start of the Tour, Astana's German, Matthias Kessler, and Caisse d'Épargne's Italian, Marco Fertonani, tested positive for testosterone.[24]

On 5 July, the Thursday before the prologue of the Tour de France, in the ExCeL Centre next to the Thames where the Tour had its London headquarters, Vinokurov and Klöden appeared before the press. They were asked questions solely about suspicious controls and their relations with Michele Ferrari.

The following day, Eusebio Unzue opened the Caisse d'Épargne press conference with a condition: 'We are only going to answer sporting questions.'[25]

A German journalist wielding photocopied pages of the Operación Puerto summary asked Valverde the first question: 'Do you appear in these documents? Do you recognise yourself in any of the codenames of Operación Puerto?'

The interpreter answered for the Murcian cyclist: 'We are here to talk about the race that starts tomorrow'. A French journalist, invited to ask the next question, announced, 'If you don't want to talk about this, we have nothing to do here.' At which a dozen or so journalists stood up and walked out.

To those who stayed, Valverde admitted, 'This hounding makes it more difficult to concentrate.'

Óscar Pereiro commented, 'It's always the same questions. We'll answer when they present us with something official, not rumours.'

Despite being the previous year's winner, Pereiro had not been awarded dossard number one. The Tour had decided to start the race numbers at eleven.

'That's two ones,' Pereiro joked.

The president of the Spanish Olympic Committee, Alejandro Blanco, demanded 'respect' for Valverde, 'who, without being implicated in Operación Puerto, is being persecuted . . . he has nothing to do with Operación Puerto.'

The national cycling coach Francisco Antequera blamed the CSD for, as he put it, building the house starting at the roof, and having no exit strategy. 'They gave names and data with no legal basis for any punishment. Only twenty cyclists have been released when we all know that there were many more blood samples. The others have not come out, they have been covered up.'

The first week of the Tour was marked by a crash 23 kilometres from the end of stage five, when Vinokurov's chain broke, sending him somersaulting through the air until he landed on his knees. He carried on with stitches in both knees and excruciating pain as he pedalled. Meanwhile, in an interview with the *Süddeutsche Zeitung* with Jan Ullrich's mentor, Rudy Pevenage, he sought to make a virtue of the German's sins by asking, 'Why don't the Spaniards and the Italians also confess?'

Bala's Tour beginnings were unhurried. He lay twenty-fifth overall before the first mountain stage, over the Col de la Colombière to Le Grand Bornand. He finished tenth, in the same group as Vinokurov. Sporting as always, he said, 'I'm happy the crash hasn't affected his performance. Vinokurov is fine. The race is on.'

9

The Absence of a Rope

On 15 July 2007, the day of stage eight, Denmark's Michael Rasmussen, King of the Mountains in 2005 and 2006, attacked alone
at the foot of the Cormet de Roselend, the first of three climbs in
the last 85 kilometres. He won the stage by 2 minutes 47 seconds,
with Iban Mayo second and Bala third at over three minutes.
Rasmussen took the yellow jersey and declared that he intended
to keep it to Paris.

Descending on his bike from the stage finish at Tignes, the
T-Mobile rider Patrik Sinkewitz crashed into a 78-year-old man.
Both ended up in hospital. Sinkewitz was transported to hospital in Hamburg, where he learned that a surprise test by the
German Anti-Doping Agency on 8 June, when he was training
in the Pyrenees, had found six times the permitted level of testosterone in his body. The German TV channels ARD and ZDF
immediately suspended their Tour coverage. The chairman of the
German Bundestag's sports committee, Peter Danckert, said the
government would consider blocking financial support for the
world championships in Stuttgart and, within weeks, Deutsche
Telekom announced that, while it would honour the financial
terms of its sponsorship contract, it was severing all other ties
with the team and removing the T-Mobile name and branding.[1]
With that, another major sponsor followed Liberty Seguros and
Discovery Channel out of the sport.

The day after Sinkewitz's positive test became public, a letter from the Danish cycling federation to Michael Rasmussen, dated 29 June, was leaked to the press. Rasmussen, who had a Mexican wife and often trained in Mexico, had twice failed to submit his quarterly whereabouts information, in March 2006 and June 2007. If it happened again, he would face automatic suspension. Meanwhile, his federation was banning him from the world championships in Stuttgart from 25 to 30 September and also from the 2008 Olympic Games in Beijing.

Christian Prudhomme, the race director, pointed his finger at the UCI. 'Why is a letter dated 29 June being released on 19 July?' he asked.

On stage nine, seeing Vinokurov breathing hard on the Galibier, Bala launched a long-distance attack six kilometres from the summit and 43 kilometres from the finish in Briançon. The Colombian Mauricio Soler won the stage, but Bala was next across the finish line. Vinokurov arrived at the finish line three minutes after Bala, weeping with pain and rage.

Bala moved into second place overall, which meant that, had Rasmussen been excluded from the Tour de France, Valverde would have been race leader: 'Yes, I did think at breakfast that Rasmussen could be kicked out. Of course, I didn't want that to happen. And, obviously, I wouldn't have worn the yellow jersey.'

While Bala flew high in the Tour standings, Green Party activists on Stuttgart city council raised a motion to cancel the approaching world championships. Baden-Württemberg's Sports Minister Helmut Rau added, 'If the World Cycling Federation does not want to or cannot implement the strict anti-doping requirements of the federal government, the state and the city, the event may not happen.' Germany's Interior Minister Wolfgang Schäuble told a newspaper, 'If necessary, it will have to be cancelled.'

As Germany, recoiling from the T-Mobile affair, called on participants in the world championships to put integrity above mere sporting success, Spain, seen through German eyes, seemed to be doing the opposite.

In stage thirteen, a 54-kilometre time trial around Albi, Bala conceded 6 minutes 8 seconds to the stage winner, Vinokurov, over three minutes to Rasmussen and nearly four to Contador. He dropped to eleventh in the general classification. His Tour had come apart.

Two days later, on the final ascent of stage fifteen, Contador launched six stinging accelerations. Rasmussen responded every time. Despite finishing more than five minutes behind the victorious Vinokurov, Contador and Rasmussen increased their lead over Valverde and their other rivals by 56 seconds.

The second rest day of the 2007 Tour was in Pau. At 2.30 p.m. the UCI announced that, after winning the stage thirteen time trial, Vinokurov had tested positive for a blood transfusion. He and his team were withdrawn from the race.

On the morning of the last day in the mountains, stage sixteen from Orthez to the Col d'Aubisque, a group of riders on teams belonging to the new Movement for a Credible Cycling held a sit-down protest against Vinokurov's positive test result. Six and a half hours later, in the final kilometre of the stage, Rasmussen rode away from Contador to disapproving whistles from the crowd. After the stage, one of the morning's protestors against doping, the Cofidis rider Cristian Moreni, descended the Aubisque in a police car. Shortly after finishing the stage 41st, 21 minutes 36 seconds behind Rasmussen, Moreni learned that a sample taken from him on Tuesday 19 July had tested positive for testosterone. While the police searched his hotel, his team also withdrew from the Tour.

The Rasmussen subplot received new impetus when the former professional Davide Cassani, commentating on the Tour for RAI, told Italian viewers that he had met Rasmussen in the Italian Alps before the Tour. At the time, the Dane had claimed to be training in Mexico. It meant a third breach of the whereabouts rules, and two missed surprise tests. That evening, Rabobank withdrew the yellow jersey from the Tour for failing to comply with the team's internal regulations. Rasmussen later revealed that, if there had been anything with which to make a noose in the mountain hotel to which he had been banished, he would have hanged himself. But for the absence of a rope, the Tour de France would have seen its first suicide.

Stage seventeen went ahead with no yellow jersey although Alberto Contador now led the race. Prudhomme commented, 'The only good news is that the leader's team has sacked him. Contador is more credible – at least, as credible as the rest of the peloton, which means he's just as suspicious.'

Contador defended his race lead in the final time trial, although it was the tightest podium in history, with Cadel Evans second at twenty-three seconds and Levi Leipheimer eight seconds behind him.

After the race, Bala said: 'The most important thing is that I've learned a lot from this Tour.'[2] But, in the hierarchy of Spanish cycling, he had been definitively displaced by the 24-year-old Contador.

In the pages of *El País*, José Miguel Echávarri contrasted Rabobank's capitulation with his resistance in the 1988 Tour, when the race director, Jean-Pierre Courcol, had pressured him to withdraw Delgado because of his positive for probenicid. Echávarri had stood firm, Delgado won the Tour and Courcol had resigned.[3] From the standpoint of 2007, it put Reynolds and its leader on the wrong side of history.

The initials A.C. appeared together with those of the other eight Liberty Seguros riders who raced the 2005 Tour on Document 31 of the Operación Puerto summary, published by *El País* on 30 June 2006, which showed alleged doping doses established by Fuentes, although for A.C. and L.L., whom some suspected to be Luis León Sánchez, now provisionally suspended by his team, the prescription stated: 'Nothing or the same as J.J.' Next to J.J. – meaning Jörg Jaksche – Fuentes had written: 'Corticoids and hormones'.[4] On that basis, the one-day Vattenfall Cyclassics race around Hamburg on 19 August barred Alberto Contador from starting – not that he ever had any intention of taking part. It was an indication of the mood in Germany.

As well as showcasing the sport, the world championships generated essential funds for the UCI. To prevent Stuttgart and the German government carrying out their threat to suspend the championships Valverde's exclusion was a price worth paying,[5] and, on Wednesday 29 August the UCI asked the Spanish federation to open disciplinary proceedings against him. In an official statement it explained, 'After a thorough reading of the six thousand pages of the Operación Puerto dossier, the UCI has concluded that several documents might prove Alejandro Valverde's involvement.' Citing article 9.2.002 of its regulations, according to which a rider under investigation is not allowed to start at the world championships, the press release continued, 'In accordance with UCI rules and to protect the atmosphere and reputation of the World Championships, Alejandro Valverde will be denied participation in the upcoming World Championships (25 to 30 September).'[6]

The Spanish institutions refused to play ball. On 7 September both the RFEC and the CNCDD, the competent body for doping matters within the RFEC, announced that they would not be starting proceedings against Valverde. The RFEC secretary Eugenio Bermúdez, in charge of administrative proceedings, said, 'The UCI is talking about documents that we have already looked at. In any case, the German rider Erik Zabel is riding, and he has confessed to doping.'[7] The RFEC announced that it would be appealing to the Court of Arbitration for Sport and to the ordinary courts.[8]

The same day, WADA filed its own appeal against the RFEC's decision with CAS in Switzerland. Four days later, the UCI did the same. Stuttgart's Sports Mayor, Susanne Eisenmann, said of Valverde's inclusion in the Spanish team: 'I think it's a mistake from the point of view of a new start.'

The Spanish national coach, Francisco Antequera, retorted, 'There is no reason why Valverde cannot take part in the world championships. He has already ridden in the Tour de France, and there the case was examined to the last millimetre.'

On 26 September, the Wednesday before the Sunday of the elite men's road race, CAS published its ruling allowing Bala to take part. 'A ban on a rider who has not been found guilty of doping from participating in a World Championship would constitute a form of preventive sanction'. McQuaid commented, 'This does not mean that Valverde is now clean in the eyes of the UCI, but we bow to the law and if Valverde wins the World Championship, we will allow him to wear the champion's jersey.'

The following day, German Interior Minister Wolfgang Schäuble froze a €150,000 subsidy to the championships. 'When the world championships themselves refuse to embrace the opportunity for a fresh start, they must assume the consequences.' The national TV channel ZDF announced, 'Our focus will be on journalistic coverage of the current situation in cycling. We are limiting our live coverage in favour of information about the background to the events.' The channel resolved to show only the last quarter of an hour of the elite men's road race.

Of Eddy Merckx, Gianni Bugno, Dietrich Thurau and Rudi Altig, all former world champions expected in Stuttgart, the organising committee declared, 'They are not welcome. We are for a new cycling, where there is no room for doping tolerance.'[9]

In the event, the elite men's title was won by another rider who had had to take legal action to reach the starting line. Paolo Bettini, who had refused to sign the pre-Tour Geneva Oath, calling it 'an intrusion into my private life', won his second consecutive world championship. Bala, after all the fuss, came in fifty-seventh, 2 minutes 47 seconds behind him.

With sponsors fleeing and its institutions at each other's throats, the entire economy of professional cycling was in crisis. A representative of France Télévisions, the state broadcaster, was of the opinion that the Tour de France would not survive a third consecutive year of scandals. Cycling needed a game-changer, something to force a paradigm shift.

10

Epoch-making

On 23 October 2007, day two of the International Meeting against Doping in Cycling, organised by the French Sports Minister, Roselyne Bachelot-Narquin, the presidents of the UCI and WADA, Pat McQuaid and Dick Pound, signed a protocol in Paris to implement the first biological passport.[1] Working alongside traditional, direct methods of substance detection, the biological passport took a different approach. By monitoring selected biomarkers – haematological, initially, to detect blood doping through transfusions or EPO, but, later, steroidal and, eventually, endocrinal – it sought to uncover the effects of doping indirectly. Samples would be collected, values fed into a statistical model, and a physiological profile would gradually emerge for each individual athlete. If a test threw up a value beyond the expected range, or showed suspicious changes, the passport would be submitted to a panel of experts who would consider the data and the athletes' explanation. If they considered that doping was the likely cause, they would pass the case to another panel, which would rule whether an anti-doping rule violation had been proven.

The plan was to carry out blood tests on 500 riders between January and July 2008. It was an enormous logistical challenge, and a working group was created to solve it in time to allow all potential participants to have passports in time for the Tour de France. A scientific group was convened to analyse the results and be able to decree a temporary suspension or even a sanction for doping. As Pound said in his presentation, 'In a few years' time, historians will remember that cycling was on the brink but that on this day, 23 October, in Paris, it decided to step forward and clean itself up.'

It would take years to build up profiles and refine the scheme to make prosecutions possible. But one of the world's leading anti-doping investigators, Renzo Ferrante of the *Nucleo Anti-sofisticazione e Salute* (NAS), the food and medicine unit in the Public Health Command of the Italian Carabinieri, told me:

> The biological passport's introduction was an epoch-making step forward for anti-doping, and not only in cycling. It made life much more difficult for those who decide to cheat and have the resources to evade ordinary testing. As anti-doping science became more refined in its ability to detect traces of prohibited substances and methods in biological matrices collected during testing, doping science discovered new methods to frustrate the efforts of laboratories. An example of this is the abuse of EPO and the adoption of microdoses, a system that reduced the windows of detection of EPO metabolites, especially in urine, to just a few hours. It is much more difficult to defraud the biological passport. I personally have seen proof of this during investigations, when even the doping 'sorcerers' have had no choice but to surrender in the face of passport evidence. They curse the biological passport, and the experts who administer it.

Four weeks after the gathering in Paris, an even larger international meeting took place in Madrid. The World Conference on Doping in Sport brought 1,500 dignitaries and delegates to the Spanish capital to review the world anti-doping code and elect a new president of WADA.[2] Pat McQuaid took the opportunity to pass Jaime Lissavetzky a report drawn up by Mario Zorzoli,

Right At Port d'Envalira in stage 9 of the 2003 Vuelta a España, Bala took the seventh win of his career and his first Grand Tour stage win. Another stage win, third place overall, and a World Championships silver medal, await.

Below At the 2004 Vuelta a Murcia, a five-day race in those days, Bala took the win overall and Kelme-Costa Blanca the best team. Their controversial general manager, Vicente Belda, joins the podium shenanigans.

Above At Plasencia, before stage 17 of the 2004 Vuelta a España, Bala - second overall, five seconds behind Roberto Heras - looked relaxed. That afternoon, on the climb to the stage finish at La Covatilla, he conceded 2'10" to Heras, and held onto his podium place by one second.

Opposite page below
Lance Armstrong, second, congratulates Bala on his stage win at Courchevel Altiport on 12 July 2005. Armstrong reflected: 'A guy like him could be the future of cycling. He's a complete rider, a patient rider and smart.'

Right Fifth in the Prologue around Strasbourg, Bala started stage 3 of the 2006 Tour de France seventh overall, 16" from the race lead. Nineteen kilometres from the finish at Valkenburg, Bala went down, breaking his right collarbone. Two Tours started, two abandons.

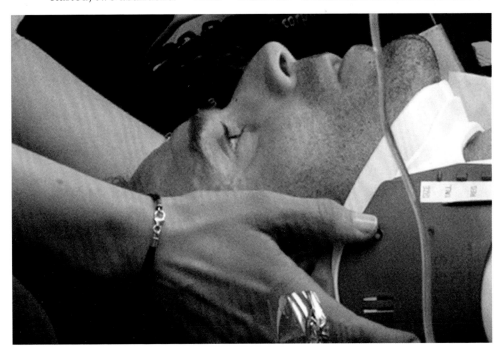

Above Seven kilometres into the Prologue of the 2017 Tour de France, Bala believes his career is over. The impact with a crowd barrier has shattered his left kneecap, and caused other fractures in his left leg.

CONTRÔLE ANTI-DOPAGE

Above After his suspension, despite being subjected to a targeted testing regime, Bala was the same rider with a comparable win rate. There was never the slightest hint of a biological passport issue. Could it be that the early doping did not make the slightest difference?

Left The architect behind the Illes Balears cycling sponsorship deal, Iñaki Urdangarin, husband of the Infanta Cristina de Borbon, in court at Mallorca, declaring before the judge in Noos Case.

Above Left to right:
Eufemiano Fuentes,
José Ignacio Labarta,
Vicente Belda and
Manolo Saiz stand
in court during the
Operación Puerto
trial in 2013.

Right The 2009 Vuelta
a España was Bala's sole
Grand Tour win, but
one of twenty where he
finished in the top ten
(twelve at his home
tour, the Vuelta, a
record for that race).

Above 30 September 2018: world champion at last! Bala celebrates with Juan Carlos Escámez, a former rival who retrained as a physiotherapist and became Valverde's confident and confessor.

Above The final podium place of Bala's career: third in the Tre Valli Varesine, 4 October 2022, behind Tadej Pogačar and Sergio Higuita.

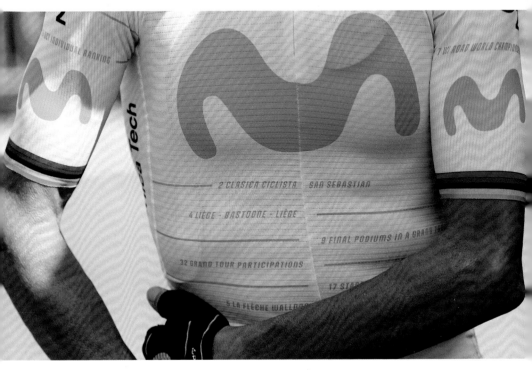

Above Bala and his teammates rode his final Grand Tour, the 2022 Vuelta a España, with the stand-out statistics of his long career printed on their jerseys.

Above Innsbrück, in full flow. 'It was a very long sprint. They left all the responsibility to me. When there were three hundred metres to go, I said to myself, "It's my distance. Full gas to the finish line."'

the UCI's chief medical officer, which showed, by measuring reticulocytes, that blood doping was still going on in Spain and Portugal. The conversation then turned to Valverde.

'Proof, proof, proof,' Lissavetzky told him. 'Without proof you can't punish anyone. Valverde is not implicated in the Guardia Civil's report. And the Court of Arbitration for Sport agrees.'

At nine o'clock in the morning of day one, Jacques Rogge, the president of the International Olympic Committee, called on investigating magistrate Serrano to hand over the blood bags to the UCI for DNA profiling.[3] At seven the same evening WADA secretary general David Howman added: 'CAS has only agreed with Alejandro Valverde in the World Championships case. We have indications of his involvement in Operación Puerto. Everyone knows that the nicknames of those involved corresponded to the names of their dogs, and everyone knows that Valverde's dog is called Piti, like the name on a bag.'[4]

The message seemed to be that there could be no peace as long as Alejandro Valverde continued to race uninterrupted.

The new year brought wonderful news for Bala: the birth, on 4 January 2008, to his wife Ángela González, of twins, Iván y Alejandro.[5] Five days later came less heartening tidings.

As Ferrante explained, 'Initially, the investigations in Italy only examined Italian athletes and support staff involved in the activities of Dr Eufemiano Fuentes and people associated with him. Later, it was decided to extend the investigation to foreign athletes who had doped abroad prior to competing in Italy; this approach was based on a ruling by our Supreme Appeals Court in the case of the footballer Gaddafi, the son of the former Libyan dictator, who played in Italy's Serie A. Valverde was one of the athletes who were included.'

A double procedure – criminal and sporting – began, which could potentially have led to a criminal conviction as well as a ban from competing in Italy. Given that July's Tour de France entered Italy for a stage finish at Prato Nevoso, a rest day in Piedmont, and a stage start in Cuneo the following morning, and the Italian town of Varese was hosting the world championships in September, two of Bala's season goals were suddenly under threat. Also on his list were the Vuelta, and victory in the hilly Olympic road race around Beijing, although the developing face-off between the race organisers, dominated by the Tour de France organisers ASO, and the UCI's ProTour, threatened to make the season decidedly gap-toothed.[6]

Ferrante had been working on the Valverde case as part of a broader investigation that took its cue from the evidence of Operación Puerto. Two investigations were opened in Italy, one in Busto Arsizio and another at the Rome Prosecutor's Office, the latter with investigations delegated to Ferrante's office in Florence.

Bala's season started as usual, in Mallorca. During the Challenge, he was the subject of a frantic exchange of letters between the Court of Arbitration for Sport in Lausanne, the Spanish cycling federation, the UCI, WADA, and his own lawyers. Rumour had it that the Court of Appeal in Madrid was soon to decide on the closure of Operación Puerto. If confirmed, there was a real chance that the contents of blood bag eighteen would be disposed of. On 13 February, WADA asked CAS to send Serrano an urgent request to release all or part of blood bag eighteen for DNA profiling. The following day, Valverde's lawyers wrote to CAS complaining that blood bag number eighteen had been misattributed and, in any case, CAS's jurisdiction had not yet been established. Aware of this intense legal activity or not, their client finished third in the Trofeo Calvià, the last of the Challenge de Mallorca races, on 14 February.

Later the same day, the High Court in Madrid ordered Serrano to reopen Operación Puerto and investigate the way the 200 blood bags had been stored to determine whether it amounted to a crime against public health.[7] With its tightly delimited remit, it could have been worse for Valverde.

At the end of February, WADA chair John Fahey announced that a new test capable of detecting human growth hormone would be ready for use before Beijing. In *El País* he elaborated on his mandate's motto 'Weed out the cheats.'

Carlos Arribas asked him, 'When you talk about weeds, do you mean Alejandro Valverde?'

Fahey began, 'I can't comment on individual cases that are before the courts.' But he added, 'As a matter of principle, WADA has no choice but to work with the courts to ensure that information about doping is shared by all federations and anti-doping bodies.'[8]

The comment seemed directed at Serrano.

The fact was, the sanctioned riders were, in many respects, the lucky ones. Ivan Basso's two-year ban expired on 24 October 2008, after which he would be back racing. Michele Scarponi's eighteen-month ban ended on 1 August 2008. There were riders for whom a temporary ban would have been far better than the current impasse. There were no proceedings against them, and they still had racing licences,[9] but the ethical codes of the Pro-Tour and the three-week races prevented them from taking part. Joseba Beloki, David Etxebarria and others had opted to retire. Others were racing in Portugal or the USA for €15,000 a year. In May, it would have been two years since Operación Puerto started, and there was still no end in sight.

In February, the Giro d'Italia had defied UCI ProTour rules by announcing that it would not be inviting Astana. Tour de France organisers ASO followed suit. Alberto Contador was the target of the first snub to the reigning champion's team in the race's 105-year history. The snub extended to the first ProTour stage race of the year, Paris–Nice. Two weeks before it was due to start, Pat McQuaid wrote, in a letter to the teams: 'Paris–Nice will be a feral event, a private race unintegrated into organised sport or the Olympic movement. As a UCI licence holder, your team is not permitted to participate.'

On 5 March, the day Bala finished fourth in stage two of the Vuelta a Murcia, the arbitration panel at CAS resolved to send Serrano yet another urgent request to release all or part of blood bag eighteen to CAS or a suitable laboratory, to be agreed by all parties. On the seventh, the day Bala won the Vuelta a Murcia time trial in the Sierra Espuña mountains, the RFEC suggested that the blood bag remain in Barcelona.[10] Valverde's legal team agreed.[11] WADA and the UCI wanted the blood bag transferred to Lausanne, and CAS was of the same opinion. On 8 March, Bala won the Vuelta a Murcia overall for the third time.

Meanwhile, on 7 March, two days before the start of Paris–Nice, it was still unclear whether it would take place or not. In the nick of time, the teams reached an agreement with the organisers of Paris–Nice.[12] McQuaid wrote another letter, this time to the riders, reminding them that, if they took part, they faced a €10,000 fine, a six-month suspension and a ban from the world championships.

Complaining that the threats were illegal or abusive, the riders' union and a number of teams asked CAS to make a ruling.[13] The UCI and ASO both refused to recognise the arbitration court's jurisdiction, at which the court declared itself incompetent and so the teams elected, with fifteen votes in favour and eight abstentions, to take part.

The dispute between ASO and the UCI escalated. When the French Sports Minister expressed his support for ASO, Pat McQuaid questioned his democratic legitimacy: after all, should a political representative be supporting a private business, whose goal was to turn cycling into a league with a single dominant organiser, against a democratically constituted body representing the collective interest? ASO chairman Patrice Clerc responded by claiming that the UCI had exceeded its statutory role and become an economic actor. He added that the conflict was caused by Pat McQuaid, who was trying to prevent Alejandro Valverde from racing in the world championships one minute, and defending Contador's participation in the Tour the next.[14]

Either way, Paris–Nice went ahead without Astana and Contador. Mid-race, on 14 March, the UCI announced that it was suspending all contact with the AIGCP, the International Association of Professional Cycling Teams, although McQuaid said, 'I hope this situation is only temporary'. The same day, CSC, the team of Fabian Cancellara, the Schleck brothers and Carlos Sastre, announced the team's termination at the end of the year.[15]

If the atmosphere was not poisonous enough, while the peloton negotiated stage one of Paris–Nice, the wife of the Belgian rider Kevin van Impe gave birth to a son. Six hours later, the child died. Two days later, while the rider was arranging the funeral, anti-doping inspectors paid him a visit. The bereaved father asked to be excused, but the inspectors insisted. The news caused shockwaves in Belgium. The Flemish Sports Minister, Bert Anciaux, commented, 'The law is the law, but the controls must be more humane.' At Paris–Nice and the Italian stage race, Tirreno–Adriatico, the riders staged five-minute protests pre-stage.

Paris–Nice was not on Bala's schedule. At the start of March, he rode to seventh place in the Critérium International, with third place in stage two, leading the chasers in, 99 seconds behind Jens Voigt and stage winner Simon Gerrans. The following day, CAS dispatched its request for the blood bag to Serrano.[16] Ten days later, on 11 April 2008, midway between the GP Miguel Indurain, where Bala finished thirtieth, and the Klasika Primavera de Amorebieta, where he was second to Damiano Cunego, Serrano replied. The answer was still no. His reasoning this time was that, as a private law foundation, CAS was not included in the Convention on Mutual Assistance in Criminal Matters between the Member States of the European Union. He preferred to take this line than to consider Spain's commitment, made with the ratification in February 2007 of the 2005 UNESCO International Convention Against Doping in Sport, to 'cooperation between anti-doping organisations, public authorities and sports organisations within their jurisdiction and those within the jurisdiction of other States'.

On 15 April, as he came into form for Ardennes week, Bala took his third win of the season, in Paris–Camembert. Three days later, a preliminary hearing took place before CAS in Lausanne in the appeal, by WADA and the UCI, against the Spanish cycling federation, for its refusal to open proceedings against him (known as Valverde I). Its goal was merely to decide procedural matters raised by Valverde's legal representatives: whether CAS had jurisdiction, whether the UCI had lodged its appeal within the time limits set by its own regulations and whether Valverde should provide a biological sample for tDNA profiling (in all three cases, Valverde's lawyers argued that the answer was no).

Two days later, at the Amstel Gold Race, Bala passed under the flamme rouge perfectly positioned, third in a single file of eight riders. With 350 metres to go, Fränk Schleck accelerated, with Damiano Cunego on his wheel. Alongside Thomas Dekker, Bala began to slip back. Rising out of the saddle, he repositioned himself onto Davide Rebellin's wheel, then darted past. But by then, Cunego had won the race, with Schleck second. He had been hoping for much more, but his third place still made Bala the first Spaniard to finish on the podium of the Amstel Gold Race.

Four days later, in pouring rain, he rode an anonymous Flèche Wallonne to twenty-first place. But, at Liège–Bastogne–Liège, two days after his 28th birthday, he was a different rider. On La Roche aux Faucons, a climb new to the race, he bridged across to the leading group, made up of the Schleck brothers, Davide Rebellin and his teammate Purito Rodríguez. As Rodríguez dropped out of contention, Andy Schleck attacked, forcing Bala and Rebellin to chase. On the slopes of St Nicholas, with six kilometres left, Andy Schleck was caught. His brother Fränk counterattacked, but Rebellin closed down the move. He, Fränk and Bala entered the final kilometre together. With 200 metres to go, Bala unleashed his sprint to win Liège–Bastogne–Liège for the second time.

Ever honest in his self-appraisal, he admitted, 'Fränk Schleck was the strongest, as in the Amstel Gold Race. But me and Rebellin were faster.'

Third in the 5.6-kilometre prologue to the Dauphiné Libéré on 8 June, and first in stage one after a 300-metre sprint, Bala took the lead after stage four, a 31-kilometre mountain time trial, his second stage win. Third place in stage six to Morzine, and fifth the following day at La Toussuire, ensured he won the race 39 seconds ahead of Australia's Cadel Evans.

Two weeks later, in 40-degree heat, Bala's finishing speed made him the Spanish national champion for the first time, a second ahead of Óscar Sevilla, *persona non grata* in the ProTour, so riding for the American team Rock Racing.

The 2008 Tour de France started on 5 July at Brest, on the westernmost tip of Finisterre in Brittany. Valverde started among the favourites.

'To be good in the third week, I have to try to expend as little energy as possible in the first two weeks', he said.[17]

But it was a smokescreen. On day one, finishing on the famous climb at Plumelec, he won the stage and took the race lead.

Setbacks followed: twenty-second in the flattish, 29.4-kilometre time trial in stage four, he dropped to seventeenth overall, 1 minute 27 seconds behind the winner, Stefan Schumacher.

Then, 85 kilometres into stage five, the longest of the Tour at 232 kilometres between Cholet and Châteauroux, Bala's Tour de France demons struck again when a protruding cat's eye brought him down with two or three others. Bala took a heavy blow to the right knee, calf and collarbone, the one he broke during the 2006

Tour. Treated on the road by the race doctor, he finished the stage then went to hospital for an ultrasound scan which ruled out serious injury.

The following day, 1.5 kilometres from the finish in Super Besse in the Massif Central, in a section with an average gradient of 10 per cent, the Italian veteran Leonardo Piepoli attacked, with the American Cristian Van Der Velde. Pereiro chased them down before Piepoli's teammate Riccardo Riccò, the new phenomenon of Italian cycling, darted off his wheel to win the stage.

Bala, second in the stage, moved up to eighth overall.

The same day, CAS issued its decisions following the preliminary hearings to Valverde I. It ruled that, yes, the appeal lay within its jurisdiction, and yes, the UCI's appeal was within the stipulated time limits, and no, pending the release of the blood bag, there was no need for Valverde to provide a DNA sample just yet.

Given that Serrano had so far refused the request to release the blood bag, there was understandably no great urgency on the part of WADA and the UCI. On the one hand, the ruling noted, in a tone of mock-confusion, that Valverde claimed to want a quick solution on the grounds that the uncertainty was causing him harm, notably in the loss of contracts. Yet, if he would only release the blood bag and take a DNA test, the uncertainty could be resolved in an instant. He professed to object because the burden of proof was not his. As a result, awaiting further clarification whether blood bag eighteen or part thereof would become available, the court stayed proceedings for up to six months. If, after that period, no formal response from Serrano had been received, the case would resume. In the meantime, Valverde rode in its shadow.

Back in France, Valverde was fifth in stage seven, finishing in a group of twenty-two riders six seconds behind his fellow Murcian Luís León Sánchez. It was the day the race registered its first doping positive, the Spaniard Manuel Beltrán having tested positive for EPO on stage one. Beltrán had been one of a group of riders who, according to the French anti-doping agency, had been targeted for extra testing after showing suspicious parameters in the blood tests carried out before the race. As stipulated by the contract between the teams and ASO, Beltrán's team, Liquigas, expelled him from the race, while the French police arrested Beltrán and searched his room.

On stage nine to Bagnères de Bigorre on 13 July, Riccardo Riccò took his second stage win, finishing alone, 1 minute 17 seconds ahead of the Valverde group. Going into stage ten, the hardest mountain stage of the race, from Pau to Hautacam over the towering Tourmalet, Bala lay sixth overall, 1 minute 12 seconds behind the yellow jersey held by the Luxembourger Kim Kirchen. He crossed the Tourmalet 50 seconds behind the other favourites, Cadel Evans, Denis Menchov and Carlos Sastre. Then, on the final climb to Hautacam, those 50 seconds became 3 minutes 35 seconds. That the stage was won by the Italian Piepoli, with his teammate Juan José Cobo second, in the same time, was incidental. Bala dropped to fourteenth overall, 4 minutes 41 seconds behind the new yellow jersey, Cadel Evans. His bid to win the Tour de France was over for another year.

On the morning of stage eleven in the Pyrenean town of Tarbes, a young Spanish rider, Moisés Dueñas, nineteenth overall, just over six minutes behind the yellow jersey Evans, became the second doping positive of the Tour when it emerged that traces of EPO had been detected in a sample taken on stage four. Calling Dueñas an idiot, McQuaid added: 'Spain is the last frontier of doping. I think this country is slow to get the message. I can't say that the Spanish sports authorities are very effective, or their anti-doping policy. Two years ago a new law was passed there but I still haven't seen a single athlete brought to justice. It's business as usual.'[18]

Mundo Deportivo found some consolation, reflecting: 'It is a stroke of luck, at the very least, that Beltrán and Dueñas ride for foreign teams.'[19]

Two days later, Barloworld, Moisés Dueñas' team sponsor, announced that it too would be pulling out of cycling after the Tour.

On the morning of stage twelve in Lavelanet, Riccardo Riccò, the leader of the mountain and best young rider competitions and the winner of two stages, was arrested after testing positive, also on stage four, for a new, long-acting variety of EPO known as CERA. Later it emerged that the pharmaceutical company Roche, CERA's manufacturers, had secretly introduced a molecular marker that made it detectable in a test of their own devising, made available to the anti-doping authorities. Riccò was the first to be caught out. His team, Saunier Duval, withdrew from the Tour.

Six days later, on 20 July, Caisse d'Épargne lost its first rider of the race. Descending from the Colle dell'Agnello, just before a hairpin bend, Óscar Pereiro was hit from behind and sent flying over the safety barrier. After falling five full metres, he stretched out an arm to break his fall. The impact shattered his left humerus. Bala fought his way back into the top ten when he finished seventh over the Italian border at Prato Nevoso.

The Tour teams spent the next two nights and, in between, the second rest day of the Tour, in Italy. Late that evening, and early the following morning, CONI's anti-doping officers descended on the Tour de France. On rest day morning, at Caisse d'Épargne's hotel, the Albergo Cannon d'Oro at Chiusa di Pesio, they collected urine samples from each of the team's eight riders still in the race, and labelled the samples for two tests: standard testing and for EPO. They also took one blood sample. Marked 278350, the blood was labelled for two tests: '3P', meaning the three parameters haematocrit, haemoglobin and reticulocytes, and HBCOs, for Haemoglobin-Based Oxygen Carriers (products like Hemopure or Oxyglobin), sometimes called blood substitutes or artificial blood. The blood was Valverde's. At the Hotel Giardino dei Tigli in nearby Fossano, where, among others, the

CSC team was staying, they took thirteen urine samples and two more blood samples.

The riders signed the standard sample collection form, on which the CONI logo was prominent. It noted that the donor could be sanctioned for 'violating the organisation charter'. The wording indicated that 'all information related to anti-doping controls, including but not limited to laboratory results and possible sanctions, shall be shared with the relevant bodies in accordance with anti-doping rules.' Valverde signed his form and the samples were couriered the same day to the anti-doping laboratory in Rome.

The following day, after finishing thirteenth at Jausiers, he moved up to eighth in the general classification. That left stage seventeen, the final day in the high mountains from Embrun, over the Galibier and the Col de la Croix de Fer to Alpe d'Huez. The day belonged to a Spanish rider, but not Bala. Even before the first of the twenty-one hairpins on Alpe d'Huez, Carlos Sastre had attacked, obliging the race leader, his teammate Fränk Schleck, and Frank's brother Andy, to hold back. For seven kilometres, the Schleck brothers, Samuel Sánchez, Denis Menchov, Bernhard Kohl and Bala sat on Cadel Evans's wheel while Sastre gained an average of 15 seconds per kilometre. Over the next 4.5 kilometres, his gains were four seconds per kilometre, although, in the final 1.5 kilometres, as the attacks started behind, he conceded 24 seconds of the lead he had built up. Even so, his stage winning margin of 2 minutes 3 seconds over Andy Schleck and Samuel Sánchez, and a further ten seconds over Bala, fourth, and Fränk Schleck, fifth, earned him the yellow jersey with an advantage of 1 minute 24 seconds.

Cycling lost yet another sponsor on Alpe d'Huez day when Saunier Duval announced that it was terminating the team with immediate effect. Moments after Riccò's arrest on the morning of stage twelve, his teammate Leonardo Piepoli had told his director Joxean 'Matxín' Fernández: 'I have done the same as Riccardo.'

The expected positive result materialised on 7 October, when the French anti-doping agency announced that Piepoli, together with Stefan Schumacher, the winner of stages four and twenty and the yellow jersey for two days, had tested positive for CERA. By then, Riccardo Riccò, the winner of stages six and nine, had been given a two-year ban by the Italian National Olympic Committee.

On 27 July, Sastre celebrated victory in Paris. Bala, ninth at 7 minutes, 12 seconds, had again been upstaged by compatriots – Sastre, but also Samuel Sánchez, seventh overall, 47 seconds ahead of Valverde. Six days later, Bala won the Clásica San Sebastián in a sprint against nine others. Caisse d'Épargne's flamboyant chairman, Charles Milhaud, the team's main supporter within the bank, was there to witness the victory, which gave Bala the lead in the UCI ProTour rankings. The day after the Clásica, he flew to Beijing for the Olympic road race with Carlos Sastre, Óscar Freire and Samuel Sánchez. Alberto Contador arrived later. The dream team, as the Spanish press called it,[20] was subjected to intensive anti-doping checks. Valverde, Sastre, Freire and Sánchez were given three tests in four days. Contador, who arrived later, had two in two days. In the race, Valverde stayed close to Bettini, while Sánchez and Rebellin attacked with Andy Schleck over the final climb. Cancellara led the Russian Alexandre Kolobnev and Michael Rogers of Australia across the gap. On the steep finish, Kolobnev started the sprint early, but Sánchez eased past to take the win, with Rebellin second and Cancellara third. Bala was twelfth.

Two days later, the rider Maribel Moreno, who had arrived in Beijing for the women's road race on 10 August, was immediately tested, suffered a panic attack and travelled back to Spain the same day. She tested positive for EPO, becoming the first participant to test positive for a banned substance at the 2008 Games. Samuel Sánchez said, 'It's a shame because it continues to tarnish our sport.'

*

At Jaén on day two of the Vuelta a España, Purito Rodríguez attacked, allowing his teammate Bala to bide his time, then pounce to take the stage and leader's jersey. He stayed in the top five until stage twelve, an attritional stage from Burgos to Suances on the northern coast. On the category-two Alto del Caracol, 60 kilomètres from the finish line, the peloton crumbled and, through bad positioning, Bala began to shed time. By the end of the stage, Contador led him by 3 minutes 50 seconds in the general classification. All his hopes of winning the Vuelta were frustrated.

Mundo Deportivo diagnosed 'Monachil syndrome', a relapse into the condition that had allowed Vinokurov to ride away near Granada in the 2006 Vuelta. *ABC* saw 'blank spots' in 'Valverde's mental cartography . . . black holes, a fog, as if he is suddenly dissociated.' Eusebio Unzue said it was punishment for 'not being where he should have been, a recurring mistake'. In the heat of the immediate post-stage, Óscar Pereiro commented, 'A man of his category and experience cannot lose the Vuelta on a stage like this. Once again a stage race has slipped away from him because of stupidity.'

Two days later, Alberto Contador won on the Alto de l'Angliru. It effectively sealed overall victory. Bala, second in the stage, 42 seconds behind Contador, slotted into fifth place overall, which is where he finished in Madrid. Having won the 2007 Tour de France and the 2008 Giro d'Italia, Contador became the first Spaniard to win all three Grand Tours. Bala completed a different transition from Spain's greatest Tour hope to its latest disappointment.

September was not all bad news though. On the twenty-sixth, five days after the Vuelta, Judge Serrano closed down Operación Puerto yet again.

In the world championship road race at Varese on 28 September, Bala stayed with his nemesis, Paolo Bettini, who, in his last race as a professional, knowingly dropped out of contention, allowing his teammate Alessandro Ballan to ride to victory. Valverde came in thirty-seventh, 4 minutes 53 seconds behind Ballan, in the same group as Bettini, who had outfoxed him again. Of the Spaniards, only Purito Rodríguez made the decisive split, finishing sixth.

On 20 October, UCI president Pat McQuaid and the former rider Vittorio Adorni made what must have been an uncomfortable visit to Caisse d'Épargne's Paris headquarters to present Eusebio Unzue with the award for the world number one ranked team, and Bala with the trophy for the world number one ranked cyclist. In spite of his personal disappointment, he had still enabled Caisse d'Épargne to end the season as the world's number one team.

The previous day, three of Caisse d'Épargne's top executives, including its 65-year-old president and architect, Charles Milhaud, had resigned after a €600 million stock market loss.[21] The sponsorship contract, worth €8 million a year, ran until the end of 2010. Team sources were quoted in the press as saying, 'In the short term, we have no doubt that it will continue. The medium term depending on how the crisis evolves, which is another story . . .'

11

Match Point

As the proceedings in Spain slipped into frustrating inertia, the Guardia Civil discreetly passed on to their Italian colleagues some strategic information: the dates of Antonio Serrano's annual vacation. Timing his application to reach Madrid in Serrano's absence, CONI's anti-doping prosecutor Ettore Torri wrote to Court No. Thirty-one in Madrid on 6 November with yet another request for access to blood bag eighteen. His faxed letter included in the margin a *nulla osta* or certificate of no impediment from Paolo Ferraro in the office of Rome's public prosecutor. This approved the application on behalf of the judicial authorities. Ferraro followed this up with a confirmation letter on the tenth. Anticipating a positive response, the public prosecutor's office in Rome ordered the Italian police to seize from Rome's Anti-doping Laboratory the blood samples collected during the 2008 Tour de France's brief stay in Italy.

On 22 January 2009, Serrano's holiday cover, investigating magistrate Ana Teresa Jiménez Valverde, authorised the request as a matter of routine. Things moved fast. On 30 January a police scientist, Dr Tiziana Sansolini, accompanied by Marco Arpino, the director of the Italian Olympic Committee's anti-doping office in Rome (whom the public prosecutor in Rome had rapidly made an 'auxiliary of the judicial police') and two members of the Carabinieri, flew to Barcelona and collected samples from blood bag eighteen. Among them was the Carabinieri investigator

Renzo Ferrante, who recalled, 'The critical moment was the loading of the samples into the aircraft cabin, given that they were biological material. Our Guardia Civil escort interceded on our behalf, and we were allowed to take them on board. This proved to be crucial as the chain of custody was later debated at length in the CAS proceedings.'

On 2 February, with the authority of the public prosecutor's office in Rome, the Police Scientific Service analysed the DNA of the samples collected in Barcelona and compared the results with the DNA of the three samples collected during the Tour de France. On 10 February it informed the public prosecutor that sixteen genetic markers in one of the samples matched those of blood bag eighteen. The number would have been considered more than sufficient in many countries' criminal proceedings. CONI was asked to consult the documentation which would identify the sample, numbered 278350. 18 – VALV. (Piti) and Alejandro Valverde proved to be one and the same, to no one's great surprise.

CONI informed the UCI and WADA. Valverde's legal team complained bitterly about the release of the plasma but, given the substantive fact of the DNA test, their procedural stalling could be seen for what it was.

The same day as the DNA match, 10 February, Bala crashed in the Trofeo Pollença, the third race of the Challenge de Mallorca, although he was not seriously injured. At one o'clock the following afternoon, the accountant of the Caisse d'Épargne team, Javier Valera, received a call from Marco Arpino summoning Valverde to CONI headquarters in the Olympic Stadium in Rome at twelve o'clock on Monday the sixteenth.[1] For the first time, Valverde faced a formal and direct accusation of doping, almost three years after the Guardia Civil had dismantled Fuentes' blood transfusion ring.

According to a Caisse d'Épargne statement the rider was 'surprised and indignant' and protested: 'I have expressed on multiple occasions my willingness to contrast my blood values with the evidence in the judicial investigation, provided that the competent authority for this purpose requested it.'[2] But this was skating round the facts. At Valverde's request, the hearing was rescheduled to the nineteenth.

Back from his annual leave, Serrano can only have been incandescent with rage. It was the second time in six weeks that his authority had been undermined. The first was on 12 January when, two years and seven months after the arrests of Fuentes and his associates by the Guardia Civil, and four months after Serrano had ordered the case to be closed, Madrid's Provincial Court ordered the reopening of the Operación Puerto file and the preparation of hearings. The order noted that, according to the National Institute of Toxicology, 'autotransfusions have a series of risks for the patient which are increased in this case as the technical requirements and minimum conditions for obtaining, preparing, conserving, distributing, supplying and therapeutic use of the blood and its components have not been fulfilled.'[3]

According to the Provincial Court ruling, this could constitute a crime. 'They were not carried out in suitable premises, they were not transported in suitable containers, there was no clear identification of the donors, there was no guarantee of maintaining the conservation temperatures of the blood and its components, which were kept in refrigerators and freezer chests in private flats and without being able to guarantee the maintenance of the cold chain in the event of a simple power cut and without any record of the temperature graduation system.' And, the order continued, 'The whole procedure was clandestine.'[4]

The ruling effectively quoted Annex Six of Royal Decree 1088 (16 September 2005), which laid out the minimum safety standards for blood transfusion, although the decree laid out medical guidelines, not criminal law.[5] Even so, having twice dismissed the case on the grounds that there was no evidence of a crime, Serrano was obliged to set the entire operation in motion again.

The order releasing blood bag eighteen was his second humiliation. On 18 February, the day before the hearing in Rome, the Fifth Section of the Madrid Court of Appeals revoked the authorisation releasing blood bag eighteen to CONI, regarding the office of CONI's anti-doping prosecutor as 'nothing more than an administrative body under the Italian Ministry of Culture [whose] proceedings are neither public nor criminal but private [and] subject to appeal not before the courts but before CAS, a private body under the International Olympic Committee.'[6]

When CAS reviewed the decision, it took a different view: 'The request for cooperation came from a judicial authority (the public prosecutor of Rome), not from CONI or another non-judicial body.'[7]

In any case, the Madrid Appeals Court ruling was poorly drafted. It invoked, erroneously, the 2000 Convention on Mutual Assistance between EU Member States. In fact, cooperation in criminal matters between Italy and Spain was governed by a 1959 European Convention that did not allow any Order of Revocation.[8] True, in ratifying the 1959 Convention, Spain had reserved the right not to authorise requests unless the offence in question was punishable under Spanish law.[9] But once authorisation had been given, there was no way of rescinding it and, in any case, judgments had effect only in the country in which they were issued.[10] The moment the plasma drawn from blood bag eighteen entered Italy, it became subject to Italy's rules of evidence, not Spain's, and in Italy it was perfectly legal to use evidence obtained in a criminal investigation in sports proceedings. The same applied to the documents mentioning '18 – VALV. (Piti)' found during the Operación Puerto investigation. Acquired quite legally by the UCI, they had been passed on to the Italian authorities, and now lay beyond the reach of Court No. Thirty-one.

All this will have been perfectly clear to Serrano, whose reaction was empty bluster. CONI went through the motions of appealing Serrano's order, but it made no difference. The genie was not going back in the bottle.

The collection of Valverde's blood at the 2008 Tour de France marked an important step in the developing relations between the anti-doping authorities and the police, which was soon consolidated. Renzo Ferrante told me, 'When, at an international level, cooperation between anti-doping and investigators was still barely spoken of, something important was already moving in Italy. Thanks to far-sighted leaders such as Dr Arpino, the first NAS Carabinieri were trained as anti-doping inspectors under WADA rules. This gave us a way of interacting with anti-doping controls. Thus was born the coordination between inspectors and doctors of CONI, the national anti-doping organisation, the Italian Sports Medical Federation (Federazione Medico Sportiva Italiana or FMSI) and investigators of the Carabinieri Command for the Protection of Health, which led, during the anti-doping controls carried out during the Italian leg of the 2008 Tour de France (in Cuneo and its province), to the possibility of carrying out targeted controls. In this way, samples were collected that were later used in DNA matching. This type of collaboration is now established practice in Italy.'

On 19 February, Valverde arrived in Rome for the four o'clock hearing with his team manager Eusebio Unzue, the team lawyer, Francisco Fernández, Valverde's Spanish lawyer, José Rodriguez Garcia, and his lawyer in Italy, Federico Cecconi. The Giro d'Italia director Angelo Zomegnan had already made it known that Valverde would not be welcome at his race. Before the hearing began, the NAS officers notified Valverde in person that the Public Prosecutor of Rome had placed him under criminal investigation.

Valverde's group left the building forty-five minutes after they had entered it. Cecconi told journalists gathered outside that CONI's case was useless: it lacked the 'where, when and how' of the alleged crime. Standing on the same steps, Torri retorted that Valverde and his lawyers had refused to discuss any substantive details of the case. They had limited themselves to purely procedural matters, arguing, among other things, that Valverde had already been completely exonerated in Spain, which was stretching the truth. Torri explained that CONI's proceedings were entirely legal, based, as they were, on national legislation and the Italian justice system. He added that the violation, 'attempted doping', the same committed by Ivan Basso, took place between May 2004 – presumably 4 May 2004, the date on document 114 – and 23 May 2006, when the Guardia Civil seized the bags of blood and plasma. Valverde's legal team was given fifteen days to prepare its defence.

On 20 January the new presidency of the Spanish Cycling Federation had again asked Serrano to release the blood bags.[11] The UCI was still demanding access to blood bag eighteen, without success. Ten days later, acting on the instructions of the Madrid Court of Appeal, Serrano asked the private parties to the Operación Puerto proceedings to submit the charges they wished to see brought against the accused.

The RFEC, WADA, UCI and Jesús Manzano limited their claims to offences against public health under Article 361 of the Criminal Code, which targeted 'Whosoever manufactures, imports, exports, supplies, brokers, markets, offers or places on the market, or stores for any of these purposes, medicines ... without the necessary authorisation required by law, or medical products without the required documentation, or in a state of deterioration, or out of date, or otherwise failing to comply with the technical requirements relating to composition, stability and efficacy, thereby creating a risk to life or health ...'

CONI took a more adventurous approach, seeking their prosecution for fraud, unlawful association and offences against the Public Treasury. They wanted the defendants prosecuted for breach of contract and non-payment of tax.

But, far from relaunching the case with renewed vigour, the ruling started twenty-eight months of stasis. Four years later, the trial judgment noted that 'the truly significant paralysis of proceedings [belonged to] the period between the Order of Abbreviated Proceedings of January 30, 2009 until the date on which the written accusations were presented, two years and four months later.'[12]

In a twenty-one-page document submitted on 5 March 2009, Valverde's lawyers asked CONI to pass the DNA test data and the rest of the file to the Royal Spanish Cycling Federation and the Spanish sports justice bodies, on the grounds that these were the only bodies with jurisdiction.[13] It is worth considering what might have happened had the request been granted. Serrano would presumably have ruled the DNA match inadmissible and exonerated Valverde. The damage, not just to the rider and his team's credibility but to Spanish sport and justice, would have been catastrophic. It might even have put Spain in open conflict with the World Anti-Doping Agency, rather like Russia some years later. After all, the DNA match was the best evidence allowed by the nature of the case. It was hard to see how the ad-mission of the DNA match could reflect adversely on the fairness of any court proceedings. The insistence on procedural fidelity risked making justice a prisoner to the law. The case exposed a deficiency at the heart of the Spanish legal system.

Meanwhile, Bala continued to train and race. He took his first win of the season on 25 March. The day after finishing twenty-second in the time trial at the Vuelta a Castilla y León, he responded to accelerations by Contador and Menchov on the uphill finish at Alto de San Isidro, bridging the provinces of León and Asturias, and launched an unanswerable sprint in the final 200 metres. Fourth the following day at the Laguna de los Peces, close to the Portuguese border, he won the flat sprint in Valladolid on the final stage and ended the race ninth overall. But, on 4 April, he could not follow the decisive move on the final climb of the GP Miguel Indurain up to the Basílica de El Puy in Estella, and came in eleventh.

April 2009 was a cruel month for doped cyclists. On the seventeenth, Tyler Hamilton learned that he had tested positive for the anabolic drug DHEA in a spot test in February. Finally, perhaps wearily, given that he had just turned 38, he admitted his guilt and announced his retirement.[14]

Eleven days later, on 28 April, *La Gazzetta dello Sport* revealed that, in the International Olympic Committee's review of samples from the 2008 Games, six participants had tested positive for CERA,[15] the third-generation EPO that had played its part in the downfall of Riccò, Piepoli, Schumacher and Bernhard Kohl at the 2007 Tour. Davide Rebellin, a Gerolsteiner teammate with the last two, and 38 like Tyler Hamilton, was one of them.

On 12 April, Bala bounced back with his third victory in the Klasika Primavera de Amorebieta, which he had won in 2003 and 2004. Two days later, at Paris–Camembert, he opted to take no risks on a dangerous final descent and finished thirty-fourth. He said after the race, 'I preferred to keep in mind the great classics of the Ardennes, which are more important to me.'

His Ardennes week was forgettable, though. In the Amstel Gold Race on 19 April, he missed the decisive break and came in twenty-first. Three days later, at Flèche Wallonne, he was never on the pace on the Mur de Huy and finished seventh without sprinting. Then Andy Schleck won Liège–Bastogne–Liège with a solo attack. Bala's teammate Purito Rodríguez followed in second place. Bala settled for nineteenth. Third in the prologue of the Tour de Romandie on 28 April, and second in the stage four time trial around Yverdon-les-Bains, Bala went into the decisive fifth stage in fourth place overall. But after working hard on the lower slopes of the final climb to eliminate potential rivals, he was unable to follow an acceleration by Roman Kreuziger, who took the stage and the race lead overall. Bala ended the race fourth in the general classification.

On 7 April, Valverde announced legal action against Ettore Torri for impersonating a criminal prosecutor in order to trick the substitute judge in Madrid into allowing him access to blood bag eighteen. Then, at 10.15 a.m. on 11 May, his lawyers, led by Federico Cecconi from Milan, arrived at the Olympic Stadium in Rome for the hearing, although Bala did not attend.[16] At the end of a long and acrimonious day, the Italian Olympic Committee's Anti-Doping Court banned Valverde from watching or participating in sporting competitions organised on Italian territory by Italian sports federations and other entities, for two years.[17] With the 2009 Tour de France due to enter Italy's Aosta Valley on stage sixteen, the race director, Christian Prudhomme, quickly announced, 'If he is suspended in Italy, he cannot start the Tour de France.'

The Caisse d'Épargne team described the decision as 'unjust, obsolete and made by a manifestly incompetent body, after a procedure riddled with irregularities, and in which the minimum guarantees of defence that any athlete should have were not respected'. Abarca Sports announced its intention to 'seek compensation for the damages suffered by it and its sponsors against those personally and institutionally responsible for to-day's decision'.

But none of these complaints prospered. Suspension in Italy seemed to help Bala's racing form elsewhere. His first post-ban appearance was at the Volta a Catalunya on 18 May. In the pro-logue at Lloret de Mar, he finished second behind the previous year's winner, Thor Hushovd. After finishing seventeenth in stage two and taking the race lead overall, he complained that 'The situation doesn't let me concentrate. If nothing was going on, my concentration and physical shape would both be better.'[18] Even so, in stage three, he accelerated on the last climb of the day to thin out the group, then won the sprint.

Third in stage four to Andorra behind two breakaway riders, Bala defended his overall lead in the three remaining stages. At the foot of the podium in Barcelona on Sunday 24 May, he said, 'I dedicate this victory to my father, who is very affected by what is happening and who, for the moment, is in hospital. I only hope that this injustice will end soon and that I can focus on racing without any external distractions. This victory is very important for me, given the context we all know.'[19]

At the end of May, the anti-doping inspectors visited him twice in one day,[20] presumably suspecting that he was taking forbidden products the moment the inspectors left his house. But the double visit had no repercussions.

The Spanish press framed June's Dauphiné Libéré as a duel between Cadel Evans and Alberto Contador. They finished the 12.1-kilometre prologue around Nancy first and second, in that order, with Bala third. Bala was lying eighth overall on 10 June, the day CONI published its reasons for his ban.[21] Most of the twenty-four-page document discussed jurisdictional matters. Only a couple of paragraphs addressed substantive issues, to wit, the DNA test, but no more was needed.

Even so, the following day, with 9.3 kilometres to go to the summit of one of cycling's sacred places, Mont Ventoux, he spoke to Contador, then attacked with the Polish climber Sylvester Szmyd. They worked together and, with a kilometre and a half to go, Bala was the overall race leader on the road. On the final corner, Szmyd, who had never won a race, ground to a halt. 'I was about to get off and throw up,' he said afterwards. To gift him the stage, Bala almost had to come to a complete halt.[22] After the stage, Szmyd said, 'Valverde was a real gentleman.'

Overall, Bala led Cadel Evans by 16 seconds.

On the Col de la Madeleine, the final climb of stage seven, Briançon to Saint-François-Longchamp, Evans made his bid for victory. As Bala described it the following morning, 'Evans must

172

have attacked fifteen times on the last pass, but I was ready. This was the most important stage, and the team helped me.'

He sealed victory at Grenoble on 14 June. The win moved him, his team and his country to the top of their respective world rankings, although the Italian ban, the prospect of missing the Tour, and Valverde's ongoing divorce meant there were no smiles on the podium.[23]

He revealed to the press, 'I'm furious about what is happening to me. It's unfair, and I'm convinced it will be resolved in my favour sooner or later, but I'm going through a difficult moment.'

The Tour de France started in Monaco on 4 July. Valverde filed an appeal against the ban with CAS on 17 June, making the usual claims: CONI had no jurisdiction, the evidence from Spain was inadmissible, the chain of custody of the plasma from blood bag eighteen had been broken, there was no proof of any payment or doping plan connecting Valverde and Fuentes, and that CONI's proceedings violated the defendant's rights to equal treatment, to know the charges against him, to question all witnesses and not to testify against himself, as well as numerous international agreements.

Faced with the impossibility of obtaining a decision before the start of the Tour, the team announced on Tuesday 23 June that Bala would not be taking part. Five days later, in the Spanish national championships, he finished third, worked over by two former Kelme teammates, Rubén Plaza and Constantino Zaballa,[24] both implicated in Operación Puerto and riding in Portugal, both of whom had been complaining for years that Valverde had not been made to suffer the way they had.

Zaballa, second, commented after the race, 'The road has done justice to the exiled,' although Carlos Arribas noted in *El País* that, unlike Valverde, neither of the two was part of the UCI's biological passport scheme, which perpetuated cycling's travails before the Tour could begin when disciplinary proceedings were opened against five riders whose samples were considered suspicious.[25] To compound matters, the Rabobank rider Thomas Dekker then tested positive for EPO.

Away from the Tour, Bala finished second in the Vuelta a Madrid on 19 July, then won the Vuelta a Burgos for the second time since 2004, despite finishing fourth in the final stage, won by the 35-year-old Ezequiel Mosquera of Xacobeo-Galicia.

The 2009 Vuelta a España featured four mountain finishes in consecutive days, three more mountain stages, and four tricky medium mountain stages dotted through the race. Eusebio Unzue called it 'the hardest in history.'[26]

CONI's dismissal of Valverde's appeal came during stage six. Even so, a good time trial performance around Valencia in stage seven left Bala seventh overall. Fifth place in the mountain stage to Aitana the following day lifted him up to second place overall behind Cadel Evans. Third place on the Xorret de Catí, 40 kilometres north of Alicante, gave him the race leader's gold jersey, swapping places with Evans, over whom he now had a seven-second lead. It meant Bala would wear the leader's jersey to his home town, Murcia, the following day.

During his rest-day press conference on 10 September, on the eve of three consecutive mountain finishes, Bala said, 'I think that whoever leads on Sunday, arriving at La Pandera, will be the winner of the Vuelta, even if there is still the Sierra de Madrid to go, and the climbs on the penultimate day.'

The next day, on the Alto de Velefique, Bala finished sixth, in the same time as his rivals Evans, Basso, Cunego and Tom Danielson. On the twelfth, at Sierra Nevada, he finished third, five places and 1 minute 12 seconds ahead of Evans. Then, three kilometres from the punishing finish at La Pandera, he seemed to have a crisis. Basso, Evans and Robert Gesink forged ahead to take advantage of Valverde's momentary lapse, gaining a hundred yards on him.

Then, just as suddenly, Bala started to accelerate while his rivals slowed down. As he put it gleefully after the stage, 'I went up and my rivals went down.' He finished fifth, 18 seconds ahead of Evans and 26 seconds ahead of Basso. He now led Basso by 1 minute 28 seconds and Evans by 1 minute 51 seconds in the general standings.

For the next ten days, he defended his lead until, on Sunday, 20 September, the Spanish press room erupted in a standing ovation when Alejandro Valverde entered for his last press conference of the race.

'I've been looking forward to winning one of the big ones,' he joked. 'I knew I could do it with a bit of luck. After this Grand Tour victory, I believe that, with the same focus, I can get on the podium of the Tour de France and, why not win it? Right now, Alberto Contador is very strong, but a man can try.'

The 2009 world championships were held in Mendrisio, in Italian-speaking Switzerland. Valverde's presence was controversial: the German riders Tony Martin and Bert Grabsch both said he should not have been there.[27] Instead of flying to Malpensa in Italy,[28] the Spanish moved their race headquarters from Como to Lugano, 'to preserve due calm' in their words,[29] and followed the two-hour flight to Zurich with a three-hour bus ride.

Exiting the bus, Valverde, in good spirits, quipped, 'The journey was more tiring than the Vuelta.'

On 27 September he finished only ninth in the elite men's road race, won by Cadel Evans. Even so, as the season closed, three Spanish riders – the Tour de France winner Alberto Contador, Alejandro Valverde and Samuel Sánchez – led the world rankings. But it was not all good news. Contador was still waiting to know if the UCI would grant his Astana team a ProTour licence, while Valverde was staring down the barrel of not one but two imminent CAS hearings.

12

Weightlifting

To distinguish it from the case surrounding the RFEC's refusal to start disciplinary hearings against him in defiance of the UCI and WADA, known as Valverde I, Alejandro Valverde's appeal against the two-year suspension in Italy is referred to in the case papers as Valverde II. Valverde II was heard at Lausanne's sumptuous Hôtel de la Paix, with splendid views of Lac Léman, on 12–14 January 2010. Each party was allocated a floor of its own. While maintaining that evidence from the criminal proceeding in Spain was inadmissible, Valverde's legal team had nonetheless summoned the lead Guardia Civil investigator, Enrique Gómez Bastida, to testify that his enquiries had found no proof of any payment, blood analysis data or doping plan connecting Valverde to Fuentes. There was an element of humiliation in this. Gómez Bastida, whose affinities naturally lay with the other camp, gravitated towards CONI's floor and his Carabinieri colleagues who, with regret, had to ask him to leave.

He was heard after the opening presentations before lunch on day one. The afternoon session examined the chain of custody of the plasma samples taken from blood bag eighteen. Day two started with the DNA tests. After lunch, Echávarria, Unzue, Bala's room-mate José Luís Arrieta, and then Jesús Manzano were heard, before the journalist Enrique Iglesias and the photographer Jesús Rubio were asked to confirm the name of Bala's dog. The day ended with Valverde, who, by telephone from

Australia, where he was competing in the Tour Down Under, denied knowing Fuentes or owning a dog called Piti.

Day three started with a session on Italian legal procedures, then moved onto the final statements. Given Valverde's objections to the DNA match, the CAS panel, without disputing the reliability of the DNA match, invited the parties to agree to a new DNA test. Predictably, the proposal went nowhere, so CAS announced that it had no choice but to rule on the basis of the file as constituted.

In Australia, Bala, below par, helped his teammate Luis León Sánchez finish second. In February, back in Europe, he won the five-stage Tour of the Mediterranean by finishing second on Mont Faron in stage five.[1] Meanwhile, in a misconceived gesture of solidarity, the Vuelta a Murcia, scheduled for 3 to 7 March, decided not to invite any Italian teams because 'Alejandro Valverde, a citizen of Murcia, is not authorised to race in Italy.'[2] In an editorial, *Mundo Deportivo* said the fault lay with the Spanish courts, not the foreign riders: 'What fault is it of the Italian teams that Operación Puerto has been a real disaster due to the ineffectiveness of the Spanish justice system?'[3]

In the prologue of Paris–Nice in March, Bala conceded 29 seconds to the winner, Lars Boom, and 23 seconds to his compatriot, Alberto Contador. The following day, Caisse d'Épargne broke up the group, then took advantage of a fall affecting Contador three kilometres from the finish to position Sánchez fourth overall, 15 seconds ahead of Bala, who moved to within four seconds of Contador.[4] On stages two, three and four, the young Slovakian prodigy Peter Sagan finished second, first and first.

Bala responded by finishing second, third, second and third in stages four to seven, but it was only good enough for second place overall, behind Contador, with Sánchez third. The result left Sánchez at the top of the world rankings, ahead of André Greipel, Alberto Contador and Valverde himself.

Two days after the race finish, on 16 March 2010, CAS upheld

CONI's ban. Eusebio Unzue called it 'a cold shower'.[5] Valverde complained that one of the CAS panel of arbitrators, Prof. Ulrich Haas, a professor of civil law at Zurich University, had worked for WADA – he was the chair of WADA's independent observer team at the Athens Olympics in 2004. In fact, Valverde's request for Haas's recusal had been considered and denied in November 2009. Curiously, in April 2011, Alberto Contador's defence team selected Haas as their member of the three-person tribunal for his appeal.

The same day, Valverde's lawyers travelled to Switzerland for the other CAS hearing, Valverde I, regarding WADA and the UCI's complaint against the Spanish Federation for its failure to sanction him. This was the hearing where CAS would decide whether to extend his ban worldwide and expunge his results all the way back to May 2004. His career in the balance, Valverde assured *El País*, 'Whatever happens, I will still be the same person. If [the decision] is favourable, I will carry on racing, and hopefully more relaxed. If not, no problem. I'll come back and keep winning. It's not complicated.'[6]

The situation did nothing to encourage potential team sponsors. Unzue, pessimistic, expected a sanction. 'I would like to be able to move on, secure a new sponsor and plan for Valverde's future, but there is no news. We are waiting for a response from the possible sponsors. The economic crisis is causing a lot of damage but we are confident that the quality of our proposal will be enough for the team to continue. Valverde is a great team leader and without him things won't be the same.'

Before the ruling came, at least one decision went Bala's way. In stage one of the Vuelta al País Vasco on 5 April, the commissaires disqualified Oscar Freire for an irregular sprint and awarded the stage victory to Valverde.[7] It was his first stage win of the year. His second came the following day, although at the end of the week he had to settle for second place overall, beaten in the time trial by veteran rider Chris Horner.[8]

After the stage, Bala commented, 'I'd like to ride like that at 38 years old.' With the decision that would decide his future looming, it must have been a heartfelt wish.

Years later, he remembered of that spring, 'I was winning races, but I didn't even want to be a cyclist any more. It wasn't living. I read the newspapers and looked on the internet each morning to see what else had come out. It was one surprise after another.'

Four days before the Amstel Gold Race, the Icelandic volcano Eyjafjallajökull released an ash cloud that led to the closure of most of Europe's airspace. With flights cancelled, Bala missed the race, which saw Philippe Gilbert give Belgium its first victory in sixteen years. Valverde and Sánchez set off from Murcia by car. With the journey still in his legs, Bala could finish only eighth in Flèche Wallonne, won by Cadel Evans.[9]

Liège–Bastogne–Liège took place the day after Bala's thirtieth birthday. With 16 kilometres to go, Aleksandr Vinokurov escaped with the Russian Alexandre Kolobnev. In the last 500 metres of the final climb at Ans, Vinokurov opened a gap, leading Kolobnev home. Bala led Gilbert and Evans, 1 minute 4 seconds down.[10]

From Belgium, the riders made the familiar journey to Switzerland for the Tour de Romandie. On Tuesday 27 April, Bala finished twelfth in the 4.3-kilometre prologue, seven seconds behind the winner, Marco Pinotti. Three days later, Bala finished second to Richie Porte in the 23.4-kilometre time trial, and moved into second place overall, two seconds behind Michael Rogers. On the tough final day on 2 May, taking in three first-category passes, including the Ovronnaz, 20 kilometres from the finish line, Bala won the stage and the race overall.

Celebrating, he said, 'I was able to make the most of the condition I had in the classics, even though I started to feel the fatigue from racing in January. Now I'm going to take a short break to rest with my family before returning to training and preparing for the Dauphiné Libéré, which will be my next objective.'

His short family break would last until 17 January 2012.

On 31 May, CAS published its decision. Bala's suspension was made worldwide. His 2010 results were expunged. He was removed from his position at the top of the world rankings. He would not be eligible to race again until 1 January 2012.

The judgment agreed that, in principle, an athlete could refuse DNA profiling. However, by signing the 'Rider's Commitments to a New Cycling' in June 2007, Valverde had committed himself to exactly this type of cooperation. The CAS ruling observed:

19.9 ... That statement read: I declare to the Spanish Law that my DNA is at its disposal, so that it can be compared with the blood samples seized in the Puerto affair. I appeal to the Spanish Law to organise this test as soon as possible or allow the UCI to organise it.
19.10 Having regard to Mr Valverde's conduct throughout this arbitration, it is clear that no attempt was ever made on his part to follow through with this commitment.[11]

The panel called his bluff, as if to say, no one likes to be played.

In a press conference on Wednesday 2 June 2010, he insisted, as he has ever since, that he was the target of an inexplicable witch hunt, although he admitted, perhaps surprisingly, that, with the suspension, 'a weight has been taken off my shoulders'. He vowed to continue training as he always had, alternating cycling with swimming and gym work.

In 2005, when, after abandoning the Tour de France, he finished second in the world championships, he had said, 'I have shown that by working at home and doing well, you can get in shape.'

Now he had two years in which to apply the same philosophy.

In May 2011, mid-suspension, he joined a group of friends and teammates – Beñat Intxausti, José Joaquín Rojas and the Catalan rider Xavier Tondo among them – in the Sierra Nevada for a training camp. Tondo, 32, shared Bala's sunny attitude towards life. In January he had taken the new Movistar team's first win in the individual time trial at the Tour de San Luis in Argentina. In April he had added victory in the Vuelta a Castilla y León.

Tondo was also a hero of the antidoping movement. In December 2010, on receiving an e-mail offering cut-price EPO, growth hormone, nandrolone and clenbuterol, he had contacted the Mossos d'Esquadra, the Catalan police. On 18 February 2011, seven members of a criminal gang selling banned substances were arrested, and 12,000 doses seized.

Tondo hired a flat for the training camp. On the morning of 24 May, he stepped out of his car, which moved slightly and trapped him against the automatic garage door causing lacerations to the neck. He bled to death.

Three and a half weeks later, at the Tour de Suisse, another teammate, the Colombian Juan Mauricio Soler, hit a pothole at something over 70 kph and slammed his head into a fence post at the roadside. His injuries were career-ending and life changing.

Bala was undeterred.

Looking back on the suspension, he said, 'I decided I was going to make the most of it.' His third son, Pablo, was born in January 2010 to his second wife, Natalia. 'I decided I was going to enjoy the first two years of my son's life.'

Even today, he says, 'In the end the sanction for me was a good thing during the suspension. I enjoyed being with my family. I enjoyed training. I didn't need to compete. So, I went to the beach for two months and I trained with my group at the beach, I discovered new things, new freedoms, a new tranquillity.'

Even so, he still cannot help adding, 'It was a witch hunt against me. They were going to get me one way or the other.'

13

The Armstrong Connection

Even before CAS had published its decision, another storm had begun to blow over the sport. In July 2009, Floyd Landis, financially ruined and romantically abandoned, had called Johan Bruyneel to ask for a place on Armstrong's new team, Radio-Shack. Bruyneel had rejected him. In March 2010, Armstrong and RadioShack were, of course, welcomed to May's Tour of California, while the small team Landis was riding for was refused entry. Landis instructed his lawyer to contact the United States Anti-Doping Agency and, on 30 April, Landis dispatched a 1,080-word email to USA Cycling and the UCI giving precise details of his own doping, and accusing other former US Postal Service cyclists, chief among them Lance Armstrong, of doing the same. Journalists at the *Wall Street Journal* caught wind of the email and, on 20 May 2010, published a report under the title 'Cyclist Floyd Landis Admits To Doping, Alleges Use By Armstrong'. On 13 July, the day of stage nine of the Tour de France, the *New York Times* reported that Armstrong was the subject of a federal investigation into possible fraud charges led by Jeff Novitzky, the top federal agent in the 2002 BALCO probe into the Bay Area Laboratory Co-operative (BALCO), a San Francisco operation supplying anabolic steroids to professional athletes, including the Olympic sprinter and long jumper Marion Jones. The report added that grand jury subpoenas had been issued to witnesses.

Then, in an anti-doping control on 21 July, the second rest day of the Tour de France, one day before the stage up the Tourmalet, the race leader Alberto Contador produced a sample that contained minute traces of the steroid-like chemical clenbuterol. A repeat analysis on 8 September confirmed the result. On 29 September, it became public that he had been suspended as a precautionary measure by the UCI. Contador attributed the finding to a sirloin steak consumed on 20 or 21 July. In October 2010, the *New York Times* reported that plastic residues, consistent with the material used in blood bags, had also been found in his blood, although the test had not been officially validated, and Contador argued that plastic residues were so widespread that there was too much doubt about how they got into an athlete's body. Funding for the test to detect these chemicals was discontinued in November 2011.[1]

Both cases raged through Valverde's suspension. On 6 February 2012, the CAS decision found that, on the balance of probability, Contador's clenbuterol most likely came from a contaminated food supplement. Even so, the rules of strict liability applied, in other words, the athlete is responsible for whatever is in the athlete's body. His 2010 Tour de France win, and all his results from 25 January 2011 to the date of the decision, which included victory in the 2011 Giro d'Italia, were annulled. He was able to return to racing in August 2012.

On 3 February 2012, three days before the CAS ruling on Contador, the US prosecutor for the Central District of California, André Birotte Jr., terminated the investigation of Armstrong's affairs and sealed all evidence in the case. He offered no explanation for his decision. There was speculation that Armstrong's closeness to political power may have affected the legal process. In former President and fellow Texan George W. Bush, he had a connection at the very highest level. They had met on many occasions: in August 2001, after his third Tour win, Armstrong had presented President Bush with a bike. In August 2005, after his seventh, they went mountain biking together through sunflower fields on the President's ranch in Crawford, Texas. With good humour, the President imposed two rules: do not overtake the President and do not push the President too hard. Armstrong joked, 'I told him that I wanted to be governor of Texas.' Over dinner, they discussed how the President might support Armstrong's cancer foundation. Armstrong told ABC Television, 'I have never asked for so much money from anyone before. The President promised to help us.'

Again, in April 2011, he joined President Bush and fourteen servicemen and women wounded in Iraq or Afghanistan for the George W. Bush Presidential Center's first Social Enterprise Initiative, a hundred-kilometre mountain bike ride.

Yet, whatever the reasons for the closure of the criminal case, the sealing of the evidence meant that the sporting case was likely to collapse. Even so, eleven months later, in the course of two ninety-minute segments broadcast on the Oprah Winfrey Network on 17 and 18 January 2013, Armstrong admitted that he had doped to win all seven of his Tour de France titles. What had changed? The answer had everything to do with the relationships forged among the law enforcement agencies during Operación Puerto and the Valverde investigation.

The Italian Carabinieri had spent years investigating their own Fuentes: Lance Armstrong's coach, Dr Michele Ferrari. The relationship between Armstrong and Ferrari went back to 1995. Tyler Hamilton had worked with Ferrari in 1999, 2000 and 2001, before moving onto Fuentes.[2] In October 2004 the Carabinieri investigators had achieved a conviction against Ferrari for 'abusively exercising the profession of pharmacist' and 'having doping substances administered to athletes to achieve a result different from that resulting from the correct and fair conduct of sporting competitions'. Ferrari had been fined, sentenced to one year's imprisonment and banned from practising as a doctor for eleven months and twenty-one days, even if the sentence was suspended for five years.[3] Armstrong, at the time the winner of six consecutive Tours de France, said he was 'disappointed to learn of the Italian court's ruling against Ferrari.'

In his second autobiography, *Every Second Counts*, Armstrong wrote of his relationship with Ferrari: 'He was a friend and I went to him for occasional advice on training. He wasn't one of my major advisors, but he was one of the best minds in cycling, and sometimes I consulted him.' While awaiting the outcome of Ferrari's appeal, 'the US Postal team and myself have suspended our sporting collaboration with Dr. Ferrari.'[4]

Ferrari was acquitted on appeal in May 2006, but the Carabinieri remained vigilant. At the same time, as well as working on the Valverde case, the Carabinieri had taken their cue from Operación Puerto and launched a parallel investigation into the wide network of Italian athletes and support personnel implicated in Operacíon Puerto, directly or tangentially. These enquiries, codenamed Puerto Connection, led to months of meticulous fact-finding, although in the end it was never prosecuted. Even so, the Italian NAS officers who worked with CONI, and the Spanish SECOMA officers led by Gómez Bastida, had formed a relationship of trust, as had CONI and WADA, who, as civil parties at the CAS proceedings against Valverde, had acted together. This cooperation led to the creation of a WADA-CONI working group in 2011, involving officers who had worked on Puerto and Valverde.

These close personal ties were an important addition to the anti-doping movement. At its foundation in 1999, WADA's aim was to harmonise anti-doping policy and law across sports and between countries, to establish a collaborative worldwide movement for doping-free sport.[5] But WADA's decisions only applied to the sports movement, so the national governments who were WADA's members could not be bound by its rules. This weakness was addressed in 2005 in the UNESCO International Convention Against Doping in Sport, after which signatories began to enshrine WADA principles and frameworks in national law.[6] However, missing was the human touch: the personal contacts and relationships of trust among the law enforcement agencies on which policing the written agreements was going to depend. The relationships forged during Operación Puerto and the Valverde investigation created the first of those links.

In 2010, rumours started that Ferrari was working with athletes in Saint Moritz and Teide, on the island of Tenerife. But any investigation was going to need more than just gossip. Later, in a signed and sworn statement, the former Saeco, Liquigas and Lampre rider Leonardo Bertagnolli confirmed to police that he had met Michele Ferrari in Saint Moritz, where the doctor had explained the best way to take EPO without testing positive.[7] Then, a very well-known cyclist who cannot be named here, facing doping charges and cooperating with the court in Padua in exchange for a reduced suspension, signed a statement to the effect that, as well as going to Saint Moritz, riders were going to Teide 'to get bombed' – that is, to dope. This gave investigators the power to act.

To investigate Ferrari's activities in Teide, the Carabinieri asked for the Guardia Civil's help. The Guardia Civil shadowed Ferrari on his next visit to Tenerife, gathering among many other details, the contact information Ferrari was using. This led the Carabinieri to a company in Switzerland called Health and Performance, whose registered accounts showed consultancy payments to Ferrari. Witness interviews and the company accounts revealed that, while some of Ferrari's clients paid him off the books, others made bank transfers to Health and Performance. Armstrong was one of the latter.

The Health and Performance bank statements showed payments of more than a million dollars. Armstrong's claim to have severed all ties with his former doctor was plainly untrue.

Soon after Landis's email at the end of April 2010, the US prosecutor for the Central District of California had opened a grand jury investigation into the US Postal Service team. This put three federal agencies on Armstrong's tail: the Federal Bureau of Investigation, the Food and Drug Administration and the Bureau of Criminal Investigation of the US Postal Service. Their predicament was a familiar one: doping was not a crime in the United States, so the US investigators had to find ways he and his team could have violated federal laws.[8] They considered wire fraud, conspiracy and drug-trafficking (given that the team had transported controlled substances across state and international borders).

In November 2010, the lead FDA investigator Jeff Novitzky, the CEO of the US Anti-Doping Agency (USADA) Travis Tygart, and representatives of the other American agencies, visited Interpol in Lyon, France, for meetings with French, Spanish and Italian police officers. The US Department of Justice in Los Angeles then made formal applications to all of those countries for information about the relationship between Armstrong and Ferrari. Italy provided telephone transcripts, emails and the Health and Performance accounts, and the investigators were persuaded to adopt the same strategy used in Germany against Jan Ullrich. Like Ullrich's T-Mobile agreement, the US Postal Service team's major sponsor contracts had clauses outlawing doping. Novitzky and his colleagues pursued the line that Armstrong and the US Postal Service team may have violated their contracts and, by so doing, criminally defrauded their sponsors. Given that there were continued allegations of impropriety against Ferrari, and that the money Armstrong had paid him ultimately originated with the US Federal Postal Service, he could potentially be accused of using federal funds for illegal business.

Novitzky and his colleagues were building what they considered a strong case against Armstrong when Birotte closed it down. With the investigators shellshocked and the evidence sealed, Tygart resolved to continue the sporting case. After all, although the file containing the telephone transcripts, emails and accounts was sealed and out of reach in the USA, it still existed in

Italy, although it was unclear how he could get hold of it.

The opportunity arose when WADA joined the proceedings in Padua. As Renzo Ferrante explained in an affidavit on 27 September 2012, 'WADA was admitted by the prosecutor as a party in the investigative proceedings and was given access to the file in order to review and obtain documents and other information relating to Dr Ferrari, his clients and relatives, and others involved in the potential violation of sport's anti-doping rules.'[9]

It was also an absolute legal novelty. WADA then legitimately shared this information with its member agency, USADA, handing a copy of the file to William Bock III, USADA's general counsel, who took it back to America. Tygart was now in possession of the same file that had been handed over to the federal investigators after their Interpol meeting.

Things then moved very quickly. On 24 August 2012, USADA issued public notice of its intention to sanction Armstrong. On 10 October the same year, it published a 164-page Reasoned Decision explaining its revocation of Lance Armstrong's competitive results from 1 August 1998, and to rule him ineligible from sporting competition for life.

On the same day, USADA uploaded a shortened form of its Reasoned Decision, and a mass of witness statements – including eyewitness, documentary, first-hand, scientific, direct and circumstantial evidence – incriminating Armstrong, Ferrari and the US Postal Service team onto its website.[10] With this barrage of evidence in the public domain, Armstrong had little choice but to admit his guilt.

14

The Second Coming

Even before the Valverde ban, Caisse d'Épargne's interest in cycling had begun to cool. It had started merger talks with another major French banking group, Banque Populaire, in 2008.[1] On their fusion in June 2009, the new combined group, BPCE, announced they would be focusing their sports sponsorship on the French Olympic teams at Vancouver 2010 and London 2012. It was almost a rebuke for Caisse d'Épargne's unpatriotic use of French money to back a Spanish team. In January 2010, they spelled it out: the sponsorship deal would be allowed to run, but would not be renewed at the end of the year.

Years later, on 28 December 2014, the feast of the Holy Innocents, the Spanish equivalent of April Fool's Day, a blogger joked, 'From 1 January Mariano Rajoy will be the new sports director of Movistar Team. After a long conversation and meditating, which is the ambition of his life since he was a child, the Galician ex-politician will lead the team for four seasons and will have Pedro Delgado from Segovia as his right-hand man.'[2]

Like any good April Fool's Day joke, it was strangely plausible. Mariano Rajoy, variously, between 1996 and 2003, Minister for Public Administration, Minister for Education, Culture and Sport, Minister of the Interior, government spokesperson, Minister for the Presidency and deputy prime minister, and then, from 2004, president of the Partido Popular, was also a well-known cycling fan. But it was while in opposition in mid-2010 that he made a personal request to Movistar's mother company, Telefónica, to take on the sponsorship of Spain's top cycling team. Telefónica had recently acquired the Brazilian communications provider Vivo and announced half-year net profits of €3.8 billion.[3] Its executive vice-president, Luis Abril, was largely responsible for Banesto's decision to continue its sponsorship of Indurain and the Banesto team after the Bank of Spain bailout in December 1993.

Although fully privatised in 1999, Telefónica retained close links to the political parties. Proximity to power was part of its heritage. Founded in 1924 and given the monopoly in telephone services by Primo De Rivera, the prime minister and dictator from 1923 to 1930, Telefónica, or, properly, the Compañía Telefónica Nacional de España, was initially controlled by the International Telephone and Telegraph Corporation of New York. With generous subsidies and no tax obligations, it made fortunes for Primo and the oligarchs around him.

From 1940 Telefónica paid President Franco a monthly remittance of 10,000 pesetas (about €100,000).[4] Five years later, the Spanish state took an 80 per cent stake in it and, by 1960, it was the country's largest company. In 1995, in the spirit of popular capitalism, 15 per cent of Telefónica was sold off, reducing state participation to 15 per cent. The rest was disposed of in two share offers, one in 1996, the other in 1999.

Telefónica's chairman César Alierta consulted Luis Abril, then accepted Rajoy's appeal. It was well judged: in December 2011 Rajoy became prime minister, a post he would hold until June 2018.

In August 2010, Unzue's management company published a press release announcing that the team would continue under the name of the Telefónica brand Movistar: 'Abarca Sports would like to thank Telefónica for the trust placed in this project and especially for the personal commitment of its president, César Alierta, to make it possible . . . we would like to thank the support of all those who have helped us to achieve this goal.'[5]

By coincidence, Bala, who had, like Urdangarin, made good money from the coffers of the People's Party in Valencia and the Balearic Islands, would return to racing in the pay of Telefónica, again, like Urdangarin. As Banesto had Miguel Indurain to distract the public from its troubles, Telefónica would have Alejandro Valverde.

On 21 January 2012, on Old Willunga Hill Road, 50 kilometres south of Adelaide, Bala took the long way round the final curve to ease past Simon Gerrans and win stage five, the toughest stage, of the Santos Tour Down Under.[6]

It was a brilliant start to his second sporting life, and as he later recalled, speaking of himself in the third person, 'To go to Australia and win in the most important stage meant that Alejandro Valverde had taken care of himself, he'd been training properly. It showed that, after everything that had happened, I was the same or much better.'

As a rider with a suspension in his past, he was targeted for intense testing. A UCI anti-doping inspector who met Valverde after his comeback, told me:

> I did several Tours de France with him, and I actually felt sorry for him. I was getting him up at six o'clock in the morning three, four, five days in a row, and then calling back for more of the same at night. He didn't seem to mind. He'd open the door at six in the morning, look out with his little eyes and he'd go, 'Oh, it's you, come in,' always courteous, always polite. I went from never having met him and absolutely hating him, saying he's bad for the sport, the devil incarnate, a horrible man, to feeling sorry for him. In 2019, when I saw him in his world championships jersey, I made a point of going over and I said, 'Fantastic race, well done,' and I shook his hand. So I went from hating him to thinking, he's a genius on the bike.

My informant added, 'I honestly think the only intelligence they had on Valverde was, one, that he had had a ban in the past, and, two, he was winning. We are the grunts on the ground and they don't tell us what the intelligence is, but from what I could see I was basically bullying him for no real reason at all.'

Bala's infinite cordiality won him great affection in the peloton and among sponsors and race organisers. And, to the disappointment of those who suspected that he was a mere product of doping, the relentless testing made no difference to his results. He emerged into a cycling landscape dominated by a new player, Team Sky, which had set itself the task of winning the Tour de France with the track and time-trial specialist Bradley Wiggins. It pursued this goal by contracting, and paying handsome wages to, hugely talented riders with meticulously selected abilities, and drilling them to sustain a pace so high, so far into the stage, that it became nigh on impossible for others to attack. It was technically brilliant, and intended, quite deliberately, to suffocate the very moves that made cycling so compelling.

The temporary decline in Bala's win rate – seven in 2012, four in 2013 – was perhaps related to this new development. Even so, he was one of the few riders to defy Sky's stage-race dominance, along with Vincenzo Nibali, Nairo Quintana and one or two more. In any case, the downturn in the number of victories was offset by near misses. Second overall in the 2012 Tour Down Under, he won the Vuelta a Andalucía a month later, then finished third in Paris–Nice in March with a stage win. On stage two of the Volta a Catalunya, a water bottle on the road in the feed zone brought him down, and he did not start the next day.

He was second at the Klasika Primavera de Amorebieta behind his teammate Giovanni Visconti, who called him 'an idol to me . . . To have him help me like he did today is an honour that I hope to repay in the coming classics.'

However, in the 2019 documentary *Un año de arcoíris* ('A rainbow year'), he revealed that he woke up one day in March

2012 to some sort of panic attack which left him giddy and nauseous, and with altered perception. The condition lasted a year, during which, training on straight roads, he suffered a nagging anxiety. He did not dare drive on the motorway.

'I rode the Amstel Gold Race at the back of the group, following as it grew thinner and thinner, but always at the back, with Pablo Lastras at my side, afraid of suffering a bout of dizziness.'

He finished twenty-second in the Amstel Gold and forty-sixth in Flèche Wallonne, and nowhere in Liège–Bastogne–Liège, after a mechanical problem climbing La Redoute lost him all hope of victory.

Psychotherapy left him feeling worse. 'The one-hour sessions felt ten hours long. I was bombarded with questions I didn't know how to answer.'

The psychiatrist diagnosed depression rooted in a variety of post-traumatic stress. In Bala's understanding, his stage win in Australia released the trauma his body had stored up between 2008 and 2011, 'the years of persecution until the sanction'. After a year of psychotherapy and medication, he recovered.

Encapsulating his ordeal in a sentence, he said, 'For there to be good moments, there have to be bad ones.'

Even so, it would be seven years before he felt able to talk about his depression. 'The rainbow jersey played a role in my decision to go public,' he said. 'In doing so, I have freed myself.'

At the Tour de Suisse, he worked for his teammate Rui Costa. When Costa's closest rival, Fränk Schleck, 14 seconds behind him in the GC, raised the pace on the Glaubenberg climb in the final stage, then attacked alone and led at the summit by nearly a minute, Bala took it on himself to manage Costa's pacing. On the finish line, Bala celebrated Costa's victory with him.

At the 2012 Tour de France, with Alberto Contador suspended until 5 August, the principal Spanish contenders were Valverde and Samuel Sánchez.

In his pre-race press conference, Bala said, 'There is no question that Wiggins and Evans are the favourites, but I'm here with the idea of fighting for the overall and getting on the podium.'[7]

A fall in stage six to Metz, two crashes on stage seven to La Planche des Belles Filles, and another on stage eight through the Jura mountains to Porrentruy, ended his hopes of a podium finish.

The final mountain stage, number seventeen, took place on 19 July between Bagnères-de-Luchon and Peyragudes. Bala joined the breakaway on the first climb of the day, the Col de Menté. When Vincenzo Nibali, who was third overall, reached the leading group on the descent, Bala himself asked him to sit up, which he did.

'I told him that the breakaway had no chance of success if he was in it, and he understood.'

Then, on the Port de Balès, with 35 kilometres to go, Valverde attacked. Chris Froome went after him on the final climb and might have won the stage had he not been ordered by his team to desist and wait for Wiggins, who had begun to lose position. Bala took the win by 19 seconds.

After stage twelve, the winner, David Millar – the co-owner of his team, Garmin – had adopted a tone Valverde never could: 'I cheated, I paid and now I'm racing clean and proud.' Millar continued, 'Our passion is to change the sport, and show that it can be done in a different way.'

The same day, Bradley Wiggins had written in the *Guardian*, 'the attitude to doping in the UK is different to in Italy or France maybe, where a rider like Richard Virenque can dope, be caught, be banned, come back and be a national hero.'[8]

Now, with Wiggins and Froome first and second overall, the post-stage media room was packed with British journalists. Persuaded of their fellow countrymen's propriety, they used the post-stage press conference to stage a rematch of the 2007 bout between Valverde and the Tour de France press corps. Trying to control the narrative, Valverde said the victory 'erases everything that came before'. But when he was pressed to talk about his own experience of doping, he could only find it in himself to say, 'Of course I'm against it. Cycling is beautiful and we have to carry on and enjoy it. The fans are enjoying it.' He added, 'You have to fight. What more can I say? Full gas.' It was as excruciating to hear as it must have been to say. Even *Mundo Deportivo* called it 'a missed opportunity'.

Bala finished the Tour twentieth, 42 minutes 26 seconds behind Bradley Wiggins, who many thought of as robotically riding according to prescribed power output figures.

At the Olympic road race in London on 28 July, Luís León Sánchez finished fourteenth and Bala eighteenth. The disappointing result at least forestalled another torturous post-race skirmish with the press. Then, at the Clásica San Sebastián on Tuesday 14 August, Joaquim Rodríguez and Bala marked each other so tightly that, with 15 kilometres to go, Sánchez saw the opportunity to dart away and take the win.

The Hispano–British culture clash continued at the Vuelta a España. With no less than ten uphill finishes, six in the high mountains, two in the medium mountains and two more on short, steep ramps, it was a race for climbers. The three stages before the second rest day visited the Puerto de Ancares, Lagos de Covadonga and a long and exceptionally steep climb called Cuitu Negru. Bala was suddenly not the best climber on his team: the Colombian Nairo Quintana, 22, the winner of the 2010 Tour de l'Avenir, was in his first season as a professional, and had already won a stage and the overall at the Vuelta a Murcia, and a stage and the overall at the Route du Sud in the French Pyrenees. In between, on the Morzine stage of the Dauphiné, he had ridden away from Team Sky's formidable mountain train at its strongest.

The race started in oppressive heat. Movistar won the opening team time trial in their home town, Pamplona, and Bala emerged from stage two in fourth place overall. At Arrate in the Basque

Country at the end of stage three, Bala took the win and the race lead in his home Grand Tour. Normal service had been resumed.

A day later, in windy conditions, Team Sky formed an echelon. Contact between Team Sky's Juan Antonio Flecha and Movistar's Imanol Erviti brought down Erviti and his captain, the race leader Valverde. In the grey area of cycling's unwritten rules, the Team Sky-led peloton did not wait for the race leader but pressed on, the Sky riders saying later, unconvincingly, that they had no idea Valverde had fallen. Bala limited his losses on Froome, Rodríguez and Contador to 55 seconds, but after the stage he sought out the Sky bus and took his anger out on the door.

'They didn't have the balls to stop, they chose an unsporting way,' he said. 'Sky formed an echelon and they're perfectly within their rights to do that. I'm not cross that I lost the lead because of this, but because there was no respect.'[9]

The incident helped define his anti-Team Sky role. Over the coming years, the instinctive Bala would be cast as the antidote to the robotic Sky style. Fans who had turned against him in the years before his suspension gradually came to admire him after it for his free-spirited approach. It gave him a way back, even as he persisted in his silence about Fuentes and the DNA match.

Stage sixteen finished on Cuitu Negru. With six kilometres to go, repeated accelerations by Alberto Contador dislodged Valverde from the tiny group of Contador, race leader Joaquín Rodríguez and Quintana. Nairo waited for Valverde, shepherded him back to the group, then moved to the front. With 2.5 kilometres to go, on gradients exceeding 20 per cent, the group of four was in deadlock. Hoping to destabilise Contador and Rodríguez, Nairo launched a stunning acceleration, and established a lead of ten bike lengths. Contador took the bait. With Rodríguez on his wheel, he gave chase. If Bala had had the strength to take advantage of the inevitable recovery period that followed, the ploy might have worked. But he was not a born climber like Nairo, and had no choice but to allow the opportunity to pass.

Two days later, at the foot of the Collado La Hoz with 53 kilometres to go, Contador shot away from the group of leaders like a bullet, with his former Astana teammate Paolo Tiralongo. They worked perfectly together and led the race leader Rodríguez and Bala by two minutes at the foot of the final 17-kilometre climb. With ten kilometres to go, Bala had dropped Rodríguez and gained 20 seconds on Contador. Valverde passed the flamme rouge thirteen seconds after Contador, and closed to within six seconds of him at the finish line. He finished the stage second overall, 1 minute 52 seconds behind Contador, the new leader. Bala continued to claw back seconds, but, when the Vuelta ended four days later, the gap was still 1 minute 16 seconds.

Then, at the 2012 world championships in Valkenburg, Holland, Bala was sitting too far back in the group when, on the final ascent of the Cauberg, with 1.7 kilometres to go, Philippe Gilbert attacked. Valverde ended with the fourth medal, and the second bronze, of his career, in the wake of second-placed Edvald Boasson Hagen.

15

The Trial

The first four months of 2013 saw the Operación Puerto trial, which took place in Madrid from 28 January to 2 April. The case had taken so long to pass through the courts that one of the defendants, José Luis Merino Batres, now 72, had succumbed to Alzheimer's disease and was no longer fit to testify, and another, the bag man Alberto León, had hanged himself. Valverde was more than a spectral presence: he was at its very heart, even if unnamed. When Jesús Manzano testified that 'doping was practised by all of the Kelme riders, with one exception: Juan Miguel Cuenca Martínez,' Valverde's name hung heavy in the air.[1] As well as passing verdict on Fuentes and his fellow defendants, the judge would decide the fate of the blood bags. At stake was whether other riders would suffer Valverde's fate, or whether the treatment meted out to him was to remain unique. He cannot have been indifferent to the outcome.

The charges to be answered by the defendants had been decided by sleight of hand. CONI's January 2009 request for charges of fraud, unlawful association and offences against the Public Treasury to be included in the prosecution was quietly ignored. The Order declaring the Oral Trial open, issued on 21 November 2011 by the Madrid Investigating Magistrate's Court No. Thirty-one, that is, Serrano's Court, mentioned only one offence, against public health under Article 361 of the Criminal Code. With the trial approaching, Criminal Court No. Twenty-one noted this omission and, on 31 July 2012, asked Madrid Investigating Magistrate's Court No. Thirty-one for clarification. The Investigating Court's response came on 10 October 2012. It took the shape of an express, after-the-event decision to dismiss CONI's application. CONI of course appealed, although this was rejected on 26 November 2012 by the Madrid Provincial Court, perhaps inevitably, on the grounds that levelling a completely new set of charges at such a late stage would have constituted an abuse of the rights of the defendants. The exclusion of the charges was a fait accompli,[2] and the trial began with the narrowest possible focus.

Fuentes insisted that the large quantities of medicines, many of them past their use-by date, uncovered during the police searches, mostly belonged to his mother, father, siblings and daughter.[3] The defence strategy was to have the medicines excluded from the case. That left the bags of blood and other bodily fluids, which, they would argue, could hardly be considered medicines or medical products. Since he was being charged with offences against Article 361 of the Spanish Penal Code, which – to repeat – targeted 'Whosoever manufactures, imports, exports, supplies, brokers, markets, offers or places on the market, or stores for any of these purposes, *medicines* . . . without the necessary authorisation required by law, or *medical products* without the required documentation, or in a state of deterioration, or out of date, or otherwise failing to comply with the technical requirements relating to composition, stability and efficacy, thereby creating a risk to life or health . . .' (my emphasis). If blood was not a medicine, the case could be made to dissolve into thin air.

A serious and inexplicable oversight by the prosecution had the effect of ruling the medicines out as evidence. In December 2006, the Spanish Medicines Agency was commissioned to investigate the medicines and their potential side effects in elite athletes. The report might have been central to any prosecution under Article 361. However, for reasons that never became clear, no report was ever delivered.

That left the blood bags. Fuentes' position relied on keeping two near-contradictory stances well apart. The first of these was a group of arguments aimed at de-medicalising the blood and its transfusion, based on the premise that, legally speaking, blood was not a medicine at all. The second was that, as a medical doctor, Fuentes was allowed to carry out any medical procedure he deemed appropriate. He considered himself immune to prosecution because it was logically impossible for a medical doctor to commit an offence against public health. Asked in court whether the medical authorities had authorised him and Dr Merino to operate a transfusion centre, Fuentes said that they were authorised to do so 'by the free exercise of their profession'.[4] In addition, 'as he understood it, he and Dr Merino *were* an extraction and conservation unit for blood bags . . .', purely by virtue of their professional medical qualifications.[5]

This led to long sessions of dictionary and legal analysis to see whether the words 'medicine' and 'blood products' covered whole blood. It was like counting angels dancing on a pinhead. With examples on all sides of the argument, no opinion could possibly be definitive, which played into the hands of the defence.

Even so, it quickly emerged that the blood in the bags was not simple bodily fluid. It had been chemically altered, not only by the addition of EPO or FSH (follicle-stimulating hormone), as the Barcelona analyses found, but by the addition of glycerol, an alcohol that protects and prevents red blood cells from bursting. The glycerol was added automatically by the two compact Haemonetics ACP 215 Automated Cell Processors the size of large desktop printers, that Fuentes had bought, one in 2004, the other in 2006, for €33,000 each. So advanced were they that, at the time, he believed only three clinics in Spain used them, one of them being a military hospital.[6] In recorded telephone calls, Fuentes had informed Merino and Labarta, when they were

running short of glycerol, that he had 'cheated the machine ...
a thousand times' by using smaller amounts than the automated
procedure. As well as the obvious safety implications, this showed
that Fuentes had been very deliberately manipulating the blood
chemistry.

In a questionable link between his clandestine, highly prof-
itable transfusion service and altruistic, public blood donation,
he argued that pop-up donor centres were permitted to operate
in caravans, field hospitals or schools because of Royal Decree
1088/2005,[7] which laid down the minimum standards for carrying out transfusions, and required hygienic but not sterile premises. Therefore it was legal for Fuentes to perform his extractions
and reinfusions in hotels on the same grounds. He told the court
that he kept to the standards laid down in the Royal Decree at
all times.[8]

All of which led Fuentes to claim, as the judge noted in her
judgment, that 'he was not aware of doing anything wrong.'[9] And
this, despite his accomplice, Merino, feeling something like the
opposite when interviewed in July 2006: 'He knew he might be
doing something illegal, by which he meant "he was aware that
he was doing something wrong" and that "his conduct was not
very ethical."'[10]

Labarta, the head coach at Kelme-Comunitat Valenciana took
a less sophisticated approach: he simply pleaded ignorance on
all counts. Yes, he had heard of autotransfusions and knew that
they were banned, but, no, he did not know precisely what they
were, beyond understanding that they were intended to enhance
performance. He believed (although he could not be sure) that
Fuentes used them to keep riders' red blood cell count at healthy
levels. He thought transfusions were prohibited, but what did he
know? The one thing he was sure of was that, whatever Fuentes
did, it was to protect his riders' health. For reasons of medical
confidentiality, presumably, he was permitted to exchange im-
pressions with Fuentes on the condition of the riders in order

to plan their training schedules, but not to ask direct questions about their medical health or treatments they might be undergoing. (This, despite Manzano's belief that 'Eufemiano would not have been able to treat him with blood extractions, reinfusions, and other medical treatments without Labarta's knowledge, because Labarta adapted his training programme according to Eufemiano's reinfusion schedule.'[11]) Labarta believed that the machines in the flat at Calle Caídos de al División Azul were medical, but he never asked Fuentes. He never saw any blood bags, chest freezers or medicines because he only ever went into the front room. And no rider ever disclosed to Labarta that he was undergoing autotransfusions – despite the obvious impact that this information would have had on Labarta's training schedules. That any of this could be stated in court with a straight face says something of Fuentes' and Labarta's acting skills. That the prosecution did not instantly tear it to shreds says something of their naivety.

Even so, on 29 April 2013, Judge Julia Patricia Santamaría ruled that, 'in terms of the protected legal interest, public health, we understand that blood, whether it is whole blood, plasma, red blood cell concentrates or blood products, falls under the concept of "medicinal product".'[12]

She sentenced Eufemiano Fuentes to one year in prison and four years of disqualification, with four months for Ignacio Labarta, although, given that neither man had a prior criminal record and the prison terms were less than two years and a day, the sentences were automatically suspended. Appeals were lodged immediately.

Eleven weeks later, on the morning of stage thirteen of the 2013 Tour, Bala lay second overall, 3 minutes 25 seconds behind Chris Froome. The day promised little until, after 60 predictable kilometres, a complacent breeze mustered some energy and a day of low expectations was suddenly rich with potential.

The peloton quickly split into several groups, then flew through the feedzone at speeds that made collecting feed bags a liability. One rider tried, and careered into Alejandro Valverde's rear wheel. Before it disintegrated, the Movistar leader, second overall, stopped at the roadside. Instead of swapping bikes with his teammate Jonathan Castroviejo, he took his rear wheel and fitted it himself. It ensured he would embark on the long chase on his own machine, but it cost him precious time.

Bauke Mollema, 12 seconds behind Valverde overall, set his Belkin teammates to hold off the Spaniard's return. Bala's teammates dropped back to help their leader, with only Rui Costa and Nairo Quintana remaining in the front group.

Directeur sportif José Luís Arrieta, in the team car, faced a dilemma.

'We have two riders up front, we're only fifteen seconds off the back. I tell Rui to wait, and I say to Nairo, "I need you right up front."'

Valverde never came any closer. Arrieta was philosophical. 'We were close, but we never made it, and we lost a chance of a high position overall with Rui. But those decision-making moments are like that.

'Nairo went from being Alejandro's support rider in the mountains, to having Alejandro working for him . . .'

Quintana went on to finish second in the 2013 Tour de France. That 12 July saw the end of Valverde's career as a Tour de France leader.

Then, at the Vuelta a España, won by the 41-year-old American Chris Horner, with Vincenzo Nibali second, Bala took his fifth podium finish.

'I knew I was going to climb well if I rode at my own pace, but I needed one of the rivals to fail. It didn't happen and I have to be happy with third. It's another podium in the Vuelta a España and, even if I didn't win a stage, I came close, and I've won the points jersey.'

At the world championships road race around Florence, another old rivalry boiled over into controversy. With ten kilometres to go, five men led: Italy's Vincenzo Nibali, the Colombian Rigoberto Urán, and Bala alongside a fellow member of the Spanish national team in Purito Rodríguez, who had left Caisse d'Épargne in 2009 to join Team Katusha as its stage-race leader, and a fellow Movistar teammate, Rui Costa, representing another nation, Portugal. When Urán fell on the descent from Fiesole, with 9.2 kilometres to go, Rodríguez darted away to a potentially winning lead. On a tight, right-hand bend, where it was impossible to catch his slipstream, Rui Costa accelerated after him. Nibali was unable to respond, and Valverde opted to stay with him. At that moment, Bala lost the race for himself and for his compatriot Purito Rodríguez. When Rui Costa caught Rodríguez, the Spanish rider looked for Valverde and was unable to believe he was not there.

With 130 metres to go, the Portuguese rider surged past the Catalan, who came back alongside him, but was unable to draw level and lost it by a wheel. Nibali did not even attempt to sprint against Valverde, who came in third, 15 seconds later.

Despite having two riders on the podium, there was little joy in the Spanish camp.

On the podium, Purito barely exchanged a glance with Valverde. He complained, 'He should have followed when they came after me, on the wheel . . . It's not hard. Why didn't he? We spoke about it and he told me that he was on the limit. But it's the past now. It doesn't mean anything. That's life. That's cycling.' He added ruefully, 'It would have been the race of my life if I'd won.'

The national coach, Javier Mínguez, commented, 'The gold was ours but, because of a mistake, the horse bolted. Purito couldn't understand why Valverde didn't jump when Rui Costa went for him, but Alejandro claimed he didn't have the legs.'

Valverde, already the cyclist with the highest number of medals in the world championships, with two silver medals and two bronze medals, added another bronze to his collection.

'After 270 kilometres my legs didn't respond.'

A week later, on the final climb of Il Lombardia, with 9.8 kilometres to go, Purito attacked alone, and rode away to his second consecutive victory in a race Valverde would never win. Bala was second. The win made Purito Rodríguez the world's number one rider for the second year in a row.

16

Strategic Diversions

Bala's third consecutive Vuelta a Andalucía win in February 2014 included victories in the prologue, two stages and the points competition. He would win it again in 2015 and 2016. His fourth Vuelta a Murcia in March was his first since 2008. Now a one-day race, it had been over five stages six years before. He would win it for the last time in 2017. On 8 March 2014 he went to Strade Bianche in Tuscany where, by finishing third behind Michał Kwiatkowski and Peter Sagan, he redefined it as a race where small-framed Grand Tour specialists could excel. He would finish third again in 2015, and riders like Romain Bardet, Egan Bernal and Tadej Pogačar would follow him onto the podium.

The day after the 2014 Strade Bianche he was in Rome, the home town of CONI, who had prosecuted him with such vigour before the ban, for the one-day Roma Maxima, formerly the Giro del Lazio. When he attacked in the Alban Hills, only Domenico Pozzovivo went with him. For 41 kilometres they worked together until, with the finish line in sight and the peloton bearing down on them, Bala dropped his breakaway companion and held off the sprinters to win by a second. His exhibition doubled as a gesture of defiance towards CONI. Anti-doping samples being anonymous, there was no way for the authorities to single out Valverde's for special treatment, but presumably every specimen taken was subjected to the most exhaustive analysis possible. There was not a trace of anything suspicious.

He continued his season in the same vein at the GP Miguel Indurain on 5 April, attacking alone with 15 kilometres left to win by 1 minute 2 seconds.

Fourth in the Amstel Gold Race on 20 April behind his nemesis, Philippe Gilbert, he beat Dan Martin and Michał Kwiatkowski into second and third place in Flèche Wallonne, before finishing second to Simon Gerrans in the hundredth edition of Liège–Bastogne–Liège.

Then he took his spring break, not to return to racing until the Route du Sud in France on 20 June. By then, his teammate and rival Nairo Quintana had won the Giro d'Italia, and King Juan Carlos I had abdicated. Although the Nóos Case was mentioned as one of the causes, the sports pages passed over the connection with the Illes Balears cycling team.

A series of crashes on stage five of the Tour de France took Chris Froome out of the race, so, when Alberto Contador stepped off injured on stage ten, the door was suddenly open for an outsider to win the Tour. But it was Vincenzo Nibali, not Bala, who stepped up. Having already taken the yellow jersey with a brilliant stage win in Sheffield on stage two, when Froome and Contador were still in the race, he surrendered it for one night only the rest of the Tour. While Nibali built up an insuperable lead in the mountains, Bala manoeuvred himself into second place overall at the end of stage thirteen and stayed there for five stages. However, on the climb to Hautacam, he dropped to fourth place, two seconds behind Jean-Christophe Péraud and, in the final time trial – his old nemesis – around Bergerac, he conceded 2 minutes 1 second to the Frenchman, seeing all hopes of finishing on the podium dissolve.

Even so, fourth place was his best Tour result so far. He followed it up with victory in the Clásica San Sebastián, and third place in his second consecutive Vuelta a España, behind Contador and Froome this time, a crash having taken Quintana out of the race when he – Nairo – was in the overall leader's jersey. It allowed Bala to end the season as world number one for the first time since 2008.

The 2015 season started as usual: at the team presentation in January, Bala admitted, 'Nairo is the leader for the Tour and that will be the big objective of the year for Movistar. The rest is secondary. I will try to be with Nairo at the Tour, then I will have my opportunity at the Vuelta.'

Bala started his season in Mallorca. Fortieth in the first of the Challenge races, he finished second the next day, in the Trofeo Andratx–Mirador d'Es Colomer, then won the Trofeo Serra de Tramuntana the day after that, with a 30-kilometre solo attack in cold, wet conditions.

Missing the Tour of Andalusia, he spent most of February on the Arabian peninsula, taking second place on the steep stage finish at Hatta Dam behind John Degenkolb in the Dubai Tour, getting caught in the wind and losing three minutes in stage two of the Tour of Qatar, then finishing second again at Al Bustan in the Tour of Oman, behind Fabian Cancellara.

For the second consecutive year he finished third in Strade Bianche behind two much bigger riders, Zdeněk Štybar and Greg Van Avermaet. Then, the day after riding Milano–Sanremo finishing in twentieth place, he was at Calella, east of Barcelona, for the start of the Tour of Catalunya.

The race started with an upset: three chancers made it to the finish line, 2 minutes 40 seconds ahead of the main peloton. One of them, the Belgian rider Bart De Clercq, still led the general classification after stage four. Bala attempted to restore normal service by winning stage two, before crashing on stage three on the climb at Santa Pellaia and missing the crucial split. By finishing eighth in stage four at La Molina near the French border, he moved into ninth place overall, as Tejay van Garderen took the temporary lead. The same day, descending the Alt de Coubet, Movistar's Pablo Lastras crashed and broke his pelvis. The injury ended his career.

On the morning of the following day, 27 March, there was more bad news for Telefónica. A prominent employee named Carlos Escó was taken into custody by officers from the economic crime section of the Spanish police on suspicion of embezzling €8.7 million of public funds, in connection with cost overruns for warehouse construction in Zaragoza. Even if his subsequent four-year imprisonment was reversed on appeal, his arrest was a PR disaster. Escó, the former Deputy Minister of Public Works in the Government of Aragón, had joined the company as director of international institutional relations in 2009. It was one of a long series of grace and favour appointments at the telecoms giant under its chairman, César Alierta. In 2003, Alierta had welcomed the former head of the King's Household, Fernando Almansa, onto Telefónica's advisory council for Latin America. In December 2007 he had taken on Manuel Pizarro, a close ally of José María Aznar of the Partido Popular, prime minister of Spain from 1996 to 2004. Then, Javier de Paz, the former leader of the Socialist Youth and a member of the Spanish Socialist Workers' Party executive under Felipe González, joined the company in what the press called 'a favour by César Alierta to the then [Socialist] president José Luis Rodríguez Zapatero'.

There was nothing new in any of this. Telefónica had been performing favours for its political masters from its beginnings. The historian Paul Preston tells the story of a henchman named Pere Martir Homs, the author of a series of political assassinations during General Franco's first government, who was set up with a well-funded sinecure at Telefónica for his services. Sixty years later, and fully privatised, Telefónica continued to provide safe and lucrative havens to well-connected public figures in need of a way out of the public eye. The occasional exposure or arrest of these members of its workforce kept the company communications team busy.

In 1996, newly elected Partido Popular President José María Aznar had appointed as chairman of Telefónica his childhood friend, Juan Villalonga Navarro.[1] In the summer of 2000, a scheme to collect more than €500 million in stock options for the entire management team, with its chairman the main beneficiary, was exposed, and Villalonga was forced to step down.

After Iñaki Urdangarin's appointment as a director of Telefónica International in June 2006 – not to mention as honorary president of the Interactive Generations Forum, formed by three organisations: Telefónica itself, the (Opus Dei-run) University of Navarre, and the Inter-American Organization for Higher Education – Telefónica had taken on another colourful figure: Rodrigo de Rato y Figaredo, Dominique Strauss-Kahn's predecessor as managing director of the International Monetary Fund (IMF), which *El País* called 'the highest position ever held by a Spaniard in a multinational body'.[2] Rato had acceded to the command of the IMF in June 2004 with the support of the EU bloc of nations. His term coincided with the period immediately preceding the financial crisis of 2008. A later report slated him for paying 'insufficient attention to the risks of contagion or spill-overs from a crisis in advanced economies', and for his apparent belief that 'financial markets were fundamentally sound and that large financial institutions could weather any foreseeable problem'.[3]

To the EU's considerable embarrassment, Rato left his post prematurely in 2007. The reasons he gave for stepping down were personal – 'particularly with regard to the education of my children' – although the reality, according to a senior Partido Popular official who spoke to the newspaper *El País*, was party political. 'The entire Partido Popular obviously believes [its leader Mariano] Rajoy would have a better chance in the 2008 elections with Rato backing him up.' In one of his last speeches in charge of the IMF, Rato cemented his place on the wrong side of history by cutting a section urging international action over climate change.

Then, despite Rato's support for Rajoy, the Socialist José Luis Rodríguez Zapatero won a second term.

In January 2010, in an appointment worth a reported annual salary of €2.3 million, Rato became the chairman of the public savings bank Caja Madrid, owned by the government of the Community of Madrid. Six months later, Caja Madrid was the largest of seven Spanish regional savings banks that united to form a new institution called Bankia. In June 2011, Bankia was floated publicly. On 7 May 2012, Rato announced his departure, softened by a compensation packet of €1.2 million. He reassured investors: 'Bankia has a very high level of solvency, a very robust liquidity situation and a splendid staff of professionals that serves ten million customers and 400,000 shareholders'.[4]

Before the month was out, a revised set of 2011 accounts replaced the €305 million profit shown in Rato's last report with losses amounting to €2.979 billion. Exposure to bad debt left the bank needing the staggering sum of €22 billion. It quickly emerged that thousands of small-scale investors had been persuaded to convert their savings to so-called preference shares in the new institution, with no understanding that, despite their name, they were high-risk financial products which carried no automatic right to redemption. The life savings of hundreds of thousands of small investors were lost at a stroke.[5]

As a storm gathered around Rato, help arrived from an old friend. Rato had been part of the government that had approved Telefónica's privatisation at the end of the 1990s. In July 2000, as José María Aznar's Minister for the Economy, Rato had been Alierta's main backer for the post of chairman at Telefónica. So, in January 2013, Alierta repaid the favour by taking him on as his advisor for Europe and Latin America. Over three years, Telefónica paid Rato €730,000 into the bank account of a private company with unidentified shareholders whose only activity for years was to obtain the real estate capital gain from a plot of land near Cádiz.

In June 2014 the banking oversight watchdogs learned that, for at least the period between 2003 and 2012, eighty-three directors and senior managers at Caja Madrid and Bankia had been drawing on central bank funds using unaccounted company payment cards with unlimited credit to make cash withdrawals and personal purchases, including clothes, travel and entertainment, totalling €15.5 million. The story broke in October, after which the national media published every detail of the 526 transactions between January 2010 and May 2012 in which, despite his own obscene prosperity, Rodrigo Rato spent €99,000 of other people's money on jewellery, clothing, entertainment, spas and flights. The day of his resignation, he spent €341.63 on a last supper.

When the magistrate investigating the credit card scam attributed full responsibility for the system to the former president of Caja Madrid, Miguel Blesa, and his successor, Rodrigo Rato, Banco Santander and CaixaBank, who had retained Rato as an international advisor, dispensed with his services. Not Telefónica: they kept him on until the day he was detained by police on 16 April 2015, three weeks after Carlos Escó's arrest. In February 2017, Rato was found guilty of embezzlement and sentenced to four and a half years' imprisonment. The sentence was confirmed by the Supreme Court in September 2018 and Rato started his prison sentence the following month.[6]

For a sponsor in need of a strategic diversion, Bala offered incomparable reliability. On the day of Carlos Escó's arrest, he took his second stage win in the 2015 Volta a Catalunya. Changing pace with 11 kilometres to go, he thinned out the leaders to an elite group of Alberto Contador, Rigoberto Urán, Richie Porte, Domenico Pozzovivo, Fabio Aru and Rafael Valls, then rocketed away with three kilometres left to celebrate victory alone. Forty-eight hours later, on Montjuic, the hill in Barcelona, Bala jumped with five kilometres left. Dan Martin reacted and rode straight past him. But it was too much, too early. With 500 metres to the finish, the chasing group, with Valverde in tow, caught him. Bala's final sprint won him his third stage of the Volta, and allowed him to finish second overall behind Porte.

Three days after Rodrigo Rato's detention, Bala began the best Ardennes week of his career. In the Amstel Gold Race on 19 April, he finished second to Michał Kwiatkowski. On the twenty-second, he won his third Flèche Wallonne, equalling Eddy Merckx on the record number of victories. Then, on the twenty-sixth, after chasing down Dani Moreno in the final 150 metres, he was first in Liège–Bastogne–Liège, with Julian Alaphilippe second and Joaquim Rodríguez third. He did not return to racing until 7 June at the Critérium du Dauphiné, where he finished ninth overall. On 28 June he won the national road title for the second time.

The Tour de France started badly. Bala completed the opening 13.8-kilometre time trial around Utrecht 56 seconds slower than the winner, Rohan Dennis, and only five seconds faster than his teammate Quintana. Stage two took the riders to the artificial island of Neeltje Jans in the Oosterschelde, a former estuary now dammed in by the Oosterscheldedam. Wind and rain combined to limit the vision of the riders and the TV cameras, creating a constantly shifting impression of what was actually happening on the road. The first twenty-four finishers took 15 seconds to cross the line. There were no Movistar riders among them. Bala and Nairo were in a group of sixty-five riders who finished 1 minute 28 seconds down. Bala contributed to the chase, helping to limit Quintana's losses.

Bala finished eleventh in stages three and four, in the group with Nairo. By finishing third at Mûr-de-Bretagne on stage eight behind Alexis Vuillermoz and Dan Martin, and again the following day in the team time trial finishing in Plumelec, Bala moved up to seventh overall, with Quintana ninth, nine seconds behind him. On stage ten, 15 kilometres before the foot of the final climb up to La Pierre Saint-Martin, deep in the Pyrenees, Nairo asked his teammates to raise the pace. With eight kilometres to go on the climb, Bala made two accelerations to tempt Chris Froome's teammates Geraint Thomas and Richie Porte into chasing, but they let him ride himself out. With 6.4 kilometres to go, Froome launched an unanswerable sprint. Nairo finished the stage third, over a minute behind Froome. Quintana and Valverde now lay third and fourth overall. So they stayed until stage fourteen, ending on the landing strip at Mende, atop a steep climb, where Teejay van Garderen, who started the day second, swapped GC positions with Nairo.

At Pra-Loup on stage seventeen, Bala moved up into third place overall. The final mountain stage covered only 110.5 kilometres. Nairo had reconnoitred the stage in the company of his sport director, José Luis Arrieta, who told me: 'We looked at the stage knowing that we could go into it with a couple of minutes to make up.'

First, their Colombian teammate Winner Anacona broke away early. Then, on the Col de la Croix de Fer, still some 60 kilometres from the finish, Alejandro Valverde sped out of the yellow jersey group. Minutes later Nairo made his move, joining Valverde, who, with his teammate in tow, increased the pace. Everything was executed to perfection, until the air itself turned against them. Headwinds on the descent of the Col de la Croix de Fer made the attack impossible. For the second time in the Tour, Nairo's ambitions were thwarted by the elements. At the foot of the final climb to Alpe d'Huez, the yellow jersey group of around thirty had three of Froome's teammates in the lead.

With 9.9 kilometres to go, Valverde attacked. Wout Poels looked over at his leader, Chris Froome, and let the Spaniard go.

Eight hundred metres later, Nairo crossed to Valverde, and a kilometre later, they caught Anacona, a survivor of the early breakaway. At that moment, Valverde's job was done.

Eighteen seconds after Thibaut Pinot crossed the finish line, Nairo finished in second place. Valverde skipped past Froome into fourth place, 1 minute 20 seconds later. With the time bonus for finishing second in the stage, Nairo had gained 1 minute 26 seconds on Froome, but he had lost the Tour de France by 1 minute and 12 seconds. Bala, meanwhile, had finished on the podium of the Tour de France.

Through tears of joy, he told the radio reporters, 'This is what I've been chasing all my life.'

Bala turned 36 in 2016. There seemed to be no decline in his powers, as he demonstrated by winning the third of what would end up being four consecutive editions of Flèche Wallonne, before turning his attention to his first Giro d'Italia. For the Movistar Team management, as I saw during my brief spell working with them, the year started with the distraction of the Nóos trial, which took place in Palma de Mallorca from 11 January to 22 June. On 29 January it was ruled that the Infanta Cristina would appear as a defendant, and public interest in the case went through the roof.

Embarrassingly, the Illes Balears cycling sponsorship deal was at the top of the agenda. On Tuesday 9 February José Luis Ballester took the stand for four and a half hours and gave his version of how it came about, including the fictitious budgets and false documentations that Urdangarin and his partner, Diego Torres, presented from different companies in their network, and how that first successful operation led to many others.[7]

On Thursday 11 February, Jaume Matas accepted his responsibility for ordering his government to award public contracts worth €2.6 million to Urdangarin's companies between 2003 and 2007, the so-called 'project office' of the Banesto-Illes Balears cycling team in 2003 and the organisation of two congresses on tourism and sport in 2005 and 2006, because the Balearic government was 'interested in being on good terms with him and the Royal Family'.[8]

On Friday 26 February, Urdangarin described the Illes Balears cycling team deal as atypical for the Nóos Institute and said that the team, and the €300,000 project office, was 'one hundred per cent' the concern of Juan Pablo Molinero,[9] my immediate superior at Movistar Team. Urdangarin added that Molinero did not report back to him 'unless strictly necessary'.[10]

Cross-examined over invoices and budgets, Urdangarin answered 'I don't know' thirty times, varying it on occasion with 'You should ask him about that', meaning Molinero. Perhaps he was angry that Molinero was no longer among the accused, having been made a mere witness in October 2012, despite the judge's finding that Molinero's declarations to the investigators were '*plagadas de matizaciones, rectificaciones y ausencias de claros recuerdos*' – so excessively intricate, in other words, and then so fastidiously qualified, as to be devoid of any intelligible content.[11]

Molinero himself was heard on 9 March. Contradicting Urdangarin's flattering depiction of him as the prime mover in the deal, he made himself out, rather humiliatingly, as merely 'one of the workers, with no power to decide or set prices or anything else . . . In Nóos not a single piece of paper was moved without the supervision of the bosses of the company'.[12]

On 8 March, José Miguel Echávarri, now retired, appeared by video link to supply his recollections of the sponsorship deal.[13] No wonder the management was misfiring. At the Giro start in Apeldoorn on 6 May, Molinero was back accompanying the team as its press officer, the night watchman – me – having been dismissed on 5 April.

On Tuesday 24 May, Bala outsprinted the *Maglia Rosa*, Steven Kruijswijk, to win stage sixteen, the shortest of the race at 132 kilometres, between Bressanone and Andalo. It was his first Giro stage win, and moved him into a podium position. Five days later, he completed his set of Grand Tour podiums by finishing third behind Vincenzo Nibali and Esteban Chaves.

After a Tour ridden in support of Nairo Quintana, who – lacking his usual sparkle, finished only third – Bala stood on the final podium as a member of the winning team. He joked, 'In my old age, I'm on the podium more often than when I was a contender.'

For twelve stages of the Vuelta, Bala was third or better, while his teammate Quintana moved into the race lead. Then, on stage fourteen, ending on the Aubisque on the French side of the Pyrenees, Nairo attacked with eight kilometres left to climb. Unable to follow the pace, Bala allowed the group of leaders to go. It was his customary bad day. He dropped down to nineteenth place overall, eventually finishing twelfth.

Riding all three Grand Tours for the first and only time in his career seemed to fill him with strength for the start of 2017. First in the Vuelta a Murcia and the Vuelta a Andalucía in February, he was first again in March's Volta a Catalunya and April's Vuelta al Pais Vasco, and in Flèche Wallonne (his fifth win, ahead of Dan Martin and Dylan Teuns) and Liège–Bastogne–Liège (his fourth, ahead of Martin again, and Michał Kwiatkowski). After his usual break, he returned to racing at the Critérium du Dauphiné, where he rode low key to sixth place overall, after an excellent time trial, in which he finished third behind Richie Porte and Tony Martin.

He seemed to be getting better and better. Yet, in every interview, the question of retirement was being raised. Before the Tour, he said, '[The year] 2017 has been the best season of my life so far. I've won something in every race I've ridden, except for the Dauphiné, where I rode just to see how I was doing, with no aspirations in the general classification. I hope to continue like this for a few more years. This won't be my last Tour, I hope; I think I've got a couple more left, until I'm thirty-nine. And when I'm forty I'll see if it's time to retire.'

As things turned out, he was facing the end of his career within ten minutes of the start of this Tour.

Tour de France, 1 July 2017. It is raining in Düsseldorf as, seven kilometres into the opening time trial, on the approach to a wide, left-hand bend, Bala drifts across to the right-hand side of the road, then coasts inwards towards the apex of the curve, carefully avoiding the white lines. It is not a dangerous bend, and he opts not to touch the brakes.

Later, he will say, 'I was doing the same time as [his teammate, the time trial specialist Jonathan] Castroviejo. I wanted to do a really good time trial.'

A quarter of the way through the bend, his front wheel shudders. He starts to pull his left foot out of the pedal, but his rear wheel has already slipped away. He bounces across the road on his left side and crashes into the metal barrier. His left knee makes first contact. The impact is sickening. He rebounds into the road and comes to rest in the foetal position but for his head in his hands.

Eusebio Unzue is with him in seconds. Bala is weeping and repeating, 'It's over, it's over. The bike is over. This is my last race.'

Later, when Bala is able to call his wife, he tells her, 'My career is finished.'

The impact had shattered his kneecap and scattered bone fragments around the joint. From the University Hospital in Düsseldorf, the medical report read: 'Fracture of the left patella. Injury to the left tibia.' A later report added a break to the talus, the weight-supporting bone in the ankle joint where the tibia and fibula meet the foot.

Bala had surgery in Düsseldorf the next day. It took three hours. X-rays showed the operation to have been a complete success. Within thirty-six hours, using a continuous passive motion device to flex and extend the knee joint, he was flexing his leg between 20 and twenty-five degrees, even if, he said, it felt like he was bending a steel rod. Back in Murcia, his traumatologist Francisco Esparza was persuaded that, if he ever competed again, it would be as a Paralympian.

Yet, a week after the operation, the angle of his knee reached thirty degrees, and Esparza was less concerned about the knee, which seemed to be healing fine, than an injury in the saddle area that could have made finding a comfortable position on the bike impossible, making any future career impossible too.

His first attempts at turning pedals were on an aquabike in a therapeutic pool. They had to be limited to a quarter of an hour to prevent the water opening the scars. By the time Esparza decided it was time to get back on the bike, it was August. To remove Bala's foot from the automatic pedal, Esparza had to unscrew the cleat by hand, and lift the leg out vertically. Even so, in not much more than a week, Bala was doing 50 kilometres an hour.

The speed of his recovery was dizzying. Bala resumed racing at the 2018 Challenge de Mallorca, 208 days after the crash. With the enthusiasm of a teenager, he won the Volta a Catalunya, the Route d'Occitanie, the Abu Dhabi Tour and the Volta a la Comunitat Valenciana, before starting the Tour de France as Nairo Quintana's domestique deluxe. His best stage finish was third, between Brest and the Mûr de Bretagne, in stage six. He finished fourteenth overall, 27 minutes 26 seconds behind Geraint Thomas.

In the Vuelta a España, he won two stages and fought for the podium to the end.

The best version of Valverde was back.

In Innsbruck, 456 days after his crash, he crowned his career, perhaps even fulfilled his destiny, by becoming world champion.

Bala's first victory in the world champion's jersey was on the climb to Jebel Hafeet in the Abu Dhabi Tour. It took him sixteen race days. He was not accustomed to waiting so long. Years later, he told how heavily the rainbow jersey had pressed down on him, and how the strain of honouring the title nearly tore him apart.

'I lost the desire to win. I lacked the hunger, the overriding need,' he said. 'I thought that, by winning the world championships, I had done it all.'

In his success, he mislaid his inner child.

'I forgot how to enjoy myself on the bike, which is the key. I only felt comfortable training with friends. Those were the only times I felt strong.'

If 2019 was a season of only five wins, at least one of his thirteen second places must have offered some compensation: in the Vuelta a España, where he finished between two Slovenians, Primož Roglič, the winner, and third placed Tadej Pogačar.

With no wins at all in 2020, the year of the Covid-19 lockdowns, and only three in 2021, it might have appeared that his career was winding down. But he continued to be outstanding in his beloved Ardennes with fifth place in the 2021 Amstel Gold Race, third in Flèche Wallonne, and fourth in Liège–Bastogne–Liège. His best stage finish at the Tour de France was second at Val Thorens in stage twenty, the day Egan Bernal consolidated overall victory. He was fifth again at Il Lombardia in October.

And then came his final season, in 2022. It started with wins: the Trofeo Pollença–Port d'Andratx, part of the Challenge de Mallorca, and a stage and the GC of a new race, the Gran Camiño in Galicia, north-west Spain. It was his 133rd and final win, after which he took second place in Strade Bianche and Flèche Wallonne, and seventh in Liège–Bastogne–Liège. Not the wins he had hoped for, but nonetheless results that world-class riders yearn for.

Conclusion:

Part 1. A Commitment to Silence

Valverde was no doubt already thinking of his legacy in 2013 when he created the Valverde Team in Murcia. It started with boys' youth teams, adding junior (under-19) in 2015 and under-23 in 2019, and expanding to include women's youth and junior teams in 2021.

He seemed capable of going on and on absorbing the punishment of his brutal métier, but this was an illusion. Even so, he was competitive to the last. The final four results of his career were second in the Coppa Agostoni, fourth in the Giro dell'Emilia, third in Tre Valli Varesine and, on 8 October 2022, sixth in Il Lombardia, aged 42 years 180 days. The last two of these races were both won by a rider seventeen and a half years his junior: the remarkable Tadej Pogačar, who, in the range of his talents, both resembles Bala and eclipses him. Bala's ability to climb, sprint and, to a degree, time trial, may have inspired his successors, from Julian Alaphilippe to Pogačar and Remco Evenepoel, to strive for the same full palette of skills. Bala's career no doubt encouraged them to take on races of all types, all the way through the season, with the same joy, spontaneity and ready smile he always brought with him.

Yet, when we speak of legacy, we also mean influence outside the sporting domain. It is true that Valverde has used his sporting renown to defend and strengthen local identities, a concern shared by other members of the international peloton: riders of indigenous heritage like Nairo and Dayer Quintana, Richard Carapaz and Nielson Powless, African riders like the Rwandan Adrien Niyonshuti and the Eritreans Biniam Girmay and Merhawi Kudus, and Afrodescendants like Kevin Reza, all, like Bala, courageous and outspoken in the defence of their communities, the difference being that, whatever prejudice Murcians are subjected to in modern Spain, they can hardly be said to have been the victims of any remotely comparable persecution.

And there were other issues he could usefully have championed. As Valverde's career drew to a close, climate change was no longer a remote statistical likelihood but, for every outdoor athlete, an obvious, everyday reality.

In 2022 he skipped the Tour de France, and missed the experience of riding in 42-degree heat, although he had seen worse. In October 2015, at Qasr Al Sarab, among the sand dunes before stage one of the first Abu Dhabi Tour, he raised his bike computer to show me the temperature reading. Fifty-four degrees Celsius.

In 2019 he experienced the soaring temperatures and violent storms of the first true climate emergency Tour de France, which started eight days after the village of Verargues, midway between Nîmes and Montpellier, had recorded 46°C, the highest in French meteorological history. Eleven months later, at the 2020 Critérium du Dauphiné, he witnessed giant hailstones pummelling the final climb of stage two. In August 2021 he finished second in the first Giro di Sicilia, six weeks after the village of Contrada Mortellito, 12 kilometres off the race route, had been hit by the highest temperature ever recorded in Europe, 48.8°C.

The Tour Down Under holds an important place in Bala's career, although he only rode it twice, in 2010 and 2012. But he had teammates at the 2017, 2018 and 2019 editions, all of which had stages shortened because of the extreme heat, and at the 2020 race, when the peloton rode through areas devastated by bushfires, prompting the sprinter Sam Bennett to compare them to 'the set of a film about the end of the world'.

The world needed influential public figures to support action. In the estimation of the April 2022 Intergovernmental Panel on Climate Change (IPCC) report, the years 2012 to 2020, roughly the second part of Valverde's career, saw the highest average annual global greenhouse gas emissions in human history. The IPCC co-chair Professor Hans-Otto Pörtner said, 'Any further delay in concerted global action will miss a brief and rapidly closing window to secure a liveable future.'

Other riders – Michael Woods, Vincenzo Nibali, Robert Gesink, and younger successors like Gino Mäder and Tom Pidcock – spoke freely of the climate emergency, tried to find ways of being elite cyclists while minimising their CO2 emissions, or campaigned to limit plastic waste.

Bala did his bit by supporting Abarca Sports' sustainability plan, launched in June 2020 with the goal of becoming 'the first 100 per cent sustainable cycling organisation'. Working out its own carbon footprint, the Movistar Team's management company calculated that it had produced 175 tonnes of CO2 in 2019. As a point of comparison, Deceuninck–Quick-Step announced their intention to become carbon neutral six months before Abarca Sports. Instead of calculating their own carbon footprint, Deceuninck–Quick-Step asked a climate consultancy called CO2logic to make its own, independent assessment. Unlike Abarca, CO2logic published a detailed breakdown of its findings, reaching the figure of 1,288 tonnes for 272 days of racing in twenty countries during 2019. The difference is easily explained: Abarca limited its self-assessment to emissions generated by the team's vehicles and its headquarters, a large hangar in Egüés, Navarre. It seemed a rather arbitrary restriction.

Abarca announced that it was aiming (not pledging) to reduce and offset (two rather different things) its carbon emissions by having solar panels fitted in the team's headquarters, and making 'another big effort . . . gradually [to] replace its fleet of Volvo cars with new hybrid models' – although, given that the cars come from a sponsor, this would appear not to have entailed any particular effort or expense.

Six months later, Abarca announced that it was 'expanding its Sustainability Plan with visible actions'. The accompanying press release announced that Spain's Ministry for Ecological Transition had awarded the team its Seal of Recognition for calculating its carbon footprint. Beyond a video showing Bala and other riders telling us that they were 'more than just a team', that seemed to be it.

There was no accompanying commitment to reducing air travel to races or limiting the number of trucks servicing the riders, no undertaking to partner with producers of clothing and equipment derived from non-fossil fuel, or, for instance, to source food supplements with local ingredients. No mention of contracting an independent outside agency to verify Abarca's emissions self-assessment and monitor progress towards specified targets on a predetermined schedule. No manifesto to change the structure of the sport. No sense of urgency.

In November 2021, Valverde attended the inauguration of a team project to plant a thousand trees in Navarre. If the event resembled an off-road Volvo test that turned open countryside into a car park, its goal was essentially a positive one: to offset the 2019 total of 175 tonnes of carbon dioxide. The thousand trees are expected to take forty years to do so, if they survive.

It is easy to criticise. At least Movistar was absent from the long list of race organisers, teams and cycling federations who had placed the bicycle's indisputable environmental credentials in the service of fossil fuel producers, some of which also happened to be repressive regimes. Their names demonstrate sport's role as one of the forums in which wealthy, powerful corporations negotiate their place in society and purchase legitimacy.

Cycling's oil rush started in 2002 by Tour de France organiser ASO with the first Tour of Qatar, which ran until 2016. In 2006, oil-rich Kazakhstan moved into cycling with the team now called

Astana-Qazaqstan. Team Katusha, funded by the fossil fuel producers Gazprom and Itera, and the Russian state-owned defence conglomerate Rostechnologii, joined the peloton in 2009. In 2011, Itera's chairman, the oil and gas billionaire oligarch Igor Makarov, a former member of the USSR cycling team, joined the UCI's Management Committee, where he continues to serve. In the same year, the Belgian cycling federation accepted sponsorship from Esso. The Australian chemicals and explosives firm Orica, which produces, among other things, sodium cyanide for gold extraction, funded a team from 2012 to 2017. The Giro d'Italia organiser RCS arranged the Dubai Tour from 2014 to 2018 and the Abu Dhabi Tour from 2015 to 2018. In 2019 they merged to become the UAE Tour. TotalEnergies became a team sponsor in 2016. Bahrain Victorious launched its team in 2017, with UAE Team Emirates taking over Lampre-Merida and Ineos replacing Team Sky in 2019. In June 2021, Orica's successor, Team Bike Exchange, announced a Saudi sponsor in AlUla, 'a spectacular desert destination in north-west Saudi Arabia'. In 2022, British Cycling announced an eight-year partnership with Shell.

By comparison, Abarca's nod in the direction of green policies could be seen as having potential, at the very least, until, sixteen days after Bala's last race, it announced an alliance with the Saudi Cycling Federation 'to develop technical staff, enhance cooperation on training programs, exchange experiences, hold regular workshops and support events, races and activities in the Kingdom for years to come. The cooperation between the parties aims to jointly develop cycling projects in the Kingdom at all levels.'

How the alliance squared with Abarca's claim, made in the same press release, to be 'globally recognised as a leader in sustainability practices among the cycling family', was less clear. Saudi Arabia had long lobbied against environmental action and sowed doubt and confusion around climate science. Sources close to the April 2022 IPCC report revealed that its contents had been watered down by intense Saudi lobbying for the inclusion of repeated references to unproven carbon capture and storage technologies, which would allow the Saudis to continue extracting oil and gas.[1]

Abarca's timing was impeccable: as Russian missiles rained down on Ukraine, fuel prices soared and Western governments quarrelled with OPEC+ over its decision to cut oil production. Yet, having pioneered corporate sportswashing in the 1990s, Movistar Team was late to greenwashing. The income stream it opened was presumably substantial enough to compensate for any reputational damage to Abarca, Movistar and Telefónica, although it was bad news for Bala's legacy. After all, if the climate emergency is allowed to worsen, there will be no society left in which anything of his life and example can endure.

Bala and his teammates rode his final Grand Tour, the 2022 Vuelta a España, with the stand-out statistics of his long career printed on their jerseys:

> One Vuelta a España, UCI Road World Champion 2018. Two Clásicas San Sebastián, four Liège–Bastogne–Lièges, five Flèches Wallonnes. Seven World Championship podiums. Thirty-two Grand Tours ridden, seventeen stage wins, nine podiums. Thirty-six Monuments ridden, eleven podiums. Four times, UCI individual rankings winner.

His body bore traces of his long career. The photographs of his knee after that 2017 operation were enough to make the squeamish recoil. Cycling inscribes itself in the skin with something of the same excruciating efficiency as the capital punishment device from Franz Kafka's short story 'In the Penal Colony', which uses a fine blade to carve the precise words of the law that has been transgressed into the skin of the condemned. As

Kafka tells it, the officer in charge of the deadly machine tries to convince a visiting traveller of the instrument's utility. Failing to convince him, the officer does the honourable thing and submits himself to its torture. The machine duly impales him on its nibs.

There was never any need for Alejandro Valverde to do the honourable thing. The techniques of the PR industry have moved on since Kafka's time. Using reasoned argument to try to convince anyone of anything is no longer within its horizons. At least he can say that, never having tried to convince anyone of his case, he has never failed. In the face of incontrovertible public evidence that at least part of his career involved the use of illegal substances and practices, Valverde and his entourage began with the usual crisis management reflexes of the PR industry – attacking the investigators, appealing to prejudice, setting up straw men, deflecting, obfuscating and so on. But Valverde's greatest weapon has been reticence. He has observed near-complete discretion for so long, with such unfailing discipline, that he has achieved something remarkable: a kind of absolution, attained through amnesia, not atonement. Another variety of silence to add to the inventory.

In the legal proceedings in 2009 and 2010, Bala's legal team did most of the talking. Perhaps they advised Bala to keep quiet. If so, it was bad advice. It may have played well in parts of the Spanish peloton but, everywhere else, it deepened the stain on his reputation. It lacked courage, and it is a shame because, since serving his ban, Valverde has been free to talk. Intelligent, articulate, likable, engaging, he might have done what David Millar did: confessed his sins, taken his distance from his former self, committed himself to the cause of clean sport. His failure to do so before returning from his two-year suspension can only have lowered his market value. If he were ever to change teams again, or even negotiate his future with something in his back pocket, he needed to make a public statement of the obvious: that, with

Kelme at the start of his long career, he had doped, but that he had now paid his debt.

It would not have been without a degree of humiliation. The whitest lie told often enough to people we care enough about over a long enough period, is enough to blemish a life. Yet, for someone so articulate, so capable of realistic self-criticism, it could have been done. However, even setting aside cycling's desperate need to clear the air, the spiritual benefits to be garnered from speaking out – the truth setting you free and all that – have a time limit. The truth has its moment and the moment for Alejandro's has passed. To tell it now, with no more skin in the game, would be too late.

In Valverde's defence, the two halves of his career, pre- and post-suspension, show a striking symmetry. Before the ban, he accrued 65 wins in 554 race days as a professional. Five of those wins and thirty-seven race days were expunged by CAS. If we also discount his barren first season in 2002, we are left with 60 wins in 458 race days, which equals one win every 7.6 race days, including eleven stage race wins. Between 2012 and 2021 he took 70 wins in 761 race days, including fourteen stage race wins: in other words, one win every 10.9 race days.

Of his sixty wins between 2003 and 2009, twenty-five were in races which would today be WorldTour events, with one a national championship. That made 43.3 per cent: the rest were in lower ranked races. Of his seventy wins between 2012 and 2021, thirty-four were in WorldTour races, three were national championships and one was his world championship win, making 54.3 per cent. In other words, if his hit rate was slightly lower after the ban, its quality was markedly higher.

Before his suspension, he was the world's number one rider twice, in 2006 and 2008. After it, he achieved the same distinction twice, in 2015 and 2018. He was leading the world rankings the day his two-year suspension started in 2010, and the day of his awful crash in the prologue of the 2017 Tour de France.

Without even speculating about what he might have achieved without the ban, it was an extraordinary career. Yet, even if sport depended for its social impact on mere statistics and numerical data, it would be far from straightforward deciding what, in Bala's case, they added up to. After all, top fives and tens are fine achievements, but there is a saying in cycling: eighth and eightieth are much the same. When the podium is no longer feasible, it is generally thought better to be going for stage wins or working for someone else. There is no doubting the depth of Bala's abilities, but the stats may suggest essentially a team keen on stacking up team ranking points, and short on leaders it felt it could really commit to.

Even so, he was essentially the same rider pre- and post-ban. True, in his first seasons, armed with youthful recklessness, he mixed it with the top sprinters. But there is no indication that his pure sprint speed suddenly disappeared. In later years, he tended to give the bunch sprints a pass, but for good tactical reasons. He had monuments and general classifications to target. And, as the CAS judgment that made his ban worldwide noted in 2010:

> 19.14. There is no evidence that any of the results obtained by Mr Valverde since 6 May 2006 until now was through doping infraction.[2]

The sheer symmetry of his career raises an intriguing thought: what if Eufemiano Fuentes' treatments had no effect, and Alejandro Valverde's body responded barely or not at all to the doping at Kelme? It certainly looks as though his transgression was one from which he derived no benefit.

There is no disputing that the older, wiser man was punished for the sins of his younger, more foolish self. As he said in his press conference in June 2010, 'What has happened to me is very old, from a long time ago.'

There may be another element to Valverde's ire: on 10 June 2016, while he recovered after finishing third in the Giro d'Italia, and prepared himself for the rigours of the Tour de France, the appeal court in Madrid absolved Fuentes of offences against public health law. While finding it 'to be established that Fuentes . . . supplied athletes with erythropoietin (EPO), growth factors (IGF-1), testosterone, insulin and the female hormone gonadotropin (hMG), and treated them with blood extractions and reinfusions for the sole purpose of enhanc[ing] their performance in competition, with no real medical prescription',[3] the decision ruled that '"medicine" had no legal definition in the Penal Code[4] . . . In conclusion, his conduct does not fit in with the offence charged, and he should therefore be freely acquitted, as should Mr. Labarta.'

If Ettore Torri, Renzo Ferrante and their team of Italian investigators had been able to secure access to the rest of Fuentes' blood bags, they might well have changed the complexion of sport in Europe – and globally. Instead, their prosecutions started and finished with Alejandro Valverde, who, in consequence, became the only Spaniard with a guilty verdict against his name in the entire Operación Puerto saga. He had every reason to feel resentful, regardless of his guilt.

Conclusion:

Part 2. Bigger Lies to Tell

Going back to that January day in 2012 when he took his first post-suspension win, a new soigneur, Juan Carlos Escámez, was waiting for him beyond the finish line on Old Willunga Hill. The son of a butcher from Novelda, near Valencia, Escámez had ridden against Bala through the age groups. He described Bala's comeback victory as 'one of the most exciting moments I've experienced in this world. That victory had so much meaning ... We hugged and roared together. It was a special moment.'

A cyclist since the age of seven, Escámez rode for the Escuela Atlético de Madrid, the Club Ciclista Noveldense and Fiat Zetamobil.

'I beat him once as an amateur,' he said. 'He was just as funny and friendly then. We were rivals then, and now we are team-mates, but we enjoy each other's company just the same.'[1]

Riding for Kelme's amateur team, Escámez came to within a hair's breadth of turning professional: 'I was due to ride some races with the pros the following season, but Operación Puerto wiped out everything and many riders who had nothing to do with it were left without opportunities.'[2]

You wonder what they talk about on the massage table, the rider at the heart of Operación Puerto and the rider whose career ended because of it.

*

The way we think and talk about sport has changed over recent years. Once a refuge from worldly concerns, sporting talk has evolved into one of the central ways that we explore ideas and intuitions about social life. This may explain why sport and national identity are so inseparable.

Like the black hole at the centre of every galaxy, sport lies somewhere near the heart of the culture, without being entirely subject to its laws. Yet it obviously matters greatly that sport should be conducted fairly and legally. However, as well as returning us to the lawless animal body, which we have no choice but to inhabit, it sometimes seems to reveal what is almost an alternative moral order. If our modern, dignity-derived identities are in part structured around principles that we think of as universal, sport displays the pure partisanship of warrior societies, where loyalty to the cause of victory trumps every other type of allegiance. Part of the pleasure in watching sport may lie in the contrast.

A sunnier viewpoint was articulated by President Barack Obama, for whom sport is 'one of the few places where it's a true meritocracy. There's not a lot of BS. Ultimately, who's winning, who's losing, who's performing, who's not – it's all laid out there.'

The philosopher Michael Sandel, in his book *The Tyranny of Merit*, takes Obama to task. Consider one of America's best-loved sportsmen:

> LeBron James makes millions of dollars playing basketball, a hugely popular game. Beyond being blessed with prodigious athletic gifts, LeBron is lucky to live in a society that values and rewards them. It is not his doing that he lives today, when people love the game at which he excels, rather than in Renaissance Florence, when fresco painters, not basketball players, were in high demand.[3]

In the same way, any conversation about Valverde is likely to reflect on values like integrity and dishonesty, altruism and

232

selfishness, talent and opportunity, even justice and freedom. After all, in the second part of Alejandro Valverde's career his rivals were plagued by allegations of abusing the therapeutic use exemption system or asthma medication, or of buying race wins, no new allegations were ever made against Valverde. A beneficiary of an age when the morning headlines sometimes feel like ancient history by bedtime, he earned respect for the valour he showed during his recovery from his 2017 injuries, the longevity of his career, the courtesy and warmth with which he conducted himself, but also the instinctive brio with which he raced. Indeed, in a sport increasingly dominated by Team Sky's powerful and meticulously drilled train, the few who refused to succumb – Contador, Nibali, Quintana, Valverde – became symbols of freedom and spontaneity.

For this new way of thinking about sport, Valverde might inadvertently have been one of the vectors.

In 361 tedious, repetitive, sometimes ridiculous and, on occasion, oddly emotional pages of the 2013 Operación Puerto judgment, Judge Julia Patricia Santamaría detailed the six years, eleven months that had elapsed since police surveillance of Eufemiano Fuentes started on 4 May 2006.

She noted, on page 241, that 'law must follow society and not society the law.' Both had become highly international. When material was freely available on the internet, national laws preventing its publication were close to useless. Companies and individuals were choosing to start proceedings in the country whose laws are most favourable to them. It was no longer easy for governments to control the national space. Sport too was international and, given that, in Italy, criminal evidence could be used in sporting disciplinary procedures, attempts at a national level to suppress evidence were imperilled.

The judgment was written at a time when local and regional identities were strengthening apace and the Spanish nation-state was being corroded on both sides, by transnational forces – the European Union, and international commitments like those manifest in the UNESCO International Convention Against Doping in Sport – and by local and regional identities, most prominently Catalan nationalism which, by 2017, had plunged Spain into a constitutional crisis. On a small scale, Bala's championing of his place of origin was one small symptom of how the emergence of democracy in the late twentieth century weakened the supremacy of the central state.

Not that Spain's frequently described failure to build a large, unitary nation-state is any sort of a tragedy. Of all conceivable social structures, it is not at all clear that the nation-state is the most conducive to human happiness. Our inability to think of alternative, less environmentally ruinous ways of living is perhaps another sign of the dominance of the left-brain hemisphere, which largely reprocesses what it already knows, over the right hemisphere, which directs its attention towards the new and unexpected. In Kafka's story, the officer in charge of the execution machine shows the traveller the law that the machine was about to engrave in the flesh of its next victim. The traveller pores over the document, but he can make no sense of it. It is another expression of Kafka's disenchantment with bureaucratic systems of justice.

Twenty-eight pages of the judgment are devoted to the question of whether the biological specimens and phone tap evidence collected in the criminal investigation could be released for use in sports disciplinary cases. It was a complex area. Squaring intercept evidence and DNA profiling with Article 8 of the 1950 European Convention on Human Rights, which guaranteed 'respect for private and family life', took many forms across the continent, and involved lengthy toing and froing between the national courts and the European Court of Human Rights. Spanish law was uncompromising. The 1978 Constitution, drafted as

Spain emerged from the Franco regime, proclaimed fundamental individual rights on which the state could only encroach when 'serious criminal activity' was suspected in advance. The judgment might have cited another case, closely related to Operación Puerto, to illustrate the point.

In December 2010, after a long surveillance operation that also included telephone intercepts, the Guardia Civil entered the flat of Alberto León, already known to police for his role in Operación Puerto, finding several bags of blood preserved in a fridge.[4] As part of the same procedure, large numbers of doping substances were seized, and fourteen arrests were made, including Eufemiano Fuentes (again), his sister Yolanda (again), and Marta Domínguez, the reigning steeplechase world champion and vice-president of the Spanish Athletics Federation. Phone intercepts persuaded the Guardia Civil that the blood bags belonged to athletes trained by the head of the Spanish cross-country team, Fuentes' old coach and colleague, Manuel Pascua Piqueras. The investigation, dubbed Operación Galgo (Operation Greyhound), suggested that the blood doping ring uncovered in Operació Puerto extended much further into Spanish sport.

However, fifteen months later, Operación Galgo was terminated abruptly on the grounds that 'the prerequisites for constitutional legitimacy' had not been in place. The authorisation had been issued on the basis of 'rumour, gossip or hearsay [which] cannot be considered evidence of a crime.'[5] The telephone intercept warrants had been improperly authorised. The mass of incriminating evidence they had gathered could not be used. Even statements made by the accused, in the presence of their lawyers, had to be set aside. The Guardia Civil had no right to know what they knew, and were required to unknow it, if such a thing were even possible.

Before binning illicitly obtained evidence, other jurisdictions were allowed to consider the nature of the violation, the difficulty of acquiring evidence and the public interest in discerning the truth (Switzerland), or simply consider the relevance of the evidence (English law).[6] From the outside perspective, the closure of Operación Galgo looked like the very paradigm of overvaluing the rights of the accused and undervaluing those of the public good – as if its origins in hearsay evidence was seized on as a useful pretext.

The Puerto judgment noted that telephone intercepts and DNA evidence had to be treated with special care. It reasoned that 'evidence whose collection can be authorised in one context may not be used in other contexts where it would never have been authorised'.[7] The problem is, once a DNA match exists, it cannot be simply thought out of existence.

The 2013 judgment also included a short, shrill attack on the UNESCO International Convention Against Doping in Sport, signed by Spain in 2005 and ratified in 2007. According to Article 3(b), signatories agreed to 'encourage all forms of international cooperation aimed at protecting athletes and ethics in sport and at sharing the results of research', while Article 13 reads, 'States Parties shall encourage cooperation between anti-doping organizations, public authorities and sports organisations within their jurisdiction and those within the jurisdiction of other States Parties.'[8]

After quoting the Convention's Preamble, which proclaims that 'public authorities and organisations responsible for sporting activities have additional obligations in the fight against doping in sport, in particular to ensure appropriate conduct at sporting events, based on the principle of fair play, and the protection of the health of those taking part in them,' Judge Santamaría starts her onslaught:

> Well, the truth is that just as 'not everything goes' in sport, so too in jurisdictional matters there are limits to be respected, limits constituted by scrupulous respect for the applicable legal

system and, in particular, our Magna Carta [i.e., the Spanish Constitution], and the fundamental rights proclaimed therein. This is why the request for biological samples (blood, plasma and red blood cell concentrates) made by certain Prosecutors in the terms already examined cannot succeed, without this implying an invasion of competences by the justice system in the field of Public Administration.[9]

This is not technical legal debate. The pretentious 'Well . . .' (*Pues bien . . .*), the irate 'not everything goes', the sanctimonious 'limits' ('there are limits') and 'respect' (invoked twice in the space of ten words), the appeal to the Constitution and fundamental rights, the paranoid image of an 'invasion', are all loaded with emotion. But why? For its refusal to share Operación Puerto evidence, the Spanish legal system was subjected to international opprobrium. The judgment had a responsibility to restore . . . what? Its honour? In which case, the honour-based values of the warrior society are not limited to the sporting field of play at all. They lurk just beneath the surface of modern society's most dispassionate and rational pursuits.

It seemed to me that the real Josef K. of this story was Enrique Gómez Bastida, the Guardia Civil detective whose work led to the arrest of Fuentes. Yet not even Kafka would have dared invent Gómez Bastida's boom-and-bust career. In 2010 he was reassigned to Afghanistan. His online CV says that he was sent to advise the Afghan Ministry of the Interior on terrorism and organised crime, although, among the many complex challenges facing that country, it was open to debate whether it had a pressing need on the ground for one of the world's two or three leading anti-doping investigators. In 2013 he was rehabilitated and appointed to the Spanish anti-doping agency (Spanish Agency for the Protection of Health in Sport or AEPSAD) as head of research and intelligence. Nine months later, in January 2014, he was appointed director. Consolidating the agency's independence from the federations and other forms of political interference, he was hampered by the two-year delay before the Rajoy government brought Spanish anti-doping law into line with the World Anti-Doping Code, during which Spain was sanctioned by WADA, and the Madrid anti-doping agency and laboratory suspended in March 2016.

In March 2017 he was dismissed from his post by the new Secretary of State for Sport, a former professional basketball player named José Ramón Lete. Lete had been prominent in the sports secretariat in the Partido Popular government for the autonomous community of Galicia in the years when the region funded a cycling team, Xacobeo-Galicia. In 2010 two Xacobeo riders, Ezequiel Mosquera, the runner-up in the Tour of Spain, and David García Dapeña, tested positive for hydroxyethyl starch, a drug used to boost blood pressure.

Gómez Bastida was posted to Ibiza and Formentera, where the main law and order issues were pirate taxis. It is difficult to see this as anything other than payback for contravening the unwritten laws, and thus treading on the wrong political toes.

So much for the separation of powers.

When I started this book, my aim was to fathom the depths of Bala's insatiable appetite for speed, and his implacable desire for victory, and to understand why he attributes his talent to his father, but not his mother. I would have liked to have been able to ask him when he had his first big crash on a bike, and how he processed the discomfort. Or what impact the death of Mariano Rojas had on him, and whether it was the first time he had lost someone close. I would have liked to know whether he wore the cross of Caravaca de la Cruz with any religious conviction. Whether he retains any religious faith, what his forebears thought of the *Cristo de Monteagudo* and its 1936 destruction, and where Alejandro fits into the larger perspective of the Spanish Civil War and its secular aftermath. But that would be another book.

Instead, it has been the chronicle of a Kafkaesque plot in which, working to block the prosecution of Eufemiano Fuentes, the Spanish justice system reached a pragmatic solution, limiting the charges to public health offences that were unlikely to prosper, and arranging a trial using a formula – the abbreviated procedure – that made it impossible for the accused to be sentenced for an offence other than the one identified at the origin of the case. Whatever Valverde's relationship with Eufemiano Fuentes and doping, society's most powerful actors have much bigger lies to tell. If talk of covert perversions of justice by secret organisations in the Spanish deep state sounds like a movie plot, it is in part because ours is an age of conspiracy theories, and in part because it is also an age of conspiracies, in which every party claims to be the victims. The victims of all this, caught in an opaque, incomprehensible bureaucracy where nothing is clear and there is no hope of learning the truth, is the general public, held in contempt and treated as fools. In the twenty-first century, we are all Josef K.

Acknowledgements

Books are final products. They mark endings – in this case, of a brief, undistinguished career working for cycling teams, and a seven-year residence in Spain which started with the move to work for Movistar Team. In May 2016, with characteristic generosity, Mauro Vegni, then still the Giro d'Italia's race director, welcomed me back to the Giro by creating a post for me. During the race, my dear friend and colleague Rob Llewellyn, an engineer and programmer who, for fun, worked as a driver and production manager for the VSquared TV/ITV team at eight Tours de France and, with me, at three Vueltas a España, died suddenly while working at the Tour of California. In those sad circumstances, a vacancy opened, and VSquared TV and their director, the late Steve Docherty, kindly invited me back onto ITV's Tour de France production team, initially in Rob's role. By mid-Tour I had begun to report again, and, later, I took over as the back-up race commentator.

To Mauro Vegni and the entire RCS Cycling crew, and to Carolyn Viccari, James Venner, Gary Imlach, and all at VSquared TV, thank you.

Thanks also to Duncan Steer, entertainer extraordinaire, book tour host (coming soon to a venue near you) and purveyor of dodgy French music, and Clive Marshall of Italy Bike Tours, who periodically drags me away from my laptop to lead bike-bound adventures in Italy, Spain and Colombia, allowing my poor eyes to feast on mountains and the horizon, instead of the terminal terminal. You should join us.

Thanks also to my editor, Beth Eynon, and the following: project editor Lucinda McNeile, copy-editor John English, senior designer Jessica Hart, picture editor Natalie Dawkins, cover designer Matt Thame, publicist Elizabeth Allen, and my agent, Laetitia Rutherford.

I gratefully acknowledge the Comando Generale dell'Arma dei Carabinieri in Rome for permission to interview Renzo Ferrante, and to Investigator Ferrante himself for his precious collaboration. A few of the many journalists whose work I have relied on are mentioned in the text. My apologies go to everyone I have forgotten.

My sincerest thanks go to the many other friends who sustained me during my Spanish years, in particular Carlos Arribas.

Finally, and most personally, to 陳誼玲, my companion these past ten years, *no quiero que vacilen tu risa ni tus pasos.*

一路順風, 我的天使.

Notes

Introduction: Rare Bird

1   The distributed mind – see Colin Renfrew, *Prehistory: The making of the human mind* (London: Weidenfeld & Nicolson, 2007), pp. 119–20.

2   https://elpais.com/diario/2008/09/28/deportes/1222552809_850215.html

3   https://ecoteuve.eleconomista.es/programas/noticias/9927350/06/19/David-Broncano-en-La-Resistencia-Tener-acento-murciano-es-peor-que-tener-una-ETS.html

4   http://hemeroteca.mundodeportivo.com/preview/2010/04/11/pagina-29/5517605/pdf.html

5   Baltasar Garzón, *El Fango: Cuarenta años de corrupción en España* (Barcelona: Debate Editorial, 2015), pp. 19 and 25.

6   Anil Seth, *Being You. A New Science of Consciousness* (London: Faber & Faber, 2021), p. 111.

7   https://www.cyclingweekly.com/news/latest-news/mcquaid-attacks-mafia-culture-of-euro-federations-91132

8   Bradley Wiggins, 'I could never dope because it would cost me everything', *Guardian*, 13 July 2012.

9   https://publications.parliament.uk/pa/cm201719/cmselect/cmcumeds/366/36606.htm, para 110.

10 https://elpais.com/economia/2022-05-19/telefonica-vende-el-7076-de-prisa-a-global-alconaba-por-mas-de-34-millones.html

Chapter 1: The Wolf King

1   https://www.abc.es/espana/murcia/abci-piden-retire-cristo-monteagudo-aconfesionalidad-estado-201002090300-1133656900374_noticia.html For

the local response: https://www.laopiniondemurcia.es/
murcia/2011/06/25/cristo-queda-monteagudo-32722920.html

2 https://elpais.com/diario/2008/03/01/necrologi-
cas/1204326002_850215.html

3 https://elpais.com/diario/2007/07/02/
deportes/1183327212_850215.html

4 https://elpais.com/diario/2008/03/01/necrologicas/
1204326002_850215.html

5 https://dorsal51.wordpress.com/2014/02/11/
los-inicios-de-alejandro-valverde/

6 https://elpais.com/diario/2003/06/30/
deportes/1056924015_850215.html

7 https://www.diariovasco.com/v/20100413/deportes/ciclismo/
carrera-lanzo-valverde-20100413.html
?ref=https%3A%2F%2Fwww.google.com%2F

8 https://www.ciclo21.com/
los-inicios-de-valverde-como-pistard/

Chapter 2: Two Teams

1 https://elpais.com/diario/2007/12/24/deportes/
1198450829_850215.html

2 https://elpais.com/diario/2007/01/12/deportes/
1168556408_850215.html

3 Ibid.

4 https://muhaz.org/tribunalsupremo-sala-de-lo-penal-v2.
html?page=4

5 http://hj.tribunalconstitucional.es/es-ES/Resolucion/
Show/17768

6 http://hemeroteca.lavanguardia.com/preview/1994/12/20/
pagina-85/34450750/pdf.html

7 https://elpais.com/deportes/2022-03-08/las-1000-victorias-
del-equipo-navarro.html

8 https://www.ciclo21.com/
los-inicios-de-valverde-como-pistard/

9 José Antonio Miranda Encarnación, 'La industria del calzado
en España 1860-1959. La formación de una industria mod-
erna y los efectos del intervencionismo estatal.' Tesis doctoral
dirigida por el Dr Jordi Nadal i Oller, Departamento de

Análisis Económico Aplicado, Universidad de Alicante, 1996, p. 302.

10   https://elpais.com/elpais/2019/02/22/ideas/
1550835197_031784.html

11   https://lamarinaplaza.com/2018/01/14/1985-el-ano-en-que-
disney-casi-se-instala-en-pego/

12   https://elpais.com/economia/2014/10/20/actualidad/
1413828642_793314.html?rel=mas

13   https://elpais.com/diario/2006/03/02/cvalenciana/
1141330689_850215.html

14   https://elpais.com/diario/2006/03/02/cvalenciana/
1141330689_850215.html and https://cincodias.elpais.com/
cincodias/2004/05/27/empresas/1085824742_850215.html

15   José Fernando Vera Rebollo and Isabel Rodríguez Sánchez
(eds), *Renovación y reestructuración de destinos turísticos en
áreas costeras* (Valencia: Universitat de Valencia, 2012), p. 312
(at José Fernando Vera Rebollo, Isabel Rodríguez Sánchez, p.
312 at https://books.google.es/books?id=hmP
3sHygl-gC&pg=PA310&lpg=PA310&dq=%22Terra+Mit-
ica%22+%22Economic+Research+Associates%22+%-
22Baker+Leisure+Group%22&source=bl&ots=N7u9Z-
bXyF_&sig=ACfU3U10z3osgu6-1RANXFAkR_lab-
ZmE5Q&hl=en&sa=X&ved=2ahUKEwigiIbPyM3uAh-
VFUcAKHUroAFUQ6AEwBHoECAYQAg#v=onep-
age&q=%22Terra%20Mitica%22%20%22Economic%20
Research%20Associates%22%20%22Baker%20Leisure%20
Group%22&f=false)

16   https://www.eldiario.es/comunitat-valenciana/anticorrupcion-
eleva-20-6-millones-dinero-delictivo-manejaba-eduardo-
zaplana-operaciones-corrupcion_1_9611165.html

Chapter 3: Spain's Most Endorsable

1   https://www.abc.es/economia/abci-patricia-botin-nueva-
presidenta-banesto-200202130300-77959_noticia.html

2   https://www.abc.es/deportes/ciclismo/abci-dias-confusion-
para-tropa-echavarri-200209090300-128408_noticia.html

3   https://www.abc.es/deportes/ciclismo/abci-lastras-nombre-
banesto-200209150300-129654_noticia.html

4   http://hemeroteca.mundodeportivo.com/pre-
     view/2003/04/30/pagina-37/532459/pdf.html
5   https://as.com/masdeporte/2004/03/24/polideportivo/
     1080105344_850215.html
6   https://www.elmundo.es/elmundodeporte/2003/08/06/
     ciclismo/1060156047.html
7   https://www.abc.es/deportes/ciclismo/abci-belda-
     nadie-dicho-cara-seamos-unos-drogados-
     200409040300-9623433450630_noticia.html

Chapter 4: The Only Story
1   https://elpais.com/diario/2006/05/25/deportes/
     1148508001_850215.html
2   https://www.velonews.com/news/wada-president-critical-
     of-cyclings-anti-doping-efforts/
3   http://hemeroteca.mundodeportivo.com/preview/2004/02/28/
     pagina-44/753748/pdf.html
4   Ibid.
5   http://hemeroteca.mundodeportivo.com/preview/
     2004/03/06/pagina-48/1490135/pdf.html
6   http://hemeroteca.mundodeportivo.com/preview/
     2004/03/25/pagina-45/752954/pdf.html
7   https://web.archive.org/web/20081102123646/http://www.
     deia.com/es/impresa/2006/05/24/bizkaia/kirolak/252284.
     php
8   https://web.archive.org/web/20160310074958/http://www.
     lavozdegalicia.es/hemeroteca/2006/05/28/4813397.shtml
9   https://elpais.com/diario/1976/10/06/ultima/
     213404401_850215.html
10   https://www.canarias7.es/hemeroteca/
     fani_fuentes_rompe_su_silencio-KXCSN284086
11   https://elpais.com/diario/2006/05/28/deportes/
     1148767201_850215.html
12   https://www.spiegel.de/sport/sonst/jaksches-dopingbekenntnis-
     das-gestaendnis-von-bella-a-491566.html
13   https://elpais.com/diario/2006/05/28/deportes/
     1148767201_850215.html
14   https://elpais.com/diario/2006/05/24/deportes/
     1148421604_850215.html

15 In Daniel Friebe's book *Jan Ullrich: The best there never was*, Cecchini say of Casero, 'Fuentes treated him in Spain, and Casero used to come here four or five times a year to do tests' (p. 229).

16 https://elpais.com/diario/2004/03/29/deportes/ 1080511231_850215.html

17 https://www.lainformacion.com/espana/las-acusaciones-re-nuncian-a-la-testifical-de-dario-gadeo-y-pedro-diaz-lobato_XnU1IKcj9L63d5DUD3igI4/

18 The transcript of Gadeo's interview with the Spanish Cycling Federation is online here: https://www.usada.org/wp-content/uploads/Unnamed-volume-of-documents-.pdf, on the pages marked 24 and 25.

19 Ibid., pp. 26 and 27.

20 https://www.abc.es/deportes/ciclismo/abci-valverde-y-liberty-espera-para-cerrar-fichaje-200405220300-9621616487784_no-ticia.html

21 http://hemeroteca.mundodeportivo.com/preview/ 2004/09/04/pagina-41/781085/pdf.html

22 http://hemeroteca.mundodeportivo.com/preview/ 2004/09/22/pagina-36/782132/pdf.html

23 http://hemeroteca.mundodeportivo.com/preview/ 2004/09/23/pagina-36/783887/pdf.html

Chapter 5: Sporting Royalty

1 Infanta just means 'a daughter of a King of Spain'.

2 https://elsiglodeuropa.es/hemeroteca/temaport2005/655 portada.htm

3 https://www.ara.cat/es/Los-privilegios-estudiante-Urdangarin-Esade_0_2008599378.html

4 https://cadenaser.com/ser/2009/04/22/sociedad/ 1240366411_850215.html

5 https://elpais.com/politica/2018/06/12/actualidad/ 1528790989_464827.html

6 Ibid., pp. 214–15.

7 Caso Nóos 2677/08, p. 387.

8 https://www.ultimahora.es/noticias/local/2016/02/09/ 175660/ballester-afirma-matas-ordeno-pagar-discusion-pedia-urdangarin.html

9   https://docplayer.es/4708791-Entrevista-con-juan-pablo-
     molinero-directora-marketing-y-comunicacion-movistar-team.
     html
10   Sentencia 277/2018, p. 331.
11   Ibid., p. 332.

Chapter 6: The First Tour
1   https://www.elmundo.es/elmundodeporte/2005/02/09/
     ciclismo/1107968233.html
2   https://elpais.com/diario/2005/08/05/deportes/
     1123192806_850215.html

Chapter 7: The Fifty-eight
1   https://elpais.com/diario/2006/01/29/deportes/
     1138489215_850215.html
2   http://hemeroteca.mundodeportivo.com/preview/
     2009/09/21/pagina-34/5002810/pdf.html
3   https://elpais.com/diario/2006/05/26/deportes/
     1148594401_850215.html
4   Ibid.
5   Ibid.
6   Sentencia 144/13, pp. 140–1.
7   https://elpais.com/deportes/2016/12/27/actualidad/
     1482866433_093478.html
8   https://www.abc.es/cordoba/20130305/sevp-testigo-eufemiano-
     claudica-interrogatorio-20130305.html
9   https://elpais.com/diario/2006/05/27/deportes/
     1148680801_850215.html
10   Sentencia 144/13, pp. 102 and 176.
11   Ibid., p. 176.
12   Ibid., p. 180.
13   Ibid., p. 117.
14   https://as.com/masdeporte/2006/06/23/polideportivo/
     1151100292_850215.html
15   https://elpais.com/diario/2006/05/27/deportes/
     1148680802_850215.html
16   https://www.elmundo.es/elmundodeporte/2013/02/26/
     ciclismo/1361892370.html
17   https://jurisprudence.tas-cas.org/Shared%20

Documents/1396,%201402-IA.pdf

18   https://elpais.com/diario/2006/05/26/deportes/
      1148594403_850215.html

19   Sentencia 144/13, pp. 70–2.

20   https://elpais.com/diario/2006/05/25/deportes/
      1148508002_850215.html

21   https://elpais.com/diario/2007/10/16/deportes/
      1192485606_850215.html

22   'Nelson, tal y como acordamos te envío el listado de colabora-
      dores en el festival que tiene lugar en el mes de mayo, sin otro
      particular, esperando contar con tu ayuda y colaboración,
      un saludo (el Giro). 1, Alessandro Kalc; 2, Alberto León; 3,
      Ivan Basso; 4, Marcos Serrano, 5, Michele Scarponi; 6, José
      Enrique Gutiérrez y 7, Jan Ullrich. Gracias, Eufemiano.'

23   http://hemeroteca.mundodeportivo.com/preview/
      2006/09/18/pagina-40/836363/pdf.html

24   https://elpais.com/diario/2008/02/16/deportes/
      1203116402_850215.html

25   Sentencia 144/13, p. 239.

Chapter 8: Complacent and Evasive

1   https://elpais.com/diario/2007/01/12/deportes/
     1168556408_850215.html

2   https://www.abc.es/deportes/ciclismo/abci-eufemiano-co-
     bra-bonus-euros-ganar-tour-200701100300-153838991676_
     noticia.html

3   Reproduced at https://forodeciclismo.mforos.
     com/30984/5442476-declaraciones-de-tino-zaballa/

4   https://elpais.com/diario/2007/01/19/deportes/
     1169161204_850215.html

5   https://elpais.com/diario/2007/02/03/deportes/
     1170457208_850215.html

6   https://elpais.com/diario/2007/01/22/deportes/
     1169420424_850215.html

7   https://www.abc.es/deportes/ciclismo/abci-gobierno-
     balear-abandona-patrocinio-equipo-caisse-ep-
     argne-200702270300-1631699709169_noticia.html

8   http://autobus.cyclingnews.com/news.php?id=news/2007/
     mar07/mar26news2

9   https://elpais.com/diario/2007/03/20/deportes/
     1174345201_850215.html
10   Ibid.
11   https://elpais.com/diario/2007/05/08/deportes/
     1178575202_850215.html
12   https://elpais.com/diario/2007/03/20/deportes/
     1174345201_850215.html
13   https://www.elperiodico.com/es/politica/20111115/
     el-juez-investiga-si-urdangarin-medio-en-un-patrocinio-
     ciclista-1221519
14   https://www.abc.es/deportes/ciclismo/abci-ettore-torri-lati-
     go-antidopaje-200902200300-913251264275_noticia.html
15   https://elpais.com/diario/2007/06/16/deportes/
     1181944806_850215.html
16   https://elpais.com/diario/2007/05/10/deportes/
     1178748007_850215.html
17   https://elpais.com/diario/2007/05/15/deportes/
     1179180007_850215.html
18   https://elpais.com/diario/2007/06/02/deportes/
     1180735206_850215.html
19   https://elpais.com/diario/2007/05/31/deportes/
     1180562401_850215.html
20   https://elpais.com/diario/2007/06/13/deportes/
     1181685609_850215.html
21   https://elpais.com/diario/2007/06/20/deportes/
     1182290408_850215.html
22   https://elpais.com/diario/2007/06/30/deportes/
     1183154409_850215.html
23   https://www.abc.es/deportes/ciclismo/abci-quien-atreve-
     ganar-200707070300-1634121822936_noticia.html and
     https://elpais.com/diario/2007/06/15/deportes/
     1181858406_850215.html
24   https://elpais.com/diario/2007/07/19/deportes/
     1184796002_850215.html
25   https://elpais.com/diario/2007/07/07/deportes/
     1183759209_850215.html

Chapter 9: The Absence of a Rope

1   https://elpais.com/diario/2007/11/29/deportes/

1196290808_850215.html
2   https://elpais.com/diario/2007/07/30/deportes/
    1185746404_850215.html
3   https://elpais.com/diario/2007/07/30/deportes/
    1185746401_850215.html
4   https://as.com/masdeporte/2007/08/09/polideportivo/
    1186697092_850215.html
5   https://elpais.com/diario/2007/08/31/deportes/
    1188511211_850215.html
6   https://elpais.com/diario/2007/08/30/deportes/
    1188424811_850215.html
7   Ibid.
8   https://elpais.com/deportes/2007/09/17/actualidad/
    1190013723_850215.html
9   https://www.faz.net/aktuell/sport/mehr-sport/auch-ohne-
    ehrenerklaerung-bettini-darf-bei-rad-wm-starten-1462835.
    html

Chapter 10: Epoch-making
1   https://elpais.com/diario/2007/10/24/deportes/
    1193176811_850215.html
2   https://elpais.com/diario/2007/11/16/deportes/
    1195167602_850215.html
3   Ibid.
4   Ibid.
5   https://www.laopiniondemurcia.es/comunidad/2008/01/13/
    familia-valverde-crece-33031962.html
6   https://elpais.com/diario/2008/02/14/deportes/
    1202943601_850215.html
7   https://elpais.com/diario/2008/02/15/portada/
    1203030005_850215.html?prm=copy_link
8   https://elpais.com/diario/2008/03/03/deportes/
    1204498822_850215.html
9   https://elpais.com/diario/2008/02/15/deportes/
    1203030009_850215.html
10 https://jurisprudence.tas-cas.org/Shared%20
    Documents/1396,%201402-IA.pdf
11 Ibid.
12 https://elpais.com/diario/2008/03/05/deportes/

1204671612_850215.html

13 http://hemeroteca.mundodeportivo.com/preview/
2008/03/08/pagina-34/567665/pdf.html and https://elpais.
com/diario/2008/03/08/deportes/1204930806_850215.html

14 https://www.abc.es/deportes/ciclismo/abci-contador-no-
correra-tour-no-marcha-atras-decision-
200803270300-1641748563170_noticia.html

15 http://hemeroteca.mundodeportivo.com/preview/
2008/03/14/pagina-43/573290/pdf.html

16 https://jurisprudence.tas-cas.org/Shared%20Documents/
1396,%201402-IA.pdf

17 https://www.abc.es/deportes/ciclismo/abci-
alejandro-valverde-tengo-hambre-bicicleta-
200807040300-1641982138292_noticia.html

18 http://hemeroteca.mundodeportivo.com/preview/
2008/07/17/pagina-24/591154/pdf.html

19 http://hemeroteca.mundodeportivo.com/preview/
2008/07/17/pagina-25/591156/pdf.html

20 http://hemeroteca.mundodeportivo.com/preview/
2008/08/10/pagina-16/593890/pdf.html

21 https://www.referenceforbusiness.com/biography/M-R/
Milhaud-Charles-1943.html

Chapter 11: Match Point

1 https://elpais.com/diario/2009/02/12/deportes/
1234393207_850215.html

2 https://www.abc.es/deportes/abci-italia-reabre-caso-supuesto-
dopaje-valverde-200902110300-913062503869_noticia.html

3 https://elpais.com/diario/2009/01/17/deportes/
1232146810_850215.html

4 https://elpais.com/diario/2009/02/07/deportes/
1233961201_850215.html

5 Sentencia 114/13, p. 225.

6 https://www.wada-ama.org/sites/default/files/resources/files/
cas_2009_a_1879_valverde_v_coni_en_0.pdf and https://
elpais.com/diario/2010/02/05/deportes/1265324408_850215.
html

7 https://www.wada-ama.org/sites/default/files/resources/files/
cas_2009_a_1879_valverde_v_coni_en_0.pdf, p. 7, para. 47.

8   https://www.boe.es/buscar/doc.php?id=BOE-A-1982-23564

9   Ibid.

10   https://www.wada-ama.org/sites/default/files/resources/files/
cas_2009_a_1879_valverde_v_coni_en_0.pdf, paragraph 120.

11   https://www.abc.es/deportes/ciclismo/abci-puede-
personarse-caso-y-sentenciar-valverde-
200902210300-913277103957_noticia.html

12   Sentence 144/13 p. 310.

13   https://www.abc.es/deportes/ciclismo/abci-valverde-pide-jus-
ticia-espanola-quien-estudie-imputacion-dopaje-
200903050300-913568488772_noticia.html

14   https://elpais.com/diario/2009/04/18/deportes/
1240005607_850215.html

15   https://elpais.com/diario/2009/04/29/deportes/
1240956008_850215.html

16   https://elpais.com/diario/2009/05/11/deportes/
1241992828_850215.html

17   https://elpais.com/diario/2009/05/12/deportes/
1242079208_850215.html

18   http://hemeroteca.mundodeportivo.com/preview/
2009/05/20/pagina-37/4531834/pdf.html

19   http://hemeroteca.mundodeportivo.com/preview/
2009/05/25/pagina-56/4536681/pdf.html

20   https://elpais.com/diario/2009/06/29/deportes/
1246226416_850215.html

21   https://elpais.com/diario/2009/06/11/deportes/
1244671204_850215.html

22   https://elpais.com/diario/2009/06/12/deportes/
1244757607_850215.html

23   https://elpais.com/diario/2009/06/15/deportes/
1245016819_850215.html

24   https://elpais.com/diario/2009/06/29/deportes/
1246226416_850215.html

25   http://hemeroteca.mundodeportivo.com/preview/
2009/07/02/pagina-26/4938362/pdf.html

26   http://hemeroteca.mundodeportivo.com/preview/
2009/09/11/pagina-24/4994057/pdf.html

27   https://www.faz.net/aktuell/sport/radsport-kommentar-
herzlich-unwillkommen-1853023.html

28 https://elpais.com/diario/2009/09/25/deportes/
1253829603_850215.html

29 https://elpais.com/diario/2009/09/24/deportes/
1253743220_850215.html

Chapter 12: Weightlifting

1 http://hemeroteca.mundodeportivo.com/preview/
2010/02/15/pagina-39/5348646/pdf.html

2 http://hemeroteca.mundodeportivo.com/preview/
2010/02/06/pagina-31/5323466/pdf.html

3 http://hemeroteca.mundodeportivo.com/preview/
2010/02/09/pagina-40/5332388/pdf.html

4 http://hemeroteca.mundodeportivo.com/preview/
2010/03/09/pagina-27/5414969/pdf.html

5 http://hemeroteca.mundodeportivo.com/preview/
2010/03/26/pagina-27/5469874/pdf.html

6 https://elpais.com/diario/2010/03/15/deportes/
1268607627_850215.html and http://hemeroteca.mundo
deportivo.com/preview/2010/03/16/pagina-36/5436407/pdf.
html

7 http://hemeroteca.mundodeportivo.com/preview/
2010/04/06/pagina-27/5502043/pdf.html

8 http://hemeroteca.mundodeportivo.com/preview/
2010/04/11/pagina-29/5517605/pdf.html

9 http://hemeroteca.mundodeportivo.com/preview/
2010/04/22/pagina-35/5550223/pdf.html

10 The following year, the Swiss magazine *L'Illustre* obtained
emails exchanged between Vinokurov and Kolobnev the
day after the race, which suggested that Vinokurov had paid
Kolobnev €100,000 not to challenge him in the sprint finish,
although, eight years later, a Belgian court cleared them both
for lack of evidence.

11 https://www.wada-ama.org/sites/default/files/resources/files/
cas-2007-a-1396-valverde.pdf

Chapter 13: The Armstrong Connection

1 https://www.scientificamerican.com/article/
widespread-plasticizer-clouds-doping-tests-cyclists/

2 https://www.usada.org/wp-content/uploads/Reasoned

Decision.pdf, p. 99.
3   The sentence is online here: https://sites.google.com/site/
      dopingitalia/home/documenti/sentenza-primo-grado-
      processo-contro-michele-ferrari-tribunale-di-bologna-1-
      ottobre-2004 and here: https://www.usada.org/wp-content/
      uploads/2004-10-01-Judgement.Bologna-Court.ITALIAN.pdf
4   https://www.tuttobiciweb.it/article/910
5   Julien Sieveking, 'The "Forced" Union of Science and Law',
      in Olivier Rabin and Ornella Corazza (eds), *Emerging Drugs
      in Sport* (Cham, Switzerland: Springer, 2022), pp. 63–81.
6   Ibid., p. 65.
7   https://www.usada.org/wp-content/uploads/Bertagnolli-
      Leonardo-Witness-Statement.pdf
8   Reed Albergotti and Vanessa O'Connell, *Wheelmen: Lance
      Armstrong, the Tour de France, and the greatest sporting
      conspiracy ever* (London: Headline, 2014), pp. 265 and 270.
9   https://www.usada.org/wp-content/uploads/Ferrante-
      Renzo-Affidavit.pdf
10   The documents can be viewed here: https://www.
      usada.org/athletes/results/u-s-postal-service-pro-
      cycling-team-investigation/

Chapter 14: The Second Coming
1   https://elpais.com/diario/2010/01/23/deportes/
      1264201205_850215.html and https://www.slate.fr/
      story/6827/banques-populaires-caisses-depargne-la-fusion-
      de-tous-les-dangers
2   https://ciclismopacojimenez.blogspot.com/2014/12/mariano-
      rajoy-abandona-la-politica-y.html
3   https://elpais.com/deportes/2022-03-08/las-1000-victorias-
      del-equipo-navarro.html
4   At 2010 rates.
5   https://www.rtve.es/deportes/20100812/movistar-sera-nuevo-
      nombre-del-equipo-ciclista-caisse-depargne-para-proximo-
      ano-2011/345983.shtml
6   https://www.elconfidencial.com/deportes/ciclismo/
      2014-09-05/juan-carlos-escamez-el-masajista-que-le-gana-
      ba-carreras-a-valverde-en-amateur_185867/
7   http://hemeroteca.mundodeportivo.com/

preview/2012/06/30/pagina-48/9548339/pdf.html
8   Bradley Wiggins, 'I could never dope because it would cost me everything', *Guardian*, 13 July 2012.
9   https://www.reuters.com/article/us-cycling-vuelta/valverde-angry-with-team-sky-after-vuelta-crash-idUSBRE87K0X520120821

Chapter 15: The Trial
1   Sentencia 144/13, p. 187.
2   Ibid., p. 30.
3   Ibid., p. 141.
4   Ibid., p. 141.
5   Ibid.
6   Ibid., p. 126.
7   Ibid., p. 144.
8   Ibid., p. 141.
9   Ibid., p. 132.
10   Ibid., p. 235.
11   Ibid., p. 187.
12   Ibid., p. 271.

Chapter 16: Strategic Diversions
1   https://elpais.com/diario/2007/02/05/economia/1170630004_850215.html
2   https://elpais.com/diario/2007/11/07/cvalenciana/1194466688_850215.html
3   https://web.archive.org/web/20110210092105/http://www.elpais.com/elpaismedia/ultimahora/media/201102/09/economia/20110209elpepueco_2_Pes_PDF.pdf
4   https://ep00.epimg.net/descargables/2012/05/07/bcb8d-c4b666f01dd27e2c2b7e274457d.pdf
5   https://elpais.com/economia/2012/05/20/actualidad/1337546024_438366.html
6   https://www.elmundo.es/economia/2018/10/25/5bd1a0a3468aeb546e8b45b5.html
7   https://elpais.com/politica/2016/02/09/actualidad/1455014275_285920.html
8   https://elpais.com/politica/2016/02/11/actualidad/1455178096_861184.html

9   https://www.diariovasco.com/v/20120305/politica/vueltas-ciclismo-robo-torres-20120305.html

10   https://www.europapress.es/otr-press/cronicas/noticia-urdangarin-yo-me-dedicaba-me-dedicaba-empleados-no-conocia-20160226184250.html

11   https://elpais.com/politica/2012/10/18/actualidad/1350573187_867749.html

12   https://www.elmundo.es/baleares/2016/03/09/56e01ab-ce2704e657a8b45b5.html

13   https://www.ultimahora.es/noticias/local/2016/03/09/180982/molinero-noos-habia-dos-jefes-luego-estabamos-indios.html

Conclusion Part 1: A Commitment to Silence

1   https://www.climatechangenews.com/2022/04/04/saudi-arabia-dilutes-fossil-fuel-phase-out-language-with-techno-fixes-in-ipcc-report/

2   https://www.wada-ama.org/sites/default/files/resources/files/cas-2007-a-1396-valverde.pdf, p. 59.

3   Sentencia 302/2016, p. 81.

4   Ibid., p. 70.

Conclusion Part 2: Bigger Lies to Tell

1   https://as.com/ciclismo/2018/10/01/portada/1538422975_948396.html

2   https://www.elconfidencial.com/deportes/ciclismo/2014-09-05/juan-carlos-escamez-el-masajista-que-le-ganaba-carreras-a-valverde-en-amateur_185867/

3   Michael Sandel, *The Tyranny of Merit: What's become of the common good?* (London: Allen Lane, 2020), p. 123.

4   https://elpais.com/diario/2010/12/10/deportes/1291935601_850215.html

5   Ibid.

6   Roderick Munday, *Evidence*, Tenth Edition, (Oxford: Oxford University Press, 2019), p. 39.

7   Sentencia 144/13, p. 335.

8   https://www.unesco.org/en/legal-affairs/international-convention-against-doping-sport

9   'Pues bien, lo cierto es que al igual que "no todo vale" en el

deporte, también en materia jurisdiccional han de respetarse unos límites, límites que vienen constituidos por el respeto escrupuloso al Ordenamiento Jurídico aplicable y, en particular a nuestra Carta Magna, y muy especialmente a los derechos fundamentales que en la misma se proclaman. Y es por esto que la petición de muestras biológicas (sangre, plasma y concentrados de hematíes) realizada por determinadas Acusaciones en los términos ya examinados no puede prosperar, sin que ello suponga ninguna invasión de competencias por parte de la Administración de Justicia en el ámbito de la Administración Pública.' Sentencia 144/13, p. 330.

Index

259

Index

Index

Index

Picture Credits